A

SPECTACLE

of

GLORY

ALSO BY JONI EARECKSON TADA

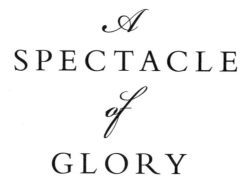

A
SPECTACLE
of
GLORY

God's Light Shining through
Me Every Day

JONI EARECKSON TADA

with LARRY LIBBY

ZONDERVAN

A Spectacle of Glory
Copyright © 2016 by Joni Eareckson Tada

Requests for information should be addressed to:
Zondervan, 3900 Sparks Dr. SE, Grand Rapids, Michigan 49546

ISBN 978-0-310-34678-4 (ebook)

Library of Congress Cataloging-in-Publication Data

Names: Tada, Joni Eareckson, author.
Title: A spectacle of glory : God's light shining through me every day /
    Joni Eareckson Tada.
Description: Grand Rapids: Zondervan, 2016.
Identifiers: LCCN 2016006359 | ISBN 9780310346777 (hardcover)
Subjects: LCSH: .
Classification: LCC BV4905.3 .M333 2016 | DCC 248.8/6—dc23 LC record
    available at http://lcnn.loc.gov/2016006359

Published in association with the literary agency of Wolgemuth &
Associates, Inc.

Cover photography: © Alejandro Moreno de Carlos / Stocksy
Interior design: Kait Lamphere

Second Printing January 2017 / Printed in the United States of America

For
Paul Buursma

Freckles, shiny blond hair, and the biggest smile on a two-year-old I'd ever seen . . . and I hardly noticed his cerebral palsy. As Paul grew, the activity that swirled around his wheelchair wasn't because of his challenges, but because of his hands-down, happy attitude. Everyone was drawn to Paul's infectious love for Jesus. And when God called Paul home at the age of thirty-two, he left a huge legacy.

Since this little book is about glorifying God in every situation,

I dedicate it to Paul.

After all, he's shown us how.

*T*hankful for These . . .

Perhaps I cannot stand on the shoulders of great saints, but I do sit on them. Take John Newton, the Anglican pastor from the 1700s, who gave us "Amazing Grace." In his book *Newton on the Christian Life*, Tony Reinke reflected on how an unconsumed burning bush was one of Newton's favorite metaphors for Christians undergoing severe suffering. He wrote, "Some Christians are called to endure a disproportionate amount of suffering. Such Christians are a spectacle of grace to the church, like flaming bushes unconsumed, and cause us to ask, like Moses, 'Why is this bush not burned?' The strength and stability of these believers can be explained only by the miracle of God's sustaining grace."[1]

After nearly fifty years of quadriplegia, and battles with cancer and chronic pain, I can say I'm a "bush not burned." I thank God and His Word for that, but also stalwart saints, like John Newton, William Law, Bishop J. C. Ryle, Jeremiah Burroughs, and contemporaries John Piper, J. I. Packer, Elisabeth Elliot, and more. Their tough take on suffering has helped deepen my walk with Christ and given me something rich to pass on to you.

Larry Libby, my longtime friend and fellow word-smith, is deserving of special thanks. In *A Spectacle of*

1. Tony Reinke, *Newton on the Christian Life: To Live is Christ* (Wheaton, Ill.: Crossway, 2015), 159.

Glory, as well as in other books, Larry has taken my rough-and-tumble words, turned them this way and that, and polished them into paragraphs that shine with truth and beauty. If anyone walks away from this book having been drawn closer to God and His Word, I have you to thank, Larry.

I'm grateful to Wolgemuth & Associates for their guidance. Robert Wolgemuth is a longtime friend with whom I have harmonized on many a hymn and collaborated on almost as many books (with his precious wife, Bobbie, who passed away from cancer). Robert and his new wife, Nancy DeMoss, have prayed me through *A Spectacle of Glory*, and their intercessions mean the world. I'm also indebted to Andrew Wolgemuth, who has been my champion on this devotional book and others—God bless you, Andrew, for opening doors for me to wheel through.

I take a bow to my publishing family at Zondervan. They put their full weight behind *A Spectacle of Glory*. From John Sloan to Alicia Kasen, *thank you*, friends, for extending the HarperCollins platform to me so I can share my heart with a new generation of readers. I feel especially close to Dirk Buursma, who did the hard work of copy editing, refining every page and paragraph. What's so special about that? Dirk is the proud father of Paul Buursma, the young "bush not burned" to whom I dedicated this book.

There were plenty of times at Joni and Friends

when I had to push away from the computer and lie down to give my body a break. It takes a team of people to not only help me research and type, but to get me sitting up in my wheelchair and moving forward. My coworkers Francie Lorey, Lisa Miehl, Deborah Gandi, Rainey Floreen, Kathren Martinez, and Tatiana Barrera deserve a round of applause for the many times they lent a hand.

Finally, special thanks to Ken Tada, who has faithfully walked beside my wheelchair for decades, seeing me through every hurt and happiness. Ken and I pray that the insights in this book will lift your spirits to new heights of confidence in our wonderfully sovereign God. So bless you for joining me on this day-by-day journey—may it help you be a flaming bush unconsumed, causing others to ask, like Moses, "Why is this bush not burned?" It will be your chance to shine… to be *a spectacle of glory*.

January

Imagine arriving at a national forest trailhead, preparing to take a long hike on a new trail. You may have read a little about the trail in a guidebook, but for you, everything will be new. Every bend in the trail, a fresh discovery. Fields of wildflowers, mountain vistas, and treacherous places too, where footing is poor and cliffs are sheer. It's a little frightening, knowing you've never been this way before. But as you tighten the straps on your pack, a quick glance ahead reveals Your Guide waiting for you. He will be with you. He knows the way. He's thought through the necessary provisions. He will teach you about natural wonders along the way, and He's prepared to take on wild animals. Today, as you face a new year, the way before you is cloaked in mystery, unknown. But Jesus will be there for every step. Protecting. Encouraging. Guiding. Providing. *Being there.*

Lord, I've never been this way before. I have no idea what this year will hold... for my health... for opportunities to serve You... for people to love and help and challenge in Your strong name. No matter whether the travel is easy or a mad scramble up a slippery trail in the dark, I know You—my Guide, my God, my Friend— will be with me.

Today's Scripture tells of a time when a large crowd gathered around the Lord, listening to Him speak the parable of the sower. After Jesus was done, you can imagine most people went home perplexed. Yes, Jesus had told a fascinating story—but what did it really *mean*? Verses 10–11 read, "When he was alone, the Twelve and the others around him asked him about the parables. He told them, 'The secret of the kingdom of God has been given to you.'" And there, away from the clamor of the crowd, Jesus revealed profound truths to them. Some had just walked away unsatisfied. But others drew near, determined to understand in a deeper way.

My friend, don't be the one who is quick to leave the Lord's presence. When you don't understand something, hang around after everyone else has gone. Crowd in close to Jesus. Let Him teach you the secrets of the kingdom.

Lord, I don't want to miss anything You have for me. Don't let me lose interest or drift away before You have finished speaking to me. Don't let me become impatient or discouraged as I wait on You for perspective and deeper understanding. When You are revealing secrets to others, Lord, tell me too!

In "Rumpelstiltskin," a children's fairy tale, an old elf sat in a room alone, spinning straw on a spinning wheel and somehow turning it into heaps of shining gold. As Christians, we have that opportunity every day! Think of your earthly problems as a pile of straw on one side of the room, and heaven's gold on the other. The spinning wheel is in the middle, and there you sit, making decisions every day about how you will work with your hardships.

When you complain or feel resentful and embittered, the pile of hay and stubble grows. But if you trust in the Lord and hold fast to His grace, then you are laying up for yourself treasure and reward in heaven. You are weaving common straw into priceless gold. As Paul puts it, our trials will "produce for us a glory that vastly outweighs them and will last forever!"[1]

How good of You, Father, to give us this—a way to turn our disappointments, sleepless nights, physical pain, and frustrating setbacks into opportunities for everlasting gain! Help me to remember these things when discouragement seeps into my soul. There are no throwaway moments in life; everything counts for eternal reward.

---

1. 2 Corinthians 4:17, NLT.

By nature, we human beings are drawn to keeping records and "gaining credit" through good works. That's the way we are wired. And that's why the gospel of grace is so difficult for some people to accept. All of us struggle with this. We mark and remember good things we've done and never seem to forget bad things done to us. Enter the first of January, when we make resolutions and keep records on ourselves! When we fail (as we certainly do), we get really tough on ourselves—or give up the good resolution altogether. At this time of year, it's good to remember today's Scripture: "The steadfast love of the LORD never ceases; his mercies never come to an end; they are new every morning; great is your faithfulness." Every day the Christian life begins with a new experience of the mercy of God. The faithfulness of God—not our own faithfulness—is our great hope.[1]

Dear God, I just want to lift my voice and sing, "Great is Thy faithfulness! Great is Thy faithfulness!" Thank You for Your multiplied mercies toward me. Thank You for forgiving me, restoring me, healing me, and resetting my life direction again and again!

---

1. Thanks to my pastor, Bob Bjerkaas, for some of these thoughts.

Arguing is usually a big waste of time and energy, but there is something to be said for arguing with *yourself*. In fact, that's a very biblical thing to do. Go ahead and speak truth and hope into your own soul! That's what the psalmist did. When he was in distress and felt himself slipping into a dark place, he spoke directly to his own heart: "Why, my soul, are you downcast? Why so disturbed within me? Put your hope in God, for I will yet praise him, my Savior and my God."

Maybe you've been listening to too many negative, hopeless voices... on the nightly news... in the car pool... or on the phone with your friends. Maybe the evil one has been whispering words of death, defeat, and futility into your ear. It's time to set the record straight! Declare the truth about who you are in Christ. Remind your soul that Jesus is your help and hope, that the Father deeply loves you, and that your future is secure in heaven.

Dear Lord Jesus, I've listened too long to cynical words, dark thoughts—and anxieties that buzz around my head like bees. Help me to speak life and peace into my own soul by the power of Your indwelling Holy Spirit.

When you were in elementary school, did you ever take a pen and write the name of someone on the palm of your hand? Maybe it was a boy or girl you liked—or someone you especially admired. The truth is, God has done this as well, only He has taken it a giant step further. In today's Scripture, He says, "See, I have engraved you on the palms of my hands." In other words, He doesn't just engrave your name on His palms, but He engraves *you*. It's all there—everything about you—your hopes and dreams, faults and failures, fears and anxieties, everything that makes up who you are. He's not just holding you; He closes His hands and feels the impression, the precious one-of-a-kind engraving. You are a part of Him, and He will never, ever overlook you and your needs.

Father, this is almost too much for me to process. You have placed me where You will always see me and set me where You will always remember me. Nothing about me escapes Your gaze. Others may look past me, forget to pray for me, or neglect to even notice me, but You never will. Not today, not tomorrow, not in a million years.

Many who struggle with severe disabilities, chronic pain, grief, or depression find themselves with a short battery life of encouragement. One day might find them cruising along on an even keel, and the next day all of that hope seems to evaporate. Today's Scripture acknowledges this, with the writer challenging us to "encourage one another daily... so that none of you may be hardened by sin's deceitfulness." The truth is, we all need daily encouragement from others when it comes to keeping a positive outlook. If we don't find that encouragement, the Bible says we're in danger of being *hardened*—not only by sin, but also by cynicism, bitterness, or despair. We need other hope-filled believers in our lives, friends who can lift us with wise words and reminders of God's goodness, grace, and power. We also need to *be* that kind of encourager, speaking confident words and letting that hope put a smile on someone else's face.

Lord, thank You for the amazing encouragers You have placed in my life through the years. I praise You for all those expressions of solid truth that lifted my heart and kept me from giving up in despair. I ask for the opportunity today to speak such words of hope into someone else's life.

A careful vineyard owner watches with great attention for signs of budding fruit. He has spent months tilling, fertilizing, pruning, watering, and testing. And now he is expecting his vines to bear big, luscious, prize-winning grapes. Don't think the Almighty is any less meticulous.

He wants *you* to bear *much* fruit. He notices every time you sow seeds in the lives of others. He keeps tabs every time you water that seed with prayer. He takes note when faith flowers and fruit ripens in the life of someone in whom you have invested for Jesus' sake. If they are rewarded, you reap. If they are lifted up, you are raised with them. Be vigilant about people in your spheres of influence. You are sowing seeds; your prayers are having an impact; and the Lord of the vineyard is paying close attention.

Lord, I see so clearly today that my life in You is all about investing in others. If I lose my life for Your sake, I find it as never before! Please show me how to invest wisely, giving my words, my time, my specific prayers, my concern, my full attention, my practical help, my smiles of encouragement, and love that is rooted in You.

Know anyone with "rough edges"? Maybe that describes you. Perhaps you've been told that you sometimes come across a little harsh, a little impatient. Today's Scripture has good advice for all of us. "Let your gentleness be evident to all." The Greek word translated "gentleness" implies an appropriate response to the people in your life. It speaks of moderation in choice of words and tone of voice, with a healthy dose of patience.

How do we manage such a thing? The answer is in the very next phrase: "The Lord is near." In other words, He's listening to every conversation. He's sitting with your family at supper. He's in the car when you're on your phone. He is *near.* And that's why we should be gentle in our words and actions. Think before you speak. Consider before you hit Send. Jesus holds us accountable for our words *and* the intentions behind them.

I'm glad You are near, Lord. I'm happy You are walking with me and listening to my conversations. I wouldn't want You anywhere else but close by. But I need the help of Your Holy Spirit to show grace and patience and kindness to the people who cross my path. Since You are near, O Lord, change my heart and touch my tongue.

Calm and matter-of-fact, the shepherd boy David described his experiences with wild animals in the wilderness: "When a lion or a bear came and carried off a sheep from the flock, I went after it, struck it and rescued the sheep... When it turned on me, I seized it by its hair, struck it and killed it." David *went after* the lions in his life. Rather than hiding from them or cowering at their approach, he pursued them. His courage tells me not to be afraid of my adversary, the devil, when lion-sized trials, heartaches, and difficulties come looking to destroy my faith or tear apart my peace of mind.

We can face our troubles head-on, my friend. Each trial gives us a chance to demonstrate to an unbelieving world that Jesus, the Lion of Judah, is greater than *any* adversary. In Him we are strong. We are overcomers. We are victorious.

Dear Lord, I need the courage of David today. There are lions in my life too! I can see them crouching in the shadows. Sometimes everything in me wants to run, hide, deny, or cower in fear. Please give me the strength to face those adversaries and take them on in Your strong name.

There is a statement I have repeated again and again through the years: "I would rather be in this wheelchair knowing Jesus than on my feet without Him." It's still true. The joy, hope, and peace I experience—not in spite of but *because of* my disability—is so much more fulfilling and satisfying than having feet that walk and run, and hands that hold, touch, and feel. The apostle Paul really sums it up for me: "For of Him and through Him and to Him are all things, to whom be glory forever. Amen."[1]

My friend, all things—even walking or not walking—find their end in Christ. To be with Him in life is *everything*. I'd rather be in the storm with Christ than in calm waters alone. As Paul wrote in today's Scripture, "For to me, to live is Christ." I wouldn't trade what I have in Christ for any other situation.

Lord Jesus, it hasn't been an easy life. At times I could have said with the apostle Paul, "We were under great pressure, far beyond our ability to endure, so that we despaired of life itself."[2] This is true, but even so, nothing, *nothing* compares to having You, the Son of God, as my Companion, Savior, Helper, and Friend.

---

1. Romans 11:36, NKJV.   2. 2 Corinthians 1:8.

Everything you face in your life and overcome with God's strength today prepares you for what will cross your path tomorrow. No matter what your disappointment or heartache, if you turn to the Lord for help, that experience will give you courage and hope for the unexpected challenges that lie ahead. In today's Scripture, the Lord says to His discouraged servant, "If you have raced with men on foot and they have worn you out, how can you compete with horses?" The challenges in your life today may be cancer, worry over a straying child, marriage tension, or an empty bank account. But whatever you have endured in your past—getting through with God's miraculous intervention—will give you greater confidence to face today's worry. Wasting nothing, God will use every hardship, every bruise, in your life to strengthen your faith and train you in godliness. You will be ready for whatever today or tomorrow will bring.

Without You, God, I could never run a footrace with anyone, let alone race against a horse. You are my strength and help. You are my inspiration and the unfailing source of my courage. All of these words about enduring and being strong are just so much talk unless You are under me, over me, beside me, and within me.

When someone holds on to joy in spite of everything, I call that "defiant joy." A person with defiant joy refuses to be squelched by negative voices or intimidated by overwhelming odds. In Jesus, we have the greatest example anyone could imagine. Today's Scripture says, "For the joy set before him he endured the cross, scorning its shame, and sat down at the right hand of the throne of God."

The joy born out of suffering is unflinching in the face of discouragement; it is unshakable when your pain screams at you to choose doubt and fear. Joy is a gift of the Holy Spirit that is far more durable, rigorous, and rugged than most of us realize. So when you pick up your cross every day, do so without wavering. Because as you do, you'll also be choosing joy.

Jesus, I am humbled—and in awe—to think You would willingly endure betrayal, the terrors of the cross, and the dark stain of all my sin. And somehow, You saw joy beyond it all. You knew Your suffering would purchase my rescue from death and open the doors of eternal life for me. Teach me, Lord, to look beyond today's pain to see heaven on the horizon.

Do you ever feel like God has called others to big plans, big visions, and important roles in His kingdom, but you're just not cut out for it? That is what Jeremiah thought. When God called his number, Jeremiah protested, claiming he was too young—and a poor speaker besides. But the Lord replied, "Do not say, 'I am too young'… for I am with you… I have put my words in your mouth. See, today I appoint you over nations and kingdoms to uproot and tear down, to destroy and overthrow, to build and to plant." What a grand-scale vision! Speak for God? Confront nations? Overturn realms? Build and plant in remote corners of the earth? It seems like too much for you and me too, doesn't it? We shrink from the task, thinking, *That's too big. Too grandiose. I can't handle that!* Yes you can! And this very day, God is calling you to a great role, bold prayers, and mighty deeds for Christ's kingdom.

Dear Lord, please don't let the enemy shrink my vision of life in Christ into something small, modest, and manageable. Lift my heart today, Holy Spirit, as You show me ways I can touch a hurting world through my prayers—and with whatever else You place in my hand to do.

Have you ever received a note or card at just the right time with just the right word of encouragement? It's like getting a message straight from heaven, isn't it? In Proverbs, Solomon writes, "A word fitly spoken is like apples of gold in a setting of silver."[1] We may minimize the words we speak or the efforts we make to lift someone's heart or brighten someone's day, but in God's hands, those few words can make a world of difference. Just as careless, sarcastic, or dismissive words have the capacity to damage, warp, and kill, so a word of kindness—"a word fitly spoken"—can change the course of a day... or a life. Knowing this, why don't we practice it even more? A notecard in the mail, a well-timed affirmation, or even a thoughtful email to a struggling soul may be among the most significant things you will accomplish—today or ever.

Thank You, Father, for those who have written timely notes or spoken words of hope and life to me through the years. Holy Spirit, show me where and how and when I can do this for others—both Your sons and daughters and those who are (for now) outside Your family. I don't want to "just talk"; I want to speak words that You can use.

---

1. Proverbs 25:11, ESV.

Today's Scripture reads, "Bless the LORD, O my soul; and all that is within me, bless His holy name! Bless the LORD, O my soul, and forget not all His benefits." But sometimes we do forget those benefits, don't we? Physical pain, illness, or grief can cloud our perspective about God's love and care for us. His great kindness and His miraculous interventions fade all too soon from our thoughts. That's why we need to continually stir our souls to *remember* those things. God has pardoned all our sin (think of it!). He has rescued us, restored us, and crowned us with His love. He has healed, protected, and encouraged us time after time. Does this make all the pain and struggle go away? No, perhaps not immediately. But just around the corner, in a few short years, the Bible promises that all of our hurts and heartache will fade like a bad dream in the morning light.

Lord, I love the bar that David sets here: "All that is within me." Let it be that way in my life today. Awaken my heart, spirit, and soul. Stir the parts of my body—even the parts that are in pain today—to bless You, praise You, and lift Your name high.

Nothing is more suffocating, more soul stifling, than feelings of hopelessness. Despair can seep into your soul like floodwaters into a basement. We've all been there when hope seems so very faint. But true hope is not a feeling; it is a fact firmly rooted in eternal truth. God never loses sight of you, never becomes distracted from your life, never misplaces your file, never allows you to slide off His radar for a single instant. When troubles come, He doesn't back away, giving Satan a free hand to harass you. In today's Scripture, we read, "God is our refuge and strength, an ever-present help in trouble." When you are in trouble, God doesn't just send help; He *is* your help. And this help is ever-present. God is closer than your troubles and stronger than your fears. Fix your thoughts on Him, and He *will* sustain you.

I'm so thankful, dear Lord, that You don't come and go in my life like a fitful breeze or a preoccupied friend. You are always here. Always in reach. Always listening. Always concerned. Always ready to help. Guard my heart, I pray, from the infection of despair. And may Your hope—Your living hope—flow from me to others.

When I was in Germany speaking at a church, a blind woman named Elizabeth served as my interpreter. You can imagine the two of us on stage—me with my wheelchair and Elizabeth with her white cane. During a break, someone placed an English language magazine on my lap. It looked like a good read, but with my quadriplegia, I couldn't hold the periodical or turn its pages.

"Elizabeth," I said, "how 'bout if you hold the magazine and turn the pages, and I will read out loud. That way we can both enjoy it." And that's just what we did. I needed her; she needed me; and together we accomplished something that blessed both of us. That is how the body of Christ should work! Our combined weaknesses become delightful strengths. First Corinthians 12 describes how we all need each other, just as a physical body needs feet, hands, ears, and eyes to move forward. If we isolate from other Christians, we impoverish them—and ourselves.

Lord, keep my mind from filling up with details about myself, my wants, my needs, my deadlines, and my schedule. Remind me of those I might help today with the abilities and gifts You have given me. If someone needs a positive word or a listening ear, move me to take notice…and take the time to respond.

Jesus describes a shepherd who leaves ninety-nine sheep out in open country to seek a lost one. On the surface, that doesn't seem like wise livestock management. What rancher turns his back on an entire flock to scour the terrain for one foolish, wandering animal? Jesus does. Yes, He loves the ninety-nine, but His heart yearns for the missing sheep, the one in eternal peril. After searching high and low, the shepherd finally finds the stray and carries it home on his shoulders. In his great joy, he even calls friends to come celebrate with him. This is how much Jesus loves and longs for that lost one you've been praying over for so long. Yes, maybe he or she is a rebel in whom others see no worth. The Good Shepherd, however, will never stop searching and calling. And that's why we should never, ever stop praying for and loving those who are lost.

Jesus, forgive me for giving up on people who have rejected You and hardened their hearts against You. Sometimes I write people off as a bad investment, but You never do. Help me not to shrug my shoulders about those who choose to ignore You or oppose You and wander into darkness. Give me a heart like Yours, Great Shepherd.

Many formerly active able-bodied people have had to learn a new pace in life after an accident or illness. Whether the condition is temporary or permanent, it isn't easy. The memory and muscles still remember what it was like to jog around the neighborhood, ride a bike on the river trail, or keep up with a busy household. But now a new reality has set in.

What happens to your relationship with God in such times? Does He leave you in the dust? Does He run so far out in front of you that you can barely see Him anymore? Not at all. God wants to walk with us, and closeness is what matters, not speed. Today's Scripture urges us to "walk by the Spirit." No matter how fast or slow you may be moving these days, God will guide you. He is at your side every step of the journey.

Father, thank You that You care more about being with me than how much distance I cover on a given day. Some days I have to take life very slowly, and on other days I can't move at all. I'm so grateful that You stay near and that Your pace will always match my ability and Your eternal purpose.

Paul's words seem like a sweet, cool breeze on a sweltering afternoon: "We know that in all things God works for the good of those who love him, who have been called according to his purpose." But what about those two wonderful, perplexing words *all things*? In his second letter to the Corinthians, Paul lists some of the experiences he includes under that heading. Severe floggings. Staring death in the face. Bloody lashings with a whip. Brutal beatings with rods. Terrifying shipwrecks. Danger from bandits. Heartaches over betrayals and false believers. Exposure, exhaustion, hunger, and thirst.[1] And the list goes on.

Most of us could say that our problems pale in light of Paul's list. Yet he could still write, "I *know* that in *all things* God works for my good."[2] What's keeping you from believing in God's goodness right now, in the midst of your difficulties, pressures, and disappointments?

Lord, I know that if You worked everything into a pattern for good in Paul's life, You will do the same in mine. I do love You, Lord, and even in today's pain and weariness, I know You called me for a purpose. Sometimes I can't imagine what that purpose might be, but right now I'm content that You know, and that's enough.

---

1. 2 Corinthians 11:23–28.   2. Emphasis mine.

One night, Xerxes, emperor of the mighty Persian Empire, couldn't sleep. This may seem like a random, trivial fact—but it's not. That one night of royal insomnia set off a whole chain of events that eventually saved Queen Esther and the whole Jewish population from destruction—while decimating their enemies. It's a reminder of how God delights to arrange "coincidences" to advance His purposes. He uses the most innocuous, everyday events to engineer the most earth-shattering and significant moments in your life. As Pastor John Piper wrote, "God is always doing 10,000 things in your life, and you may be aware of three of them."[1]

Is your heart open today? Watch for His sovereign hand at work in every life situation, and praise Him for how each incident weaves its way into His marvelous plan.

Dear Lord, how inexpressibly comforting this is! To think I can trust You with all the details of my life—right down to the frustrating delays, health setbacks, traffic jams, missed flights, and unexpected glitches. Your watch-care over my life is wonderful. Why should I be anxious or discouraged? I praise You for being Lord over all of my life.

---

1. John Piper, "Every Moment in 2013 God Will Be Doing 10,000 Things in Your Life," *DesiringGod.org*, January 1, 2013.

January 23 | Ephesians 5:15–16

There is nothing as valuable in life as an opportunity. In today's Scripture, Paul tells us, "Be very careful, then, how you live... making the most of every opportunity, because the days are evil." We sometimes talk about making the most of our financial resources with good investments. But every day we are handed twenty-four precious hours, free of charge. If you had all the money in the world, you could not purchase a single hour. So what will you do with this priceless possession? The Bible says to use it wisely. Make the most of every open door and every chance you get to speak for Jesus or help and love people in His name. Take full advantage of the hours God gives you because once time is wasted, you can't get it back.

Father, open my eyes to the doors You open for me today. Forgive me for imagining I have endless time and unlimited opportunities to love my family and friends or to impact their lives for You. Deep down, I know better. I know that time is fleeting and that open doors may not stay open. Awaken my heart to Your will and desire for me today.

When you don't walk, your shoes never wear out. My shoes can last me ten years or more and still look brand-new. The soles that have never touched dirt, gravel, pavement, or even carpet stay pristine. But I did have some sandals that got mud-stained in a monsoon in the Philippines back in the 1980s—and I treasure those stains. They remind me of the people who came to Christ that very night, in the storm, as we huddled together in a shelter. It was good to get my feet dirty bringing Good News to people who need Jesus! The truth is, even though my shoes may not get a lot of mileage, my wheelchair logs countless miles. Traveling isn't easy for me, but the Lord has sent me to visit more than fifty countries with the gospel of peace. Whatever inconvenience, difficulty, hardship, or physical and emotional wear-and-tear we experience to bring the story of Jesus to others is worth it a thousand times over.

Lord Jesus, I would love the privilege to speak for You today. I don't know how it will happen, where I will be, or whom I might encounter, but when the opportune moment comes, let me open my mouth and say a word or two that turns the conversation toward You.

At a large conference for pastors in the Philippines, a small band of blind musicians entertained the crowd inside while a monsoon rain fell outside. Suddenly, there was a loud crash of thunder, and the entire conference hall went dark. Unfazed, the musicians didn't skip a beat, even though it was pitch-black. When the song was done, the audience burst into thunderous applause. What really turned up the wattage on the praise that night was the fact that *they played through the dark.*

The same is true when we live for God and keep our spirits bright even through the dark times. People expect us to be positive and faith filled when everything goes our way. But when the lights falter and the music of our lives keeps flowing, the intensity of praise to God goes up several decibels. Keep playing the music!

Father in heaven, I pray that my song of thanksgiving won't falter when the sky clouds over with troubles and pain. How ironic that the times I least feel like demonstrating faith are the very times when that demonstration will be most powerful. I do want to be that city on the hill Jesus spoke of; I want my praise to glow in the dark.

Some people imagine that menial, mundane tasks don't rate very high in the Lord's service—whether it's cleaning up in the church kitchen, setting out Communion cups, or changing the oil on an elderly widow's car. But no task undertaken for the Lord is ever commonplace, undervalued, or wasted. Today's Scripture reads, "Always give yourselves fully to the work of the Lord... your labor in the Lord is not in vain." In other words, what you do for God—desiring to please Him and serve His people—*counts*. It makes a difference, not only here and now, but on the other side, in eternity. Could it be that angels observe our determination, sacrifice, and the hours we invest in His work? One thing is for certain: God himself sees and takes note. And what you do for Him today may have far greater implications than you could ever begin to imagine.

Lord, how good it is to remember that *nothing* escapes Your notice. Every task I have ever attempted for You, every time I worked through my pain, every time I set aside something I wanted in order to do what You wanted, has been recorded in heaven. I may feel many things in my life, but I should never, ever feel overlooked.

January 27 | Job 16:19–21

Job looks up through a fog of grief and pain and sees something in a flash of spiritual insight. He cries out, "Even now my witness is in heaven; my advocate is on high. My intercessor is my friend… on behalf of a man he pleads with God as one pleads for a friend." I love those two words—"even now."

Whatever your life situation *at this very moment*, EVEN NOW, you have a Witness, an Advocate, an Intercessor, and a Friend in heaven, making the case for you before the Father. That Friend is Jesus Himself, the Son of God and Creator of all. Whatever your circumstance, doctor's prognosis, level of pain, bank balance, or earthly trouble, you have a mighty Witness in heaven who is completely tuned in to your situation and prays for you.

Even now, Lord Jesus, I don't have to wait in line for Your attention, earn Your notice, work for Your favor, or cry out endlessly for Your mercy. Even now, You are my Advocate, pleading with God the Father on my behalf. As best I know how, I will rest in Your love today and trust You to do what's best for me.

Have you ever seen a fellow believer fall into deep sin and thought to yourself, *I would never do that?* Maybe a prominent Christian has made the news for embezzling funds or abandoning his or her wedding vows. When you hear the news, you shake your head and say, "How could someone do such a thing?" Today's Scripture has good counsel for all of us when we imagine ourselves to be above certain sins: "If you think you are standing firm, be careful that you don't fall!" In other words, don't be proud or smug when others sin, because you are *not* as strong, courageous, and godly as you think you are. Consider Noah, who stood firm in a land filled with sin—only to become drunk and disgraced in his own tent.[1] Your greatest temptation doesn't come when you feel weak and vulnerable, but rather when you feel strong, devoted, and above the fray.

Father, I know I have done this. I have seen brothers and sisters stumble, shaken my head, and thought to myself, *How could they?* But You know the truth, God. You know that sometimes I have avoided sin, not because I'm more devout, but because I lacked opportunity! Father, I admit my weakness today. I want to be strong in You—not in myself!

---

1. Genesis 9:20–23.

It's very difficult to move forward when you're locked up in physical or emotional pain. In such moments, it's a comfort to remember that the love of Jesus toward you and me can *never* be exhausted. He gives and gives and gives. Look at a typical day in His life. In Matthew 14, after a hot, dusty afternoon of preaching to the crowds, Jesus learns the devastating news about the beheading of His friend and cousin, John the Baptist. But rather than taking time to grieve, Jesus attends to the needs at hand, feeding five thousand people. Then He later rescues His disciples when a storm blindsides their boat. On the other side of the lake, He takes on more crowds and nonstop ministry with no sleep.

And so it is today. Jesus' love for you is endless. His concern never falters. He never tires of your journey. Jesus, your inexhaustible Friend, can carry your load today.

Such a Friend! Praise You, Jesus, for Your strong arm around my shoulders through the demands of my day and the occasional sleepless night. Thank You that even though I come to the end of my rope, Your rope has no end or limit! I find rest, sweet rest in You today.

When I'm in a wheelchair, riding in a special van with a raised roof, I can't see the road ahead. The scenery may be fascinating, but as the disabled passenger, I have no way of knowing. This can be a little frustrating on a long road trip.

Sometimes we're like this with God. We say to Him, "If You don't mind, please show me where I'm going. I don't need to see the whole road, but can't You at least give me a glimpse?" We long for a hint, a signpost, a whisper, or *something* to reveal where God might be taking us. Yes, He might tell us at times, but through most of life, He simply wants us to trust in Him. Today's Scripture reads, "Commit your way to the LORD; trust in him... and he will make your righteous reward shine like the dawn." God is wise and good. We can trust Him with the road ahead.

Lord, I would love to see around the bend—or just over the horizon. I'd like to have an airplane view of life, to see "how things work out." But You ask me to simply follow You step by step, hour by hour, moment by moment. I accept that today, Jesus. What matters most isn't where I'm going, but the reality that You are with me.

How do we keep going when we are hurting? How do we live? A friend once gave me some advice about living with chronic pain: *Just do the next thing.*[1] In other words, don't try to wrap your mind around a long season—or a lifetime—of discomfort and pain; just tackle the next hour, the next day, the next night. As Jesus said, "Don't worry about tomorrow, for tomorrow will bring its own worries. Today's trouble is enough for today." If you are dealing with any kind of pain today, just do the next thing. It may mean getting out of bed, getting up off the couch, getting out of the house, doing the laundry, or washing the dishes in the sink. Revelation 21:4 reminds us that very soon there will be no more night, pain, or tears. So press on as best you can and lean helplessly into His arms. You can do no more—and you can do no less.

Thank You, Lord Jesus, for reminding me that I only need to concern myself with living one day at a time, one hour at a time. I don't know what tomorrow will bring, but I know that whatever it may be, You will be there with me. And that's all I need to know.

---

1. Thanks to Dr. Michael Easley.

February

Yesterday you woke up happy and hopeful, the chronic pain evaporated like morning mist; your family was cheerful at breakfast; or God spoke so clearly to you in His Word. But today? The pain has returned; you had sharp words with your spouse; or God seemed to be vacationing in the Bahamas. It could all be discouraging, until you remember the words of Job in today's Scripture: "Shall we accept good from God, and not trouble?" In other words, God Himself is good and worthy of praise, and we will give thanks to Him for whatever the day brings. But in the meantime, don't forget to value and treasure the days that are simply *normal.* Mary Jean Irion writes, "Normal day, let me be aware of the treasure you are... let me not pass you by in quest of some rare and perfect tomorrow."[1] Today will soon enough become yesterday. Don't let it slip away without thanks.

Father, I praise You for the gift of today. I know it will never come again. I thank You for life—for another twenty-four hours to know You, to walk with You, and to let You touch other lives through me. It's only one day, Lord. But right now, it's the only day that matters.

---

1. Mary Jean Irion, "Let Me Hold You While I May," in *Yes, World: A Mosaic of Meditation* (New York: Baron, 1970), 53.

Sometimes we like to imagine swapping lives with others—lives that look more attractive and desirable than our own. The cleaned-up, airbrushed impression we get on Facebook makes us envious of their opportunities, their marriage, their vacations, or their families. But the truth is, we really don't know what's *inside* their lives, behind those smiling "selfies" they post.

At the same time, we tend to forget our own inside story. We forget how God has equipped and enabled us with special abilities to cope, grow, and thrive through life's challenges. We forget the loyal friends and wonderful people He has placed around us and the many times He has helped us, encouraged us, forgiven us, and pulled us out of trouble. We forget the incomparable, eternal purposes He has for our lives. Would we really want to swap places with someone else? How much better to be thankful and content with God's provision!

Lord, please forgive me for allowing envy into my heart. Forgive me for comparing myself, my opportunities, and my circumstances to the superficial impressions I have of other people's situations. Forgive me for so quickly forgetting all of Your many kindnesses, miraculous provisions, Holy Spirit-inspired insights, and songs in the night. Thank You for making me who I am and placing me where I am.

On a day when discouragement steals across your life like an afternoon shadow, it's a good time to stash your smartphone, turn off the TV, open your Bible, and read today's Scripture. Let the words flow across your soul. Read them out loud. One day, there will be a great shout—the actual voice of a mighty archangel—and the clear call of a trumpet. Then, in a single heartbeat, we will actually be *with* the Lord—and with all the believers who have gone before us. It will be forever! Paul concludes, "Therefore encourage one another with these words." So if your anxieties have been pulling you down or your situation is coloring your world blue, take courage from these truths. And then go out and encourage someone else. Sometimes people have been looking down for so long that they need just a little nudge to look up.

Dear God, I get so excited with the *reality* that You could call me at any moment. One minute, I'll be in my chair—and in a single blink, I'll be with You in the air, dancing in the clouds, embracing my dad and mom and so many wonderful friends who have already crossed over. I must wait for that moment, but really, I can't wait!

King Solomon wrote, "Cast your bread upon the waters, for you will find it after many days." What did he mean? Here's how I read it: When God gives you some extraordinary blessing, don't clutch it with a white-knuckled grip, or you may destroy the very thing that makes it a blessing to you. The poet William Blake wrote, "He who binds to himself a joy, does the winged life destroy; but he who kisses the joy as it flies lives in eternity's sunrise."[1]

Hold life's blessings loosely. Be thankful for the people, places, and situations God brings into your life today, but also be willing to let the blessings go, should God choose to take them away. One day He will return what He has removed—or replace it with something better.

Lord, I have lost much in life, but I have gained more. And what I have lost isn't really lost; it's just gone ahead of me. Help me to cling to You, the Giver, rather than to the beautiful gifts You've given me in Your kindness and love. With Your help, I open my hands and release my grip.

---

1. My thanks to Peter Sumner, director of the Christian Blind Mission in New Zealand, for this quotation and insight.

If you've had a long day or a nonstop, high-pressured week, you can open your Bible almost in the middle and find indescribable reassurance in these ten words: "My soul clings to you; your right hand upholds me." Consider all the things God does with His hands. He has carved out beds for great rivers, puckered up mountain ranges, ladled out seas, and dug channels for molten lava. We're talking here about very strong hands. But they are also gentle. The hands of Jesus touched a man with leprosy and made him whole, swept across blind eyes and made them see, and took the cold, dead hand of a little girl and raised her up alive. In the end, those hands were outstretched on a rough wooden beam and pierced with sharp Roman spikes for our eternal salvation. Right now, Jesus upholds *you* with His right hand. Pause, consider that, and give Him praise. And then *rest*.

Father, I remember how David said, "You are my God. My times are in your hands."[1] You cradle my days, my nights, my very life, and my eternal destiny in those hands. You shield me, comfort me, and guide me. No matter what crosses my path today, I am safe in Your hands.

---

1. Psalm 31:14–15.

In today's Scripture, Paul tells us, "Being confident of this, that he who began a good work in you will carry it on to completion until the day of Christ Jesus." Maybe you've felt paralyzed in your spiritual life. You truly long to grow closer to Jesus, but life feels more like a spinning carousel than a gallop toward a horizon. You may feel like you've been stuck for months—or years. Today is a perfect time to step off the carousel.

Begin by grabbing hold of Philippians 1:6 in faith. Start *believing* it. Ask the Holy Spirit to fulfill His promise. Quote the verse back to Him. Then roll up your sleeves and get actively engaged in your own growth. Obey God in the hard things. Persevere when you feel like giving up. Dig into the Word, even when it doesn't appeal to you. Set aside time to seek Him in prayer. Now, you are really moving.

Dear Lord, how I need that confidence Paul writes about! I want to see that I'm really going somewhere in my walk with You—and not just in circles. I do believe You have begun something strong and good in my life. Carry it forward today. You, only You, are my strength and help.

The spiritual battleground in my life isn't over a torrid love affair or road trips to Las Vegas. My paralysis prevents me from reaching for common temptations. My fight of faith is played out on the field of my thoughts. What my body can't have, my mind will shift into overdrive to deliver. But daydreams and fantasies only frustrate, bringing restlessness and dissatisfaction with God's lordship in my life. Theologian and pastor John Piper says the way you fight fire is with fire. The fire of enticing thoughts must be fought with the fire of the pleasures God offers.[1] Our battle involves more than rejecting evil; it means pursuing God with everything. When faith in Christ has the upper hand in our hearts, we are utterly satisfied with Him. He's enough. He's sufficient.

You once said, Lord Jesus, that if I drink the water You give, I will never thirst. And I would echo the woman you met at the well, "Give me this water so that I won't get thirsty."[2] I kneel at Your spring of cold, clear water—the water of Life—and drink my fill.

---

1. For a more complete discussion, be sure to read Dr. John Piper's book, *The Pleasures of God* (Colorado Springs: Multnomah, 2000).
2. John 4:13–15.

In his second letter, the apostle Peter writes, "Do not forget this one thing, dear friends: With the Lord a day is like a thousand years, and a thousand years are like a day."[1] We've all heard the adage that God looks at the last two thousand years as a couple of days gone by, but what about viewing each day as a thousand years?

In God's great wisdom and power, He can take one day of our lives and give it a thousand years' worth of impact. We should never underestimate even the smallest opportunities to serve others in the name and power of Jesus Christ. Writing a note, making a call, helping with a task, or offering a sympathetic, listening ear may resound more of God's glory than you or I could possibly imagine. And investing a few minutes in heartfelt prayer for someone is far, far mightier than we might comprehend. In fact, the echoes roll on forever.

Lord, open my eyes to the truth that even the smallest act of obedience and faith, accomplished in Your power and blessed with Your favor, can have an impact that goes far beyond the years of my life, and even beyond time itself.

---

1. 2 Peter 3:8.

As time passes and followers of Jesus grow older, we are moving in two directions at the same time. Today's Scripture affirms, "We do not lose heart. Though outwardly we are wasting away, yet inwardly we are being renewed day by day." Do you see the two directions in this passage? On the one hand, our physical abilities and strength diminish with the passing years. You can feel it—whether you are thirty or eighty. On the other hand, if we are walking with Christ, experiencing the renewal of His Spirit, our spiritual abilities and strength increase every day. This process goes on until our physical life gives out. But in that very instant, our new life in heaven begins. So if you're feeling a few aches and pains, no matter what age you are, remember that outwardly, you will fade, but inwardly, the flame in your spirit will burn brighter and brighter until God says, "It's time, dear child. Come on home, now."

Thank You, Lord, for renewing my life day by day through Your Word and Your Holy Spirit. The pain and physical struggles of today remind me of a soon tomorrow when I will be forever young and strong and filled with joy in Your presence.

The apostle Paul knew how to be joyful. This is the man who wrote, "Rejoice in the Lord always. I will say it again: Rejoice!" But he also confessed to "great sorrow and unceasing anguish in my heart" over the spiritual lostness of his Jewish race. He described Christ's apostles as "sorrowful, yet always rejoicing."[1] James advised us to "grieve, mourn and wail" when we sin and break fellowship with Jesus.[2]

The fact is, sorrow, tears, and disappointment are written into God's plan for us. Yes, He lightens and brightens our days with glimpses of paradise; He gives foretastes of the great joys to come through a thousand blessings, large and small. But we're not in heaven yet. And here on this side of life, we—along with everyone else—will experience a measure of sorrow. When those sad times come, however, we turn our gaze to Jesus—remembering that He carried our sorrows on the cross and will certainly walk with us through all of our troubles.

When I grieve, dear God, thank You for supporting me with Your presence. Let my tears help me to know You better and drive me into Your comforting arms. With the psalmist, I declare, "When anxiety was great within me, your consolation brought joy to my soul."[3]

1. Philippians 4:4; Romans 9:2; 2 Corinthians 6:10.   2. James 4:9.
3. Psalm 94:19, NIV 1984.

My friend Bob Bjerkaas tells me that Christians can learn something from sharks. Sharks almost always move forward with their mouths open. The Creator designed their gills in such a way that they have to keep moving in order to breathe, in order to stay alive.

As a Christian, you were no more designed to remain static in your walk with Christ than sharks were designed to stay suspended in the ocean. In today's Scripture, Paul encourages us to do the same: To keep moving forward! To press on. To strain toward what is ahead. The apostle had no time for relishing past accomplishments or beating himself up over past failures or missed opportunities. He forgot what was behind and moved ahead. You must move forward, making every effort to reach for the highest and best. Understand the absolute necessity of pressing ahead, daily breathing in the Word of God and the Spirit of God. Life is forward!

Lord, forgive me for dwelling on past hurts and disappointments—or faded tributes and long-ago moments in the spotlight. Fill me afresh with Your Spirit and Your Word. No matter how I feel, help me to press onward and upward, reaching for Your best.

In February, you might see farmers on their tractors, out in last year's hayfields and cornfields, furrowing the soil. There is nothing like the sweet, musty, wet scent of soil tilled deep by the plow. When the tractor passes over the dirt, it cuts a yawning channel in the field, turning over that rich, dark earth, getting it ready to receive fresh seed, water, and sun. I'm reminded of the old Scottish preacher Samuel Rutherford, who wrote, "Why should I start at the plough of my Lord, that maketh deep furrows on my soul? I know He is no idle husbandman, He purposeth a crop!"[1]

This may be a season in your life when you are being furrowed. The Spirit of God is passing over your soul, churning up channels for new seed, the water of the Word, and the warmth of the Son. It is God who is heaven-bent on producing a crop in your life, a beautiful harvest of righteousness.

Dear God, I want a rich harvest in my life. I truly do! I want to bear fruit for You during my time on earth. But I need Your grace when the plow cuts deep, when familiar things change and spring seems long in coming. Bring forth Your life in my life today.

---

1. Samuel Rutherford, *The Loveliness of Christ* (Moscow, Ida.: Community Christian Ministries, 1990), 10.

The apostle Paul was no plaster saint. He didn't walk two inches off the ground or wear a halo. He was a real human being who faced pressures, temptations, and anxieties. In today's Scripture, he took action so he would have less anxiety. Paul knew what it meant to be troubled and discouraged—but he also knew what to do about it. In the same letter, he wrote, "Don't worry about anything; instead, pray about everything. Tell God what you need, and thank him for all he has done. Then you will experience God's peace, which exceeds anything we can understand."[1] Paul isn't saying your pain will go away or the circumstances will change. We don't find peace through a change of circumstance; we find peace *in* our stressful circumstances: the rock-solid peace of knowing God is with you, He's in charge, and you are safe and secure through your salvation in Christ.

Father, I know You have the power to change my painful circumstances. And I ask You to do that if You will. But if You are calling me to walk through this trial, then I ask You to show me the actions I need to take to reduce my anxious fears and feelings so I can focus on Your presence and Your peace.

---

1. Philippians 4:6–7, NLT.

Many of us identify very closely with the apostle Paul's tormenting thorn in the flesh described in today's Scripture. We don't know what Paul's thorn might have been, but we do know that even though he pleaded with Jesus to remove it, the thorn remained. What do we learn from this? For all the many times Paul was distressed by his weakness, he had the supporting grace of Christ. He kept saying over and over, "God's grace is sufficient for me." In fact, divine power finds its full scope and strength only in human weakness.

Both exasperating frailty and great power existed simultaneously in Paul's life. That's because grace always, always meets us at our point of pain! No matter what our need, though it be as deep and wide as the Grand Canyon, His grace will forever be enough to get us through.

Thank You, Father, for giving us a way to navigate the sometimes difficult pathways through this temporary, broken world. I think of Paul's words: "We are puzzled, but never in despair... persecuted, but we never have to stand it alone: we may be knocked down but we are never knocked out!"[1] I may walk in pain, but I also walk in grace.

---

1. 2 Corinthians 4:8–9, PHILLIPS.

The movie *Braveheart* depicts the moments just before the battle of Sterling in the thirteenth century. The Scots lose heart after seeing the size of the English army; they're ready to give up before anyone strikes a blow. But then William Wallace and his band ride up from the rear, with their faces painted blue. This simple fact of "showing up" gives new heart to the Scots. They take the field and win the day. Friend, the way you respond to setbacks in your life *does* matter. It matters to those looking on. When someone demonstrates bravery in the face of suffering or loss, others can't help but notice. And courage rises in the hearts of all. So hold on to the courage of Christ. Today's Scripture shows the power of example; sometimes the steady resolve of just one person can turn the tide of battle.

Lord Jesus, here I am, knocking on Your door, needing to borrow Your courage. You know very well that I have none of my own. If You loan me Your courage and Your endurance, then I won't be afraid of this challenge. And maybe others will seek You out because I did.

Have you ever been involved in a legal battle? No matter what you think about lawyers, having a good one at your side in a courtroom is an incredible comfort. Skilled lawyers pour a great deal of time and preparation into each case. And when he or she approaches the bench and convinces the judge with the facts—what a satisfying moment!

In today's Scripture, it's as though the Judge of all the earth invites us to approach His bench. He says, "Come now, and let us reason together." God loves it when we take the time to reason with Him, explaining why we think it would be His will for Him to do a certain thing. It shows the Lord we have searched His Word and carefully thought through our requests. So the next time you pray, first think through *why* you believe something to be God's will. Because the Judge is listening.

Lord God, You are the great Judge of the universe, but You are also my Father. When I am puzzled or perplexed, when I feel under attack by accusing voices, You invite me to come to You. And when I pour out my heart, You show Your love by listening to me. And then—praise Your name!—You act on my behalf.

How well do you know yourself? You know your height, weight, Social Security number, ATM PIN, favorite movie... but do you know your own sins? In today's Scripture, David writes, "I know my transgressions, and my sin is always before me." Do you know when you're vying for attention, shading the truth, or hiding the facts? Do you know when your words ring hollow, when you secretly cut corners, or when you let that illicit fantasy dance across your imagination? Do you know when you deliberately resist the Holy Spirit's voice to go in your own direction?

David told the Lord, "I *know* I have sinned. I admit it! I need Your cleansing." It has to start there, doesn't it? Because if we refuse to acknowledge our sins, if we try to whitewash our stubborn pride, if we live in the Land of Denial, we will never run into the merciful arms of our Savior, who loves to forgive and restore.

Lord Jesus, I do run to You, right now. I've had enough of trying to hide. As best as I know how, I open my life, my thoughts, my words, and my actions to Your inspection. Forgive me and heal me, I pray, because I need You today more than ever.

February 18 | MATTHEW 13:19

Can Satan hack into our thoughts like a cyberpirate hacks into a corporate network? That's a frightening thought. But it's true. Our adversary continually tries to tap into our brains and hack into our souls. The Bible calls him "the spirit who is now at work in those who are disobedient."[1] And today's Scripture describes his access to the human soul. Those who don't understand might scoff at this, but Christians know better. We understand the subtlety and power of this invisible invader. We may download antivirus software to protect our computers, but we have the Word of God and the Spirit of God to protect our thoughts and help us stand guard.

Put a barbed-wire fence around your thinking today. Learn to recognize every suggestion and every temptation of the enemy. The Bible reminds us that "the one who is in you is greater than the one who is in the world."[2]

Lord, keep me alert today—even in the midst of pressure, a full schedule, and unrelenting pain. As You have said, "The thief comes only to steal and kill and destroy."[3] Guard me against his attacks. Shield my thoughts and emotions from his lies and deceptions. Thank You for Your presence in the very center of my being!

1. Ephesians 2:2.   2. 1 John 4:4.   3. John 10:10.

We've all endured those long stretches of highway that seem to go on and on. It's hard to keep your mind awake and your eyes on a road that seems never ending. Obedience to the Lord can feel the same way. The horizon seems hazy and indistinct at times, and there's little variation in the scenery. It might be a marriage with ceaseless struggles, a church that produces little results, or caregiving for an elderly parent or a child with a disability.

In today's Scripture, Paul offers this strong counsel: "Let us not become weary in doing good, for at the proper time we will reap a harvest if we do not give up." Oh, friend, if you are tired of obeying God and remaining faithful in a day-in-day-out routine, don't allow your weariness to detour you. Draw deeply on His strength, and persevere in doing good. A harvest awaits if you don't give up.

Dear Lord, maybe I need a reminder today that this long stretch really is *going* somewhere. It's leading to a destination with every minute, every mile. The travel may be tiring at times, but it won't go on forever. Sooner or later, I will arrive—at either a new place in life or a new life altogether in Your presence.

On a day when sadness and regret hung heavy in the air, Nehemiah told God's people, "This day is holy to our LORD. Do not grieve, for the joy of the LORD is your strength." What did he mean by that, anyway? What is this "joy of the LORD"—and how do I find it?

First, this experience of joy doesn't have the slightest connection to your current circumstances, your emotional makeup, or the mood you woke up in this morning. It isn't *your* joy at all; you can't manufacture it, drum it up, or visualize it into existence. Second, this joy belongs to God. And He wants you to have it! He offers it as a gift of His Holy Spirit. He wants you to walk in it today and experience it to the full. How do you obtain it? You ask for it and then open your life to receive it.

Lord, in spite of my circumstances today and how I feel at this very moment, I ask that Your joy will rise within me. By faith, I take joy in all that really matters most—a heavenly Father who loves me, a Lord who is both Brother and Friend, and a Holy Spirit who is my Comforter, Counselor, and the Source of a joy so much deeper and sweeter than my own.

Here's an understatement: Battling stage III breast cancer is no fun. One day when my husband, Ken, was driving me home from chemotherapy, we discussed how sufferings are "splash-overs of hell"—gritty, gut-wrenching reminders of the horrors Christ rescued us from. As Ken pulled into our driveway, we then wondered, "What are splash-overs of heaven? Are they easy, bright times when everything's going right?" After a long silence, Ken looked at me and with wet eyes whispered, "No, Joni. It's when we see Jesus in our splash-over of hell."

For reasons known only to himself, the Father calls us to intimacy with His Son on His terms—and those terms call for us to suffer, in some measure, as His Son did while He was on earth. Yes, suffering may seem like a high price to pay for having Christ as a confidant. But He is ecstasy beyond words. It's worth *anything* to be His friend.

Lord, I'm thinking about the words of a song—"I am a friend of God... He calls me friend." But being Your friend is more than a light, happy, bouncy song. That friendship came at an unspeakable price. You suffered and gave Your very life, so I could be forgiven, adopted as Your daughter, and blessed to experience Your friendship forever.

On a dry hilltop, in a classic confrontation between Baal and the God of Israel, the prophet Elijah exposed an imitation god that could never really hear or help anyone. "Shout louder!" Elijah taunted. "Surely he is a god! Perhaps he is deep in thought, or busy, or traveling. Maybe he is sleeping and must be awakened." We might cheer on Elijah here, but have you ever thought something similar? What about those dry and weary times in prayer when you wonder if God is listening at all? Do you ever imagine Him off in another part of the universe, busy with this or that, and paying little attention to your cries?

The truth is, He is never too busy! Your God is constant, and—whether or not you feel like it—you have His undivided attention. He never takes a nap, never becomes distracted, and never forgets even the smallest details of your concerns.

Lord, I guess this has been one of those times when I feel a little distant from You. Your comfort seems over the horizon somewhere, and discouragement presses in on me. Today, I declare by faith that You are with me, as close and attentive and loving as You have ever been. I choose to rest in this strong reality.

When you first believed in Christ, someone may have told you, "God loves you and has a wonderful plan for your life." So you launched out on your spiritual journey, comforted to know that God has a special purpose just for you. But then, when troubles piled up—you received a bad medical report or your marriage fell apart—did you feel like you somehow got separated from that "wonderful plan"? In today's Scripture, David writes, "I cry out to God Most High, to God who will fulfill his purpose for me." There really is a purpose for your life, and God certainly *will* fulfill it. But that plan also includes some difficulty, pain, and disappointment. Jesus made this clear when He said, "In this world you will have trouble. But take heart! I have overcome the world."[1] Hardships will come. But in Him, we *over*come.

Lord, how grateful I am that You have a game plan for my life, and that I don't have to arrange events or force outcomes to make it all happen. I trust Your heart for me today. I rest in Your wise and loving plan, even when it includes situations that seem like obstacles and roadblocks.

---

1. John 16:33.

Luke shares an account of a hemorrhaging woman who reaches out, brushes her fingers across the edge of the Lord's cloak as He walks by, and experiences instant healing. In a stunning painting capturing that moment, artist Ron DiCianni portrays her on hands and knees, one arm outstretched, desperately trying to make contact with the hem of Jesus' garment as he walks by. In a sense, it's a picture of each of us. Today. Right now. You have worries and anxieties. Maybe it's health concerns or relationship strains with someone dear to you. Maybe it's the ravages of depression. You're scared, struggling, and lonelier than you can ever remember. Never forgot that Jesus is near—so near you can almost reach out and touch Him. *Do it!* Right now. Don't let the moment pass by. Touch His robe—you've already touched His heart. Reach out in heartfelt prayer. He will not disappoint you.

Lord Jesus, do You see my hand? I'm stretching it out. I'm reaching for You. You know the issues of my life—my doubts, fears, pain, and even the longings I've never shared with another soul. I believe in Your love, Your power, and Your healing. Renew my hope today, for I am placing all my confidence in You.

Pain medications are a mixed blessing. Some remedies ease the immediate bite of pain, but they open the door to anxiety. Others create scary claustrophobia or wire-tight, jangled nerves. The best remedy, however, is one that reduces stress and anxious feelings. Isaiah has helpful counsel: "The fruit of that righteousness will be peace; its effect will be quietness and confidence forever." Nothing quiets pain better than a body at rest and a soul at peace. God's Word says this will be the result when you pursue right living. Keep in step with the Spirit, practice genuine gratitude, keep the door to prayer cracked open, get into your Bible, and give God's love to others. In short, seek out God and His ways, and the *effect* will be quietness of mind, heart, body, and soul.

Father, I've experienced anxiety again and again. Your Word says, "You will keep him in perfect peace, whose mind is stayed on You, because he trusts in You."[1] When I see Your face through my pain, the stress slips away and the tangles in my anxious thoughts unravel. Yes, it still hurts, but I don't face that hurt alone. I have You, the living God, to bring me peace.

---

1. Isaiah 26:3, NKJV.

The servant of the prophet Elisha went out for a casual stroll along the top of the walled city. What he saw made his blood freeze. The morning sun gleamed and flashed from the shields, swords, arrows, and spears of an invading army surrounding the city. Terrified, he scampered back to report the terrible news. Elisha's reply was calm: "Don't be afraid... Those who are with us are more than those who are with them." And then the servant "saw the hills full of horses and chariots of fire all around Elisha." What was true for Elisha and his servant is true for every believer. Invisible, spiritual realities surround us. Holy angels observe and protect us. David wrote, "The angel of the LORD encamps around those who fear him, and he delivers them."[1] So today, remember that there is more to life than what you see with your physical eyes. And know that you are never, ever alone.

Lord, thank You for the presence and protection of Your mighty angels. Thank You for the times they have intervened in my life—turning me, redirecting me, alerting me—when I wasn't even aware of their help. I look forward to the day when I will worship You alongside these wonderful fellow servants of Jesus.

---

1. Psalm 34:7.

Morning to night, Jesus walked weary miles, declared God's kingdom, debated hostile leaders, and performed miracle after miracle. From dawn to dusk, He confronted demons, healed broken bodies, mentored followers, and plowed the hard ground of stubbornness, hatred, and willful unbelief. But He still found time to be alone with His Father, praying before sunrise or late into the night. His prayers were earnest, honest, and filled with complete confidence in His Father.

Are you in a busy season? Follow our Lord's example by cultivating an inner walk of faith and a quiet heart. In the midst of your activities, remember that Jesus is at the bottom of the laundry basket; He's under the car hood; He's in the line of figures you're tallying and in the booth you are serving as you refill coffee mugs. Use even *those* times to sing a hymn, quote a Scripture, and breathe a word of thanks to the One who loves you.

Thank You, Lord, for Your promise in Psalm 139 that wherever we are, You are there too. In the light and in the dark. At home or across an ocean. And You are in the middle of every pressured day, every responsibility, if only I have the eyes to see. Reveal Yourself, Lord, in the busiest minutes of my day.

Whenever cucumber season rolls around, I think about my sister Jay, who lives on our family farm in Maryland. Jay's garden always produces a bumper crop of beautiful cucumbers that she boils, blanches, strains, and seals into unbelievable pickles. Her secret? Salt. Jay says the best way to preserve a pickle at its crunchiest, tastiest best is to add *a lot* of salt. Of course, two of those words have gone together for thousands of years—*salt* and *preserve*. In today's Scripture, Jesus says, "You are the salt of the earth." As followers of Jesus, we are a salty preservative in our culture, infusing godly values into life around us. We've been given the work of restraining evil and advancing good. And just as salt brings out the flavor in food, don't forget to "season" your conversations with Christ when people ask the reason for the hope that you have.[1]

Lord, please don't let me lose my flavor, my edge. You've called me to be salty, to have a distinctive tang and taste that stands out from the empty, tasteless values of the culture. Please don't allow the distractions and trials of my life to wash me out and dilute my testimony. Help me to be the salt You've called me to be.

---

1. Colossians 4:6; 1 Peter 3:15.

March

Some events in life might compare to a hammer tap; others feel like a wrecking ball. These are times when it seems the very walls and structures of life have collapsed, and nothing will ever be the same. It may be a health reversal, the loss of a child or spouse, or a sudden financial setback. How are we to live among such ruins, when everything familiar has changed? Today's Scripture offers this hope. God says, "I have loved you with an everlasting love; I have drawn you with unfailing kindness. I will build you up again, and you... will be rebuilt." God promises Israel—and us— that He will work among the ruins, and do so with loving-kindness. Life may never look as it once did, and the landscape may be changed, but if God is behind the reconstruction, He will bring beauty and purpose where you thought you would never see it again.

Lord Jesus, I want to partner with You in this. Help me not to spend the rest of my days looking over my shoulder, remembering what was—the way things used to be. In Your strong, gentle grace, renew my vision and align my heart with Your plans, Your intentions, for the rest of my life.

In today's Scripture, David writes, "I will sing of your strength, in the morning I will sing of your love; for you are my fortress, my refuge in times of trouble." David made such a *good* life choice here. Somewhere in his growing-up years, perhaps when he was just a shepherd boy watching sheep, he decided to begin his day with God. No matter what was going on in his life, he took time to reflect on the strength, love, goodness, and protection of the Lord. The prologue to this very psalm reveals that David continued this practice—even though men outside his front door were waiting to kill him! The Bible makes the point that there's something special about seeking God in the morning, especially in times of trouble. When you begin the day singing about His strength, you'll be less likely to "sing the blues" when the day is over.

How good it is, Father, to color this day with praise before any other brushes paint it in dark shades of cynicism, negative talk, and despair. Thank You for meeting me in the quiet corners of the morning. With David, I say, "You are my fortress, and my strong refuge. I sing of Your strength and love because You share it so generously with me!"

When a particular trouble intrudes into our life, it has a way of taking over. It dominates our thoughts, controls our emotions, saps our will, and drains our energy. Eventually, it crowds and bullies every good thing out of our day. As God's children, we can't let that happen. Today's Scripture tells us God has blessed us in the heavenly realms. He's given us peace of heart and mind—something the world craves but can't find. He's given us faith to pass through deep waters. He's given us the grace to give and to let go. He's given us the sweet knowledge that we have an eternal home in heaven, waiting for us just around the bend. He's given us His own Spirit as Counselor and Comforter. He's washed away our sins and forgotten our evil deeds. We have more going for us than His own angels, who have never tasted such grace.

God, there are times when I give in to my pain or surrender to my anxiety, allowing these troubles to fill my heart with dread or fear. In such times, I ask You to remind me of all the gifts You have given me. Help me to wash away the dark thoughts with fresh gratitude and heartfelt praise.

When you are homesick, what images come to mind? Maybe you think of an old house, familiar in every detail and dear to you. Maybe you remember well-loved faces and voices, now far away. It's possible you are homesick for a city, for a neighborhood, for a pet, for fireflies, for sweet summer roses, for old-favorite home-cooked meals, or for the sound of wind in the maple trees. Out of nowhere, a certain something will remind you of home and stir your longing.

Those who love the Lord and have walked with Him for years are sometimes homesick for heaven, a place where they belong but have never been. They dream of the Lord's return. They long to be clothed in pure garments, white as snow. They think about angels; a restored earth; a strong, new body; and loved ones who have already crossed over. Mostly, they think of Jesus—Savior and Friend, Lord and Bridegroom, Shepherd and King.

I'm grateful for my life, Lord. I'm grateful for my family and friends. I'm thankful for the work You've given me to do. But You know my heart. I get so weary of this sin-sick world, and deep down, I just want to "depart and be with Christ, which is better by far."[1] I want to go Home.

---

1. Philippians 1:23.

Sometimes those who deal with disabilities feel like no one understands their heartaches and struggles. They may even wonder if God Himself understands. The answer is, "Yes, He does!" He understands because He is God, but He also understands through personal experience. Jesus, the Son of God, also endured a disability through His life on earth: His was *sorrow*. Today's Scripture reads, "He was despised and rejected—a man of sorrows, acquainted with deepest grief." The suffering of earth became His lifelong disability. The shadow of the cross fell over every day of His life. The author of Hebrews writes that while Jesus walked on earth, "he offered up prayers and petitions with fervent cries and tears."[1] Jesus dealt with lifelong sorrow, knowing what awaited Him on the cross. He understands disability and carrying heavy burdens. You can open your heart completely to Him.

Lord Jesus, You truly are my High Priest. You have experienced everything I've ever faced. You even carried the shame and sorrow of my sins, paying my penalty, though You had no sins of Your own. You sympathize with my pain and discouragement. You count every one of my tears. Draw me close to You today, and be my Shelter.

---

1. Hebrews 5:7.

Friendship in Christ is more than just spending time with someone. Today's Scripture reminds us that we are to consider—think creatively about—encouraging one another in our Christian walk. Our relationships in the Lord are either moving onward and upward, or we are diminishing each other. We are to see our friends in the light of what God intends for them to become. It's a mistake to think we can let down our guard or allow ourselves to be blah, blue, crabby, or selfish just because we're with those who "already know us." Life in Christ is more intentional than that! Our friends need to see us walking with Jesus and filled with His Spirit. They need to hear wise, positive, helpful words from us, rather than empty, cynical, or complaining words. Look for fresh ways you can spur on your friends in their growth in Christ.

Dear God, help me not to become complacent or lazy about my friendships. Set a guard at my tongue, Lord, and keep me from saying empty, ungrateful, faithless words—and from using my physical difficulties or weariness as an excuse.

Well-meaning people will sometimes say to me, "Joni, God knows He can trust you with suffering. He knows your character. He knows you're strong and that you'll respond well to hardships." My reply always takes people aback a little. I will say, "You're not even close. It's the very opposite of what you are saying." I think God entrusts hardships to me because He knows that *I can't be trusted.* I fully accept that I am the least likely candidate to handle affliction well. I know how weak I can be. And how stubborn, peevish, and irritable. And this is why I run to God daily for help! "Oh, help me, Jesus! I can't face another day of quadriplegia!" When I hurry to God with that attitude, He lavishes grace upon grace on me—all because I'm so quick to realize my weakness and His strength, and that my need for Him is not partial, but total.

Lord, I know I will never forget these things—because I don't dare forget them! I need You desperately—every waking and sleeping moment. I couldn't fake being courageous and strong, even if I wanted to. You have made me helpless to show that my total help is in You. And what a good, kind, and faithful Helper You have been to me.

The Bible tells us to be perfect as our Father in heaven is perfect.[1] But how do we do that? Is that an awfully high standard? Actually, with His help, it is doable. Today's Scripture says to "avoid sexual immorality." It doesn't take much analysis. *Just avoid it.* If you want an expanded definition, it means "to keep away from, keep clear of, shun." If you find yourself enticed by wrong desires, do something about it. Turn off the TV, make your exit from the movie, hang up the phone, cancel the subscription, switch off the computer, or even walk out of the room.

Remember Joseph? He *ran*, leaving his coat behind.[2] Is it hard to do? Yes. Will God help you if you ask Him? Yes, again. To be honest, one of the most crucial priorities of our whole Christian life involves refusing to allow our desires and appetites to rule the day.

Father, even now, at this point in my life, I need to develop the habit of saying no to myself. No to the "semi-innocent" fantasies that tiptoe into my mind. No to the appetites that seek to rule me. The more I say no to the little things, the easier it will be to say no to the big temptations when they seem to rise up out of nowhere.

---

1. Matthew 5:48.   2. Genesis 39:12.

Have you ever sunk your teeth into a golden, sun-ripened peach just plucked from the tree? Once you do, it will make supermarket peaches taste like Styrofoam. A juicy, freshly harvested peach tastes the way a peach is *supposed* to taste, with no loss of essential peachiness.

Galatians 5 tells us that God's Spirit living within us will produce beautiful, flavorful fruit—far, far better than even the sweetest California or Georgia peach. This life-transforming fruit is genuine love, joy, peace, patience, and kindness. If you try to fake it and project these things on your own—faux love and plastic peace—it ends up tasting like Styrofoam, and the Spirit of Jesus will have nothing to do with it. Today's Scripture reminds us, "No branch can bear fruit by itself; it must remain in the vine." Son-ripened fruit is by far the best!

Holy Spirit, produce the sweet, genuine fruit of Jesus in me. Don't let me get away with phony peace, shallow love, and a thin veneer of kindness. I want people to taste the real thing in my life—a fresh tang that can never be mistaken for my poor efforts. And I want Jesus to receive the glory, not me—which I know is what You want too.

Driving along a two-lane mountain road at night, your headlights may fall on several of those yellow, diamond-shaped signs with black, squiggly arrows in the middle. They caution you that the road ahead—hidden from your sight—is about to twist and turn, following the contours of the mountain. But that's okay; the road will still get you to your destination.

The Bible posts many such hazard signs within its pages. We're reminded that the way ahead is filled with drop-offs, potholes, and sudden turns. Today's Scripture reads, "Your word is a lamp for my feet, a light on my path." You wouldn't drive that curvy mountain road at night without your lights on. And you don't want to race into the rest of your day—or your life—without the counsel, warnings, and illumination of God's Word.

Heavenly Father, without Your Word I really would be wandering in the dark. So many times, in so many moments, You bring the right truth to my mind at precisely the right time. Your encouragement gets me through long afternoons when pain looms and anxieties roll in like fog. Thank You for lighting my path and putting a song in my heart.

Nothing compares to the coziness of a snapping, popping campfire in the morning by a misty lake or a rushing stream. And when you've got coffee percolating and bacon sizzling over the flames, well, it's a little slice of heaven on earth. In the evening, when you come back to the ashes, there are usually a few glowing coals that can be coaxed back to life with fresh fuel and a little blowing on them. Before long, you've got a roaring campfire again. It's the same with the Spirit of Christ in our lives.

Today's Scripture reads, "Fan into flame the gift of God, which is in you." This isn't a suggestion; it's a command. We must constantly do this, or the flame within us may flicker, fade, and die. Look for those sparks, those glowing embers in your soul. If there is the slightest glow, the faintest hint of faith, take heart! It's not too late to catch fire.

Lord, please find the coals in my heart and blow on them. Restore the bright flame of Your presence and Your joy. Forgive me for letting the fire burn low. Help me to use the gifts You have given me for the good of Your people—just because I know it pleases You.

Human lives don't count for much in some places. Extremist groups in Africa and the Middle East murder whole populations. In some American cities, life on the streets can be harsh, hard, and deadly. And even Christians in our own country sometimes buy into the world's ethics when it comes to judging the value of human life. If people suffer from dementia or are in a coma or severely disabled, their lives don't seem to have much value. In today's Scripture, Jesus speaks about the incalculable value of a single soul: "What good will it be for someone to gain the whole world, yet forfeit their soul? Or what can anyone give in exchange for their soul?" Lives—no matter if they are disabled, elderly, or unborn—matter to God. Jesus scoffs at the price tags people place on an eternal human soul. The men, women, and little ones He created have incalculable worth.

Lord, I know this world is my temporary home, the place where I hang my hat. I live and work here. But I don't want to be shaped and colored by the careless attitudes around me. Please don't let me be squeezed into the world's mold. I want You to be the One who shapes my thoughts and attitudes.

It's not uncommon for someone to feel angry at God. Many believers, however, are reluctant or afraid to bare such feelings, so they bottle them up. But that's not what God wants. God can handle your questions, your disappointment, and your anger. Today's Scripture reads, "In your anger do not sin," so we know that not all anger is wrong. The next part of the passage reads, "Do not let the sun go down while you are still angry, and do not give the devil a foothold." You can either move *toward* God with your heated questions or move away from Him. The thing you never want to do is to talk badly about Him, causing others to be angry or cynical. And you don't want to nurse your anger, letting it turn into bitterness. No, rather take it all to the Lord. He is big enough to handle your anger, and gentle enough to comfort your heart.

Father, You have heard my angry prayers—prayers uttered through tears and clenched teeth. And You have never turned away from me. You really *hear* me when I pour out my heart to You. Thank You for Your patient love. Thank You for my High Priest, the Lord Jesus, who understands and sympathizes with every longing in my heart.

I find myself praying often for endurance. My quadriplegia and struggle with pain have a lot to do with it, but so does the command in today's Scripture: "Let us hold fast the confession of our hope without wavering." In the book of Revelation, Jesus says, "Hold fast... until I come."[1] And James writes, "Blessed is the one who perseveres under trial because... that person will receive the crown of life."[2]

Just how, then, do I pray for endurance? I ask God to keep me, preserve me, and defeat every rising rebellion or doubt in my heart. I ask God to deliver me from the temptation to complain. I ask Him to crush the camera when I start running mental movies of my successes. And you can do the same. Ask the Lord to incline your heart, master your will, and do whatever must be done to keep you trusting and fearing Him until Jesus comes. Hold fast! That day will come soon.

Praise You, Lord Jesus, for telling me to hold fast and then giving me the ability to do what I could never do in my own strength. Thank You, Holy Spirit, for coming alongside me, whispering encouragement, and holding my head above water when trials come in like a flood.

---

1. Revelation 2:25, ESV.   2. James 1:12.

Being in heaven with our God will never—not for one instant—be boring. Here on earth, wired as we are to live in space and time, just about anything that goes on for a while has a boredom factor. Even a great vacation at a beach resort with perfect weather and all the amenities has the potential to feel empty if it goes on too long. Not so with heaven.

Eternity is not boring changelessness, because that implies a passage of time. Eternity is timeless; time doesn't "pass." Words like *trillions of years* have no meaning there. Eternity simply *is*. We are wrong if we imagine heaven as wispy, thin, and vaporous. No, it is earth that is like withering grass, not heaven. Heaven will be more vital than anything we have ever experienced on earth. Our relationship with God will be dynamic, enthralling, ever-new, infinitely expanding, and pushing into new dimensions of joy, peace, fulfillment, and intense satisfaction.

Father, I'm so thankful You instructed us to set our sights on the realities of heaven, where Christ sits in the place of honor at God's right hand, and to think about the things of heaven, not the things of earth. You not only give us permission to dream about the next life, but You also command it!

It's one thing to mess up, neglect your duties, or out-and-out sin and be criticized for it. But what about when you're maligned for *doing good*? You may find yourself thinking, *How dare those people fault me? Don't they see my generosity? My sacrifice? My sincerity?* When these thoughts surface, it's time for a biblical reality check.

The apostle Peter says that when you do good, you will sometimes suffer for it. You will be criticized; things won't necessarily get better; and many people won't even care. Earlier in the passage, Peter says to return undeserved insults with a blessing, "because to this you were called."[1] Friend, this is your calling as a follower of Jesus. Not to hurt back. Not to nurse your resentment. Instead, to keep on doing good for Jesus' sake and in His name. Sound impossible? It is! But in Christ, even the impossible is possible.

Lord, You know my heart. I *hate* being misunderstood or taken for granted. It stings when I feel unfairly criticized. Everything in my natural self wants to defend myself or dismiss others with a sarcastic remark. All I can do, Lord, is humbly admit this—and ask for Your grace and strength to return good for evil.

---

1. 1 Peter 3:9.

All of us will lose loved ones during this life. As much as we wish it were otherwise, it just comes with the territory on this broken planet. Yes, sometimes God chooses to answer our prayers for healing and grants a reprieve. At other times, we're left wondering why it didn't happen for us. A man who recently lost his wife to breast cancer took comfort that, while his prayer for healing wasn't granted, another prayer *was* answered. In today's Scripture, Jesus prays, "Father, I want those you have given me to be with me where I am, and to see my glory." It's the heartfelt prayer of God's Son for all those who love Him. So the length of time we live on earth or whether or not we get healed isn't really the point, is it? The point is, we're all headed for heaven—the place where in the end Jesus wants us to be.

Lord Jesus, Your prayer in John 17 encourages my heart beyond all words. I hear longing in Your words to the Father. You truly want Your redeemed ones to be with You in heaven—forever! You want to show me glories I can't even begin to imagine. You are as homesick for me as I am for You. What an incredible thought!

The apostle Paul said he had "learned to be content whatever the circumstances."[1] The key word is *learned*. It didn't happen overnight. In time, however, Paul could even write those words from a prison cell. But how can *we* know whether we have learned this secret? This may be the litmus test: Are you prepared to lose what you have?

Despite Job's grief and agony, he made this strong statement about God in today's Scripture: "Though he slay me, yet will I hope in him." Though he had been staggered by blow after blow of bad news, Job took his stand on the character of God. He believed with all his heart that God had supplied him with all he needed. And even if God took it all away—including life itself—Job would remain faithful. That's the real bottom line of contentment. If tomorrow God takes away your health, your job, or even a family member, will you hold on to hope?

Being content in You, Jesus, is all I really want. You have given me many, many wonderful gifts, people, and opportunities. You have filled my life to the brim—and running over. But if You choose to remove those gifts and treasures, one by one, I will remember all You have given me in Jesus...and be content.

---

1. Philippians 4:11.

The New Testament teaches that crowns will be given as rewards when we arrive in heaven. Some people just shrug their shoulders at this. They're not excited at all. We're happy about the thought of no more tears and new, strong resurrection bodies that will last forever—but crowns? Unless you're a child, you're probably not jumping up and down at that thought. But maybe you should be, because the Bible makes much of the crowning day—even mentioning specific crowns, such as the crown of life, reserved for those who persevere under trial, and the crown of rejoicing, a reward for believers who introduce others to Christ.[1] Heavenly crowns aren't just rewards for a job well done on earth; crowns are a glorious consummation of the job itself. And don't think only of literal gold crowns encrusted with jewels. Think of a lovely mark of the Lord's favor enhancing your experience of eternity.

Father God, the book of Revelation speaks of a day when the elders will lay their crowns at Your feet, before Your throne.[2] I can't even conceive what that moment will be like, but I'm so glad You shared it with us in Your Word. You love to share Your glory, but it all returns to You—where glory belongs.

---

1. James 1:12; 1 Thessalonians 2:19. 2. Revelation 4:10.

Have you noticed how people try to tame the resurrection of Jesus with sentimental images of lilies, cherubs, and bluebirds? Could it be we've lost touch with the shocking reality of what happened on that Sunday morning? Only minutes before Mary Magdalene arrived at the tomb, this Man was stiff, gray, and stone-cold dead—a battered corpse like you might see under a sheet in a police morgue. The prophet Isaiah tells us He was barely recognizable as a human being.[1] And then the dead Man opened His eyes and sat up; the stone was rolled back; and He walked out of the grave into a dark, cool garden night—with God's glory permeating every fiber of His being. There was nothing tame or "sweet" about this miracle. This was a death-defying, victorious Christ who defeated sin, death, and hell so we might conquer sin in our own lives, live for Him all our days, and experience eternal life in heaven beyond the grave.

Because You came out of that grave, Lord Jesus, I have a hope that nothing on earth can quench. Not paralysis, not pain, not cancer, not even death itself. Because I have received Your resurrection life, I can face anything this world or Satan himself might throw at me. Because You live, I will live forever with You.

---

1. Isaiah 52:14.

Some promises are conditional. You might promise to take the children to the park—if they get their chores done. No chores—well then, no park. The Bible has conditional promises too. In today's Scripture, Jesus says, "If you remain in me and my words remain in you, ask whatever you wish, and it will be done for you." Yes, we can ask whatever we wish in prayer, but Jesus adds two important qualifiers. First, we must be living in close fellowship with Him. Second, our requests must be in line with His will. Prayer, then, is not a blank check. You can't just fill in whatever amount you like, no matter what your spiritual condition, and expect God to cash it for you. No, the most important lesson in prayer—and life itself—is to remain in close, constant fellowship with God's Son, filling your mind and heart with His words and His promises.

Lord Jesus, I see what You're saying here. If I'm thinking of You, walking with You, loving You, and sharing my thoughts with You, then what I ask of You will be the very concerns You have already placed in my heart. I'll be praying for the people You want to rescue, help, and heal. I'll be praying to You and *with* You.

Only the gospel of Mark shares this brief encounter: "A certain man from Cyrene, Simon, the father of Alexander and Rufus, was passing by on his way in from the country, and they forced him to carry the cross." Simon was heading into the city as Jesus was going out to a hill called Calvary. But then a soldier grabbed Simon by the arm and barked out his orders. As Simon lifted that heavy cross from Jesus' bleeding shoulders, the Lord must have experienced a brief moment of relief.

This story makes me think of other people who bear difficult loads. They may be about to stagger under the weight. Who will help? Like Simon, you may be going in one direction and they in another. But then your paths cross, and you have an opportunity to put the weight on your shoulders—if only for a minute.

Lord, help me remember Your words about how if I'm able to help even the least of my brothers and sisters, it's the same thing as helping and serving You. When I offer to carry someone else's cross for a brief time—praying for them, encouraging them, helping them in practical ways—You count it as if I had carried Your cross. Don't let me be in such a hurry today that I miss an opportunity to carry someone else's load.

You don't have to read much about World War II in the Pacific to know that Japanese soldiers would fight to the death for their emperor. Such dedication made them a fierce, formidable, and sometimes suicidal foe. American forces were also valiant as they fought for their country. Our soldiers and Marines, however, didn't fight for a king or emperor. To a large degree, they fought, sometimes to the death, for one another— defending one another, rescuing their wounded, and leaving no one behind.

In the same way, followers of Jesus are in a fierce spiritual war against an unseen enemy. Yes, there are battles we must fight in Christ alone, but we must also *fight for one another* through prayer, accountability, comfort, and encouragement. Today's Scripture captures our battle cry: "May the God who gives endurance and encouragement give you the same attitude of mind toward each other that Christ Jesus had."

Father, thank You for all the people who pray for me— so many I will never meet this side of heaven. Please don't let me slip into a false sense of peace or let down my guard today. Keep me alert to the attacks on my friends and loved ones and Your people who face danger and persecution around our world in this very hour.

When Jesus visited the home of Simon, his mother-in-law was suffering from a high fever. Today's Scripture reads, "They asked Jesus to help her." I love that! It was a simple and beautiful request. No fanfare, no extended discussions or wondering whether this or that was God's will. Jesus was under their roof, and they knew He had the power to help her. And He did.

You may have friends or family members who are struggling with pain, setbacks, and disappointment. But the situations are complicated, and you don't know what words to use as you intercede for them. Sometimes it's just plain hard to know how to pray. We can't go wrong when we follow the lead of Luke 4:38. It's simple, to the point, and sincere. Jesus is under your roof. He's there. He knows the needs. He cares. We don't have to make it complicated. We can simply pray, "Lord, help him. Help her."

Lord Jesus, today help my friends or family members who are dealing with illness and other distressing situations. I don't know all the details, and I'm not sure even how to form my prayers for them. But You know their difficulties right now, every one of them. Shower them with Your help and hope today.

*M*arch 25 | Luke 17:11–19

In the story of Jesus' healing of ten men with leprosy, nine hurried on their way, thrilled to be healed of their terrible, disfiguring disease. One, however, paused in the road and turned back, "praising God in a loud voice." Then "he threw himself at Jesus' feet and thanked him." Jesus wondered aloud, "Where are the other nine?" They had loudly cried for pity and help. But only one thought to give thanks, and he did so *loudly*. He was just as earnest about his thanksgiving as he was about his asking.

We cry aloud to God for His help, as we should. But when He answers, we must also cry aloud our thanks and praise. Yes, *out loud*. Let people know what God has done for you. No, God isn't deaf, but it's good for us—and good for others—when we vocalize our thanks with enthusiasm and joy.

Lord, this really speaks to me. I'm the first one pounding on Your door when I'm afraid or in pain or facing some problem I don't know how to resolve. But so many times I just take Your answers for granted. Oh, Jesus, thank You for Your care. Thank You for Your help. Starting right now, I will tell others of Your goodness and how You've answered me.

Everyone ought to experience, at least once, a very deep cavern. Thousands of tourists do so every year at places such as Carlsbad Caverns, Mammoth Cave, or Oregon Caves. It's perfectly safe on a guided tour, but at some point, the guide will usually turn out the lights just to show how *dark* darkness can really be. This is a blackness you can feel, heavy as water. Children quickly reach for their parents' hands, just for reassurance!

Perhaps you've been through some very dark times in your life. The sun may be shining, but darkness grips your mind and heart. The words of today's Scripture give great comfort: "Let the one who walks in the dark, who has no light, trust in the name of the LORD and rely on their God." Your heavenly Father will never lose you in the dark. Hold His hand; He *will* guide you through any cavern and back into the light.

Praise You, Father. You have been with me in many places that have been so very dark. I have cried out to You and reached for Your hand, and You have always been there. As David prayed, "Darkness is as light to you."[1] I won't even fear the valley of the shadow of death, because You are with me.

---

1. Psalm 139:12.

The art of growing wildly productive tomato plants requires attentive daily care. Once the main branches are healthy and producing fruit, the wise gardener will pinch off any of the sucker shoots growing up from the bottom of the plant. Left alone, these shoots will grow tall and spindly, with plenty of leaves but no blossoms or fruit to show for it. These suckers will siphon off the life-giving sap on its way from the vine to the branches. The result? Fewer and smaller tomatoes.

In today's Scripture, Jesus speaks of His Father as the vinedresser who prunes His vines so they will produce even more fruit. But we can participate by pruning ourselves! Ask the Holy Spirit to show you what needs to be pared back in your life—the activities, habits, or preoccupations that are draining away your energies from the Lord's good plan for your life. Pinch them off!

Holy Spirit, search my heart and life today. Show me where I am distracted from Your desire for me. Reveal to me what needs to be pruned. I don't want to miss Your best! I will prune my life as best as I know how, but I need Your insight and wisdom.

I wish I could adequately describe what it's like when I'm aware of the overwhelming presence and power of God's grace in my life. It's like "living above" my wheelchair in a strata of heart-splitting joy that comes with God-breathed courage to tackle whatever lies ahead! Frankly, I believe that the more aware you are of God's grace, the more joy and courage you will have. This raises the question: When *are* we most aware of God's grace? It isn't when we are riding high with a string of green lights and open doors before us. No, it's when we are needy and feeling spiritually impoverished.

Certainly, God has given you strengths and talents, and He will use them. But if you are longing to live in the celestial strata of God's joy and courage, then thank Him when you feel depleted and weak. It's your passport to a higher, fresher realm of gladness and strength in God!

Father, I'm so thankful You call us to approach Your throne of *grace.* You could have called us to a throne of judgment, a throne of harsh criticism, a throne of burning, merciless accountability. But no, You call us to a place of grace, mercy, and help in time of need. Knowing this, my God, I come.

Throughout His life on earth, Jesus had a number of special names for His followers. He called them His servants, His sheep, His little flock, His children, and His beloved. At the Last Supper, Jesus went beyond all these and actually named them as His friends. But everything changed after the resurrection. It was then that Christ referred to His disciples as His *brothers*. When He met Mary Magdalene in the garden on the day He rose from the dead, He told her, "Do not hold on to me, for I have not yet ascended… Go instead to my brothers and tell them, 'I am ascending to my Father and your Father, to my God and your God.'" He couldn't call them blood relatives until after He paid the penalty of sin. Christ's death and resurrection made it possible to share the same genes, so to speak, as the Son of God. As difficult as it is to comprehend, we are now family.

Lord Jesus, to think You have given me the privilege to call You my Brother and my Friend! I can hardly wrap my mind around that. Today, right now, I am a sibling of God's Son, the Creator of the universe. And my heavenly Father calls me His own child! What wonders these are! I am in awe of Your grace and love.

Most of us spend quite a bit of time in our cars. But whether your commute is long or short, you still have all those trips to the store, soccer practice, the post office, and on it goes. With a little planning and determination, you can make the interior of your car—whether it's a humble Subaru or a BMW—into a demon-free zone of praise and joy, where no dark spirit or discouraging words can cast a shadow over your day. Fill your car with singing and praise! Recorded music and the radio are fine, but making your own music is even better. Recite every name of Jesus you know: Master, Savior, Morning Star, Son of God, Desire of Nations. When you lift up the name of Jesus, God's favor surrounds you like a shield, protecting you from the schemes of the adversary. Remember, the name of the Lord is a strong tower!

Lord Jesus Christ, right here and now, I lift up Your mighty name, the name above every name. You are the Great Shepherd, the Word of God, the King of Kings, the Beginning and the End. You are the Author and Finisher of my faith, the Lion of Judah, the Lamb of God. I want to fill this room, this car, this day, with Your praise!

Sometimes we think about Christians serving the Lord in difficult and dangerous places—doing extraordinary exploits for Him and bringing Him glory. Then we say to ourselves, "Yes, but what am I doing? How can I bring God glory in my everyday routine?" My friend, there actually is a way to do that.

Consider this: There is a wide gap between what you would normally and instinctively do, and what you do when you are walking in His strength and Spirit. In your natural self, you might complain about your routine or difficulties. In God's strength, however, you bite your tongue and refuse to grumble, because you recognize God in those very situations. The gap between those two responses is the glory of God! And our Savior takes note, marking that gap down on our eternal account. It isn't just big acts of faith that get His attention; it's also little acts of *faithfulness*.

Father, I want You to gain glory through the way I live out this "normal" day. I pray that people will see a difference between the way I would naturally respond and the way You enable me to respond by Your Spirit. May people who observe my life see that gap and give the credit to You.

April

In today's Scripture, we read, "The bodies we have now embarrass us, for they become sick and die; but they will be full of glory… Yes, they are weak, dying bodies now, but when we live again they will be full of strength. They are just human bodies at death, but when they come back to life they will be super-human bodies. For just as there are natural, human bodies, there are also supernatural, spiritual bodies." I can hardly believe it. I, with shriveled, bent fingers; atrophied muscles; and no feeling from the shoulders down will one day have a new body—light, bright, and clothed in righteousness—powerful and dazzling. Can you imagine the hope this gives someone with a spinal cord injury, a brain injury, cerebral palsy, multiple sclerosis, or bipolar disease? As the apostle Paul writes, we can "be joyful in hope" just allowing our imaginations to think about such things.[1]

Lord, I thank You and praise You for the indescribable, almost explosive hope in 1 Corinthians 15. When I'm weary and discouraged over arms and legs that don't work, I remember that the time is very short—a handful of years at most—until I will step into a new body made to live forever. A body like Yours! What a wondrous, joyful thought!

---

1. Romans 12:12.

Facing heart surgery, Doug spoke with the surgeon before the procedure. "You might encounter some depression while you're healing," the doctor said. "It's common among heart patients." Doug, who hardly ever had a down day, didn't think so. Even so, after surgery, a deep depression did descend.

One day as he was walking around the block with his walker, he stopped and prayed, "God, please lift this depression from me. I need Your help *right now*." He had taken four steps when a car suddenly pulled over. It was his neighbor, who'd heard about the surgery and handed Doug some flowers. "These are for you," the man said and drove away. Now, Doug wasn't all that big on flowers, but from that moment on, the depression melted away. God is our "ever-present help in trouble." If you are troubled, stop where you are and call out to Him. He *is* present, and He *will* hear.

Father, You have shown Yourself strong time after time in my life. I have called, and You have come. Sometimes it's with relief for my pain. Sometimes it's with strength to persevere. And sometimes You send one of Your people through a phone call, a note, an e-mail, or a visit. Praise You, Lord, for hearing my weakest cry.

Isn't it fascinating how one little word in a Bible verse can sometimes make all the difference? Look at what the rich man asked Jesus: "Teacher, what good thing must I do to *get* eternal life?"[1] Think for a moment about that word *get*. The term implies working and striving to obtain something. No wonder this earnest young man went away disappointed! He was all about doing something good to grab something great. He didn't realize it was God who did something good in order to *give* us something great. Salvation is all about receiving, not getting. It's about opening our hands in humility to receive the mercy of God—not because we've done anything to earn or merit it, but because God did everything to give it.

Lord, have I opened the windows and doors of my life so Your refreshing breeze can blow through and drive out the stale, tired air? I need the freshness and fragrance of Your Holy Spirit swirling through every corner of my heart. I open my hands, Lord, to receive Your grace, Your gifts, Your favor, Your counsel, and Your mercy.

---

1. Emphasis mine.

Today's Scripture raises big—and honest—questions. Paul tells us we must be "always giving thanks to God the Father for everything, in the name of our Lord Jesus Christ." For *everything*? How I have wrestled with those words! The Bible says we're to give thanks, not only for the good stuff and the happy moments, but also for those hurtful, crushing, heartbreaking, out-of-control moments as well. He asks us to see life from His point of view. Paul's command begins with giving thanks to the Father and ends with the name of Jesus. All the events of our lives are bookended by the Father and the Son. Everything that touches us comes from His hand. He sees how it will all fit together. He sees right now how you will one day be healed and how the tears, bruises, setbacks, and sorrows of this life have worked for the glory of His name.

Lord, I do thank You—even for the paralysis and pain that have been my companions. I can endure whatever You allow to touch my life, knowing that my few years are cupped in Your hands, and that You love me and work every moment for my best and for Your glory.

"Whatever happens," Paul wrote, "conduct yourselves in a manner worthy of the gospel of Christ." When the apostle wrote those words to the church at Philippi, he meant, first of all, this: "Whatever happens *to me*, here in this Roman prison—whether I live or die—keep living worthy of Him." But the phrase covers much more territory than that. *Whatever happens* speaks to every possible occurrence in our lives. If you experience a devastating accident or illness. If your best friend betrays you. If your neighbor sues you. If your coworker climbs over you to get that promotion. *No matter what takes place in your life*, continue to hold on to your faith, reflect the peace of Christ, and live in the joy that bubbles up from His Spirit. Show people how someone changed by the gospel actually responds to the rough edges of life. Whatever happens, stay focused on Him.

Honestly, Lord, I can't even come close to this today. I can't live in a way worthy of You. Left to myself, I won't do Your gospel any good at all. Dear Lord, please fill me with Your power, Your perseverance, Your very life, so I can live in a way that speaks well of Your great kindness and grace.

There are Christians today, perhaps not far from where you are right now, who live in nonstop, intractable physical pain. Some are barely able to function. And yet, even in their suffering, they keep their trust in God and their attitudes bright. Yes, these friends long for the day when there will be no more pain in heaven. But in the meantime, they hold on to Jesus with a positive spirit. Could they be part of the persecuted church we read about in Scripture? Consider this: Satan and his demonic host see us when we suffer, and they needle us, prodding and poking us to doubt God, recant our faith, or slip into bitterness and despair. But like persecuted believers through the ages—right down to today—who have lost their lives, we must not deny Him. True, we may "lose our lives" every day through pain and suffering. But if we hold on to the Lord's hand through everything, He has promised a crown of life sweeter than life itself.

Deliver me today, Lord, from the unseen persecution of the adversary and his evil army. When I feel overwhelmed, set my feet in a wide and spacious place. Your name, Lord is a strong, strong tower. Here I come! I'm running through the open door. I'm taking refuge in You.

God has a strong distaste for suffering. Were you aware of that? Today's Scripture tells us that the Ammonites cruelly oppressed the little nation of Israel until the people were "in great distress"; finally cleaning up their act and getting rid of their idols and false gods, they "cried out to the LORD." At first, God said He wasn't going to help them. But then "he could bear Israel's misery no longer" and set out to deliver them from their enemies. This passage shows beyond all doubt that God's tenderness is aroused when people hurt. The fact is, He knows Your suffering today. He's touched by your tears. He aches to show you compassion. And He *will* come to your aid.

How will He come? Probably in a way you never expected. But no matter how your relief arrives, it has its origins in the Lord of the universe. Your pain has His attention, so look for His touch today.

Thank You, God, that my situation today—this very moment—has Your direct attention. I don't have to give You a long explanation, fill You in on the backstory, or pinpoint my pain level on a one-to-ten scale. You are a Physician who not only sees my chart but also loves me like the Father You truly are.

An old devotional book asks the question, "How shall God be able in heaven to dry up your tears when you have not wept?"[1] The image of God tenderly wiping away your tears describes a loving and compassionate moment in heaven between you and your Savior. Your earthly sorrows have a profound purpose in eternity: They are setting the stage for God to engage Himself wholly and completely in your eternal comfort. No wonder David prayed for God to "put my tears into Your bottle; are they not in Your book?"[2] In other words, God will account for every one of your tears. The reason for your suffering will be made plain as God reveals the unseen and unimagined purposes behind your hurts through the years. And as He dries your tears in heaven, it will showcase His intimate affection toward you personally—much more so than if you had never cried!

Lord, I am amazed You have recorded in detail every time I have cried. For some reason, You think it is important to have a complete inventory of every tear that has fallen from my eyes. Help me not to hide my tears or be discouraged over my sorrows, remembering that You take note and care about each one of them.

---

1. Citing Jose Arndt (*True Christianity*), in Søren Kierkegaard, *Purity of Heart Is to Will One Thing* (New York: Feather Trail, 2009), 70. 2. Psalm 56:8, NKJV.

In today's Scripture, we read, "Martha was distracted by all the preparations that had to be made." Martha was on the right path, even with her "*much* serving," as the King James Version puts it. Martha dearly loved the Lord Jesus, and she isn't to be chided for rolling up her sleeves to prepare a special meal for Him and His disciples. The problem was her *focus*. It wasn't that she was too busy or planned too many menu items. Martha simply allowed those things to distract her from the true focus—the Savior. She lost joy in her labor, gladness in ministering to her Lord, and delight in exercising her God-given gifts. A complaining spirit took over as she focused on her sister, Mary, along with all the pots and pans!

It takes great spiritual discipline, as well as consuming adoration for the Savior, to not become weighed down and distracted by the hard work of energetic service. Don't shrink from serving the Lord today; just be certain to keep Jesus and His glory as your goal.

Lord Jesus, may Your Spirit convict me if I become sidetracked by the demands of my Christian service, whether at home, work, or church. May You and my intimate walk with You always be my focus.

Last Sunday after church, I wheeled up front to ask for prayer. Sometimes quadriplegia coupled with pain becomes simply too much to bear. After prayer, I left church surprised by a strange, wonderful feeling of detachment from my hardships. I thought, *I can do this.* It reminded me of Patricia St. John's words:

> Stooping very low engraves with care
> His Name, indelible, upon our dust;
> And from the ashes of our self-despair,
> Kindles a flame of hope and humble trust.
> He seeks no second site on which to build,
> But on the old foundation, stone by stone,
> Cementing sad experience with grace,
> Fashions a stronger temple of His own.[1]

As discouraging as pain can be—so discouraging you can feel your face on the cold, unyielding floor— God has His face on the floor next to you. It's what *Immanuel* means: God with us. God with you.

Lord, I pray with David, "You give me your shield of victory, and your right hand sustains me; you stoop down to make me great."[2] How moving, how humbling, to know You stoop down to be near me in my need.

---

1. Patricia St. John, "The Alchemist," in *An Ordinary Woman's Extraordinary Faith: The Autobiography of Patricia St. John* (Wheaton, Ill.: Shaw, 1993), 298.   2. Psalm 18:35, NIV 1984.

We take for granted so many of the words we say, without ever considering what they might really mean. Take the words *thank you*. We'll say this phrase automatically, hardly even realizing we've spoken. In Spanish, the term is *muchas gracias*, or *much grace*. So when you're thanking someone in Madrid, you're actually saying, "You have shown me much grace. I don't deserve your favor and kindness." In French, you say *merci*, or *mercy*. When you speak appreciation to someone in Paris, you're really saying, "You have shown me mercy."

Grace and mercy, both of which have their origins in God, are the very essence of gratitude. When you truly thank and bless God from the heart, you are acknowledging, "I'm at Your mercy, Lord, and I am humbled by Your grace and favor." And with Paul, we all can say, "Thanks be to God for his indescribable gift!"

Father, it seems like I'm just water-skiing over the surface of life sometimes, without ever thinking about the depths below. I'm thankful for many, many wonderful people and things, but it all goes back to the very source of my gratitude. Without Your mercy and grace so freely offered to me in Christ, I wouldn't have real life at all. Thank You for Jesus.

What does it mean to have faith? Some may say it's seen when we "take a strong stand for Jesus." Is that true? Is faith all about *our* commitment, *our* allegiance, or *our* courage in the face of opposition? Consider this: When you place faith in Christ, you're not so much taking a stand for Him as you're acknowledging the stand He has taken for you! In today's Scripture, we read, "Through him you believe in God, who raised him from the dead and glorified him, and so your faith and hope are in God." Your stand for Jesus is only possible because Jesus stands for you. Any patience, joy, or kindness in your life is a gift from God—and it has nothing to do with your own merit. Faith means being sure of Christ's commitment to you rather than measuring your commitment to Him.

Lord, for some reason beyond my tiny comprehension, You claim me as Your own. Before the Father and the mighty angels, You have spoken my name, acknowledged me, and said, "This is one of Mine." You have stood between me and a powerful adversary who hates me and to this day wants to destroy me. I will gladly stand for You, but I can do so only because You have stood for me.

Ray, who has severe disabilities and is on oxygen, was in a group meeting at a Christian family retreat when suddenly a woman in the session began gasping for breath. Barely able to walk, Ray struggled to his feet, ripped off his oxygen mask, and began hobbling across the room toward her. "Here!" he called out, holding up his tubing. "I've got oxygen!" Without even thinking about it, Ray was ready and willing to give his own breath—his own precious air—to someone in need. Today's Scripture reads, "There is no greater love than to lay down one's life for one's friends." But this woman wasn't even Ray's friend. He barely knew her.

Jesus did the same—and so much more—for us. He surrendered Himself for His friends—and those who would be His friends. We didn't even exist when Jesus laid down His life for us. Today, take a deep breath and thank the Lord for eternal life, purchased for you at such a high price.

Lord, thank You for Ray—so willing, so eager to lay down his life for someone else, just as You laid down Your life for me. You were my Friend before I ever knew You. You were a Friend to someone who was born nearly two thousand years after You walked this earth. I can't imagine a greater love.

Moses asks the Lord, "Why have You afflicted Your servant?" It's probably a question we've all asked God from time to time. "God, why have You afflicted me—your servant, of all people? I'm on Your side!" For the believer who is really looking to understand, there *are* answers. Here's one you may not have considered: Present pain and afflictions tend to heighten future joy. When is peace the sweetest? Right after the conflict. When does a cold drink taste best? When you've become *very* thirsty. When do you appreciate rest the most? After hours of hard labor. When is joyful company most pleasant? After enduring long days of loneliness. The truth is, our recollection of past sufferings may one day enhance the bliss of heaven. Eternity with the Lord will be so much more heavenly to those of us whose faith has been tested, battered, and tried, time and again.

Dear Lord, I might also say, "When will walking across a green lawn or running up golden steps be the most joyful? After you've been in a wheelchair for fifty years!" I am thankful for life in the here-and-now, and even for the trials that test my faith. But I am so overjoyed to think about stepping through the curtain into my Father's house when You call.

My husband, Ken, must have thought our trees were looking a little undernourished, because last week, he had an arborist team come out to feed them. They pushed long poles into the ground through which they infused a rich nutrient soup (or whatever tasty meal trees like best) deep into the soil. I tried to imagine those tree roots searching through the darkness— completely unseen—with tiny hairs and tendrils extended, looking for food. And after their feeding, was it my imagination, or did those trees look just a little more satisfied and content? The Bible often refers to us as "trees" of the Lord. And like a tree, our roots are in Christ Jesus. That life is hidden in Him, deep and unseen. When we feed on Christ—take Him at His Word, repent, obey, draw on His life—the Spirit of Jesus transforms us. We change and grow into sturdy "oaks of righteousness"[1] and fragrant "cedars of Lebanon." So sink your roots deep!

Lord Jesus, no one can see my roots in You, but everyone sees the results of those roots. Am I truly growing to be more like You? Do people notice? Can they see the strength, stability, grace, and beauty of Your life flowing through me? Deepen my roots, dear Lord; I need to draw on You more.

---

1. Isaiah 61:3.

Today's Scripture reads, "Arise, shine, for your light has come, and the glory of the Lord rises upon you." These words have a special application for those who belong to Jesus. He has come into our lives, and He is our light and our glory. No matter how dark or perplexing our circumstances are, our lives are wrapped in the light and favor of God's mighty Son.

For some of us who are older or struggle with disabilities, it can be hard to get moving in the morning. Yes, we rise. But do we *shine*? We may be grateful for a new day, but we may not be grateful for the stiff joints and pain. But here's the truth: Whatever your situation today, the glory of the Lord *is* upon you, whether you feel it or not. His glory rises upon you with each new day. Repeat this verse out loud every morning: Arise! Shine!

Lord Jesus, my light truly has come, and You are that radiant, beautiful light. I invite You to illuminate my conversations, my thoughts, my actions, and even the expression on my face. Your mercies toward me today are brand-new, and I receive them with open arms and a thankful heart.

Imagine what it must have been like to have worked alongside the apostle Paul. What an experience to listen to his preaching, share his passion, witness the miracles, pray beside him, and follow him high and low, contending for the faith!

In Philippi, two Christian women, Euodia and Syntyche, were part of that inner circle of intimate Christian friends. But somehow they lost their focus and fell into a deeply personal feud against one another. News of their squabble and hurtful words even reached the ears of Paul, who was in prison at the time. These two women forgot their purpose. They didn't consider how their animosity was wounding those around them. Even the gospel of Jesus Christ took a backseat to their dispute! Paul first addressed these two women with the command to "stand firm." In other words, recapture your passion; reclaim the vision; recall your focus!

Lord, there are so many distractions out there—so many things that pull my attentions and emotions this way and that. Thank You for including the story of these two women in Scripture. I take it as a warning. Help me to agree with others "in the Lord" and keep my focus!

Today's Scripture reads, "He comes alongside us when we go through hard times, and before you know it, he brings us alongside someone else who is going through hard times so that we can be there for that person just as God was there for us." As heartbreaking as our suffering, grief, or troubles may be, they are not worthless. When you receive help and comfort from the Lord, He always makes sure to leave you with a little extra in your reservoir. Out of that place, then, He gives you the privilege of offering the sweet, healing comfort of God to someone else in his or her moment of deep trouble.

As others watch the way you handle your hard times, they may gain the courage and faith to seek God for help in their circumstances. Thank the Lord that someday all our suffering will cease. Until then, God gives this purpose to our lives. And even to our pain.

Thank You, Lord, for the privilege of holding and distributing one of the most precious commodities in the universe—the healing comfort of God. I love how You meet my needs and then tuck in a little extra to share with hurting, disoriented people who cross my path.

Today's Scripture reads, "They were at their wits' end. Then they cried out to the LORD in their trouble, and he brought them out of their distress." The expression "at their wits' end" has been around a long time and is still in use today. It's that point in life where you run into a massive obstacle or paint yourself into an impossible corner and have no idea what to do. The psalmist, however, gives us a snapshot of people who cried out to the Lord at their wits' end—and He brought them out! What has brought you to your wits' end? A family situation? Financial trouble? A health scare? A rebellious child? Here's the good news: We might come to our wits' end, but God never does. We might be out of answers, but God has answers. The solution is simple: Cry out to the Lord.

How unspeakably wonderful, God, to remember that Your wisdom has no limit. There is no knot on earth so tangled that You can't untie it. There is no situation in life too involved, too complicated, or too baffling for You. When I've exhausted my last option, when I finally arrive at my wits' end, You are able to bring me out.

Impressive-looking actors on TV commercials talk about investing in gold or silver as "the one investment that will last." And so it may—for the brief, fleeting years of your life. But what then? What will that portfolio mean when you stand before God on the cusp of eternity? It makes so much more sense to invest in heaven. The New Testament tells us again and again that one day, those who belong to Christ will stand before their Lord and be rewarded for the investment of their lives on earth. What sort of rewards? Jonathan Edwards speculated that as we lay up treasures in heaven, we actually increase our *capacity* for joy and worship and service to God for all eternity. As we seek to please Him, as we trust and obey Him and lean on Him, we stretch our capacity for all of the untold, unimagined mysteries, wonders, glories, and joys of the life to come.

Lord, sometimes I need to be reminded of these things. The way I respond to trials and tests here on earth, the way I obey You when my body and soul are pulling so hard in another direction, will one day impact my eternal soul *forever*. I want the best You have, Jesus. I want to stay faithful.

As I work in a ministry to people with disabilities, I hear the words *disabled* and *disability* over and over. Sometimes it's good to balance that emphasis by remembering that our God is *able.* Don't you love that word? It means having the necessary power, skill, resources, and qualifications. That's our God! And the New Testament declares it again and again: He is able to guard us. He is able to do more than we ask or imagine. He is able to make grace abound to us. He is able to keep us from falling. He is able to save to the uttermost those who come to God through Christ.[1] We may think we can't do His will, obey Him in the tough times, or resist certain temptations, and we may tell ourselves, "I'm not able." But He is! His abilities more than compensate for our disabilities.

Father, You know there is so much I can't do as I am. I am constantly reminded that if I am able to do anything at all, it is my God, the capable One. And You are more than willing to be my strength—and yes, my song.

---

1. 2 Timothy 1:12; Ephesians 3:20; 2 Corinthians 9:8; 2 Corinthians 10:13; Jude 24; Hebrews 7:25, KJV.

For the longest time in my walk with Jesus, I told everyone I knew Him. After all, I was saved. But truthfully, I was only *acquainted* with Jesus. It was only after I was paralyzed—after I had suffered so much—that I learned to abide by the cross. Only then did I begin to search the mystery of what His wounds meant to me. In time, my acquaintance grew into a precious knowledge. But I still have a long way to go. Even though Jesus satisfies, it's the sort of satisfaction that begs for more. The person who knows Christ wants to know Him more. You can never have too much Jesus. Your love will always keep crying for more and more of Him. It's what today's Scripture means: "Grow in the grace and knowledge of our Lord and Savior Jesus Christ." Don't settle for being an acquaintance of Your Creator and Savior; get to know Him.

Lord, I know I will spend eternity learning more and more about You, experiencing more and more of Your nearness and presence but never coming to the beginning or the end of who You are. Even so, seeking to know You is the best and sweetest part of life here on earth.

God delights in using ordinary objects to accomplish His mighty purposes. Friends of the apostle Paul saved him from a murderous ambush by lowering him in a basket through an opening in the city wall. A basket! Here was Paul, mighty apostle to the Gentiles, a man who would one day write almost a third of the New Testament, and God used what might have been someone's laundry hamper to save his life. What a reminder that God is intimately involved in your life today, protecting you and rescuing you in a thousand ways! But for the most part, you'll have no idea you're being rescued. That's because God's miraculous intervention is often so *very* ordinary. He may use a seat belt, an alarm clock, a hairbrush, a pocketknife, or a cell phone to keep you from harm and to direct You. His means may be ordinary, but His care is *extraordinary*.

Lord, I'm in awe that You never tune out of my day and all my doings. Nothing is trivial. Nothing is overlooked. Nothing is disregarded. You know how to use the most common things in my daily experience to help me, direct me, teach me, and rescue me from harm.

Sometimes the solution to a huge difficulty is so near at hand, so obvious, that we walk right by it. That may be the case with anxiety in our lives. Anxiety is distress or uneasiness of mind caused by fear. Even as Christians, we're troubled by these feelings now and again. But some people become quickly overwhelmed. In today's Scripture, Paul writes, "Don't worry about anything; instead, pray about everything. Tell God what you need, and thank him for all he has done. Then you will experience God's peace, which exceeds anything we can understand." Here are two strong commands in quick succession: Stop worrying. Start praying. It truly is the answer. If anything—*anything*—disturbs your peace, take it immediately to God. Lay it before Him, and then let it go. If you have to do this a thousand times a day, then do it! God's peace will filter back into your heart like a protective shield. That's His promise.

Lord, You know me so well. Worries and fears over the future sometimes feel like a lead weight on my heart. Why should I carry these extra burdens? I'm already weak as it is! I bring them once again to You. Like a warm blanket on a cold night, I want to feel Your peace today.

Did you ever wonder if Jesus *sang* during His days on earth? We know worshipers sang in the synagogues, and Jesus' family probably sang during the holy feast days. But did Jesus himself hum a melody or let loose with a song? The only place the Bible actually records such a time is Matthew 26:30: "When they had sung a hymn, they went out to the Mount of Olives." It was in the upper room on the night Jesus was betrayed. Of all places and times to sing, Jesus sang with His friends on the way to His arrest, crucifixion, and death. Our natural inclination, of course, is to *stop* singing when we're sad, disappointed, or in pain. But Jesus sang as He faced His darkest hour, just as Paul and Silas would one day sing while in chains in a Philippian jail. No matter what emotions you have today, follow the Lord's lead and ask God to put a song in your heart.

Lord, if I dwell on my circumstances, the music just dies away. But when I make You my song, it wells up again. Even in the dark times. Even through tears. I sing my praise to You, my Savior, Brother, Lord, and Friend. I sing my gratitude and praise for forgiveness of sins, for Your sweet companionship, and for the hope of heaven.

God hates suffering—and Jesus spent much of His time on earth reversing and relieving it. It's the same today. In answer to heartfelt prayers, He still grants babies to childless women, heals cancer, protects Alzheimer's patients from walking into traffic, and writes happy endings to sad situations. But it simply doesn't follow that God's *only* relationship to suffering is to relieve it. Yes, He will eventually banish it from His presence forever, but for now, suffering is part of our broken world, and God will still use it for His own ends.

In today's Scripture, Paul reminds us that "we must go through many hardships to enter the kingdom of God." Not just hardships, but *many* hardships. In other words, no one enters Christ's heaven who doesn't first share in Christ's sufferings. Today, determine to be no greater than Your Master. If the Lord Jesus suffered many hardships, you can expect them too—along with the comfort and encouragement of His presence.

Lord, You have always been clear about it. You have said, "In this world you will have trouble."[1] But then you offer Yourself as my Companion, Friend, and Champion through every moment. So I have hardships—but I also have You! And You, Faithful One, are enough.

---

1. John 16:33.

Today's Scripture reminds us to "keep in step with the Spirit." That's a word we Christians need to hear. It's far too easy to dash off into our day and race ahead of God—or maybe lag behind when He urges us forward. There is a certain rhythm He wants us to keep—His rhythm for the day. We need to hear His whispered words of counsel before we make a snap judgment or dash off an ill-considered email. We need to sense His gentle nudge when we need a change of direction.

Keeping in step with the Spirit means receiving fresh grace for every need—instead of trying to cruise on the grace He gave us for yesterday's tasks. Setting the pace is God's job. That means we need to check in with Him early in the day, confess sins and experience restored fellowship, and listen for His voice at the peak of our busy times *and* in the quiet moments of catching our breath.

Father, I'm ashamed to remember how many times I've raced into my day, imagining that all I need from your Spirit are "a few general directions." Oh, I need so much more. Keeping in step with You means slowing down to listen when You speak—and moving forward with boldness when You say go.

"If there is a God and He is good, as you say He is," someone asks, "why does He allow suffering in the world? Why doesn't He just get rid of it?" There is an answer to that question—if people are willing to hear it. Suffering gets its start in sin. It's just part of the "package" of living in a fallen world that has ignored God and gone its own way. So if God were to get rid of suffering, He'd also have to get rid of sin. And if He did that, untold billions of people would be burnt to a crisp in a nanosecond. Today's Scripture reads, "He is patient with you, not wanting anyone to perish, but everyone to come to repentance." God delays closing the curtain on suffering and sin because it gives more time for us to tell people who ignore God about the grace of our Savior, Jesus Christ. Let's do that today... while there is time.

Lord, please open my eyes to the opportunities You bring across my path today. If I have the chance to share a Scripture, put it into my mind. If it's just a word that's needed, help me to speak that word. If there is only time for a friendly smile, help me to smile from the heart.

Today's Scripture reads simply, "You are of Christ, and Christ is of God." Have more powerful words ever been written? Take a minute to think this through with me. God gave you to Jesus. You—yes, you—are the Father's love-gift to His Son. He assessed the price of your redemption and decided it was worth the torturous, bloody death of Jesus on the cross. Consider that for a moment. Believe me, it will shore up your heart against temptation. In fact, knowing how easily I fall into temptation, I memorized the following phrase: "I cannot *and will not* do this offensive thing, for I am Christ's." That simple phrase is all the Holy Spirit needs to pull me back from the edge of disobedience. I have committed it to memory, because I want it there, at the ready, in the moment when I'm tempted. Do your best today, my friend, to show the world around you that you belong to Jesus.

Father, thank You for paying such an unthinkable price to rescue me from an empty, hopeless life. Since You have given me to Jesus, I want to be a gift that brings delight, not grief, to His heart. I want to please Him— and You, Father—with the choices I make today.

How does a Christian who is bruised and battered by very deep trials remain tender toward God instead of becoming bitter or cynical? By remembering this: Our God suffered first, *and* He has suffered more. No other God of any other religion can claim that. It all comes into focus in the person of Jesus. He suffered first, He suffered most, and He suffered for us—the indescribable agony of the cross and the crushing burden of carrying the sins of the whole world on His shoulders. Soon, Jesus will return to earth to close the curtain on suffering—forever. In today's Scripture, we read, "They will enter Zion with singing; everlasting joy will crown their heads. Gladness and joy will overtake them, and sorrow and sighing will flee away." In the meantime, as we yield to Him in our brokenness, He authenticates our faith, refines it, and makes it strong.

Lord, You have never asked me to go where You haven't gone Yourself. If I find myself on a path of pain or sorrow, I can see Your footprints ahead of me. And I know where this path leads—to joy! Just around the bend, all of the suffering will be over forever—little more than a dim memory on a fresh, eternal morning.

May

Sometimes those who suffer from an illness, an injury, or a disability feel trapped or enclosed. The walls seem to press in, and we feel limited and powerless. Experience teaches us that one of the first things suffering does is to make us look inward. Focused on our own needs and difficulties, our souls become small and begin to shrivel. We have a difficult time looking out and looking up. Today's Scripture, however, paints a different picture. God calls on humble, even bed-confined saints to do some mighty things. With hearts full of joy and praise and a double-edged sword in our hands, we "inflict vengeance on the nations... to bind their kings with fetters, their nobles with shackles of iron." In other words, the prayers of a suffering, confined believer can shake the nations. Our prayers elevate us onto a cosmic, high-stakes battlefield of spiritual warfare. This promotes the lowliest, most seemingly "insignificant" servant into the front lines of kingdom service.

Lord, I have been on this battlefield, and I'm grateful for the privilege. Yes, I struggle with the limitations and the incessant drumbeat of pain—and probably always will this side of heaven. But how kind You are, King Jesus, to send me where the battle rages most fiercely and to place a double-edged sword in my hand.

To bless others is the very calling of a Christian. As Peter writes, "Do not repay evil for evil or insult with insult. On the contrary, repay evil with blessing, because to this you were called so that you may inherit a blessing." That's part of the mystery and beauty of life in Jesus. When you give something of value in His name—a gift, an insight, a kind word, your time and help, a prayer, a listening ear—it works its way back to *your* benefit. But rarely at the same time or in the same way! Filtered through God's wisdom and providence, it returns to you as something incredibly encouraging and helpful at a moment when you least expect it. It may not even be in this life at all, but it will accrue to your benefit and delight in heaven. But be assured of this: God is an incomparable bookkeeper, and He never loses track of one kindness done in the name of His Son.

What a delight! Bless You, Father, for making this a principle of life: "Give, and it will be given to you...pressed down, shaken together...poured into your lap."[1] What a sweetness to think that gifts given here on earth have a triple impact—first on the receiver, then on the giver, and then on Jesus Himself!

---

1. Luke 6:38.

John writes, "We know and rely on the love God has for us. God is love." The Father, Son, and Holy Spirit relate to one another in a vast waterfall of love and joy. And it's nothing short of astounding that the Trinity is driven to share that joy—with *us*! This was Christ's mission on earth. He said, "I have told you this so that my joy may be in you."[1] Soon, believers will step into the waterfall of joy and pleasure. In fact, your believing loved ones who have died participate in that Niagara Falls of delight right now in heaven. On the other side of this life, we will not only know God; we will *know* Him in that deep, personal union, that utter euphoria of experiencing Him. We will eat from the tree of life and overflow with more pleasure than we can contain.

I know, Lord, that You share Your joy on Your own terms— and those terms call for us to endure suffering, even as You suffered on earth. Remind me today that "our present sufferings are not worth comparing with the glory that will be revealed in us."[2] Be my strength and my vision, Lord, when my own strength and vision fail.

---

1. John 15:11.   2. Romans 8:18.

Have you ever driven through Kansas when the wheat was high? On a windy afternoon the wind ripples across the pale-gold grain as though it were an ocean, blowing and tossing the wheat and making the trees lining the field sway, their leaves shimmering in the sun. In today's Scripture, we read, "Let the earth be glad... Let the fields be jubilant... let all the trees of the forest sing for joy. Let all creation rejoice before the LORD." Yes, Satan has invaded our Father's world with his own dark plan, but we can still see countless glimpses of God's beautiful handiwork. And we can still sense those moments when the earth itself sings for gladness, remembering its Creator. By the way, you are part of that creation. In fact, the very centerpiece. And when you lift your voice and heart in praise to God, there is a rightness about it that rolls back the designs of the evil one.

Creator and Savior, bring my heart back into alignment today as I praise and thank You. I have felt out of tune, out of sync, and even out of sorts today, but I know Your Holy Spirit will restore me, bringing me back into harmony. I want to praise You, along with Your creation, Your mighty angels, and our loved ones in Jesus.

No doubt you've heard the expression, "It could be worse." Maybe that sounds like a cynical, too-easy reply to the hurts and troubles of the day. Perhaps. It also happens to be *true*. Things could be a great deal worse for all of us. Today's Scripture reads, "The eternal God is your refuge, and underneath are the everlasting arms." In spite of the dangers and heartbreak of this world, God is our refuge, shield, and protector. Often we don't grasp what that means. If it weren't for God's grace preserving and protecting us, our rebellious planet—and us along with it—would have spun off into chaos eons ago. Were it not for God's restraining hand, we would be inundated with a tsunami of violence, catastrophes, war, crime, and cruelty. It could be worse. Yes, and in God's plan, it *will* be worse—right before the Lord Jesus returns and makes it so that everything everywhere will be much, much better.

Father, thank You for Your restraining, protecting hand on my life. If it weren't for You, I might have surrendered to bitterness and despair years ago. If it weren't for You, all those "near misses"—in cars, airplanes, and dark places—might have turned out much differently. Praise You for Your strong arms, encircling and protecting me until You take me home.

Over the years, my wheelchair has taught me to leave "providing" to the God of providence. Although it's true my paralysis is often hard to bear, pain sears into my hip, and I feel utterly overwhelmed, the years have taught me to trust that God *will* provide. He will provide for me, just as He provided for Elijah. With a little oil in a jar and a handful of flour, Elijah outlived the famine.[1] So will I, and so will you. Yes, the sky may seem dark and threatening, but even those black clouds contain showers of mercy.

So take heart if you are struggling in much hardship. God loves you as much now as He does when skies are bright and life is a breeze. This very day, God will provide grace and a blessed escape. Today's Scripture contains some of the most beautiful words ever written: "Cast all your anxiety on him because he cares for you."

Lord, I seek to do that right now. If I'm holding on to fear, help me to release it. If I'm wrestling with anxiety, show me how to let it go. If I'm carrying weights that You never intended me to carry, help me to cast them aside. No matter what, I want to rest in You today, knowing You care for me.

---

1. 1 Kings 17:13–16.

The little boy who gave his lunch to Jesus witnessed a miracle he would never forget. His lunch (perhaps lovingly packed by his mom) consisted of five small barley loaves and two little fish. Jesus took the loaves and broke them, multiplied the fish, and gave it to *thousands* of people sitting on a hillside (with plenty left over). We ought to remember that account when we see a Christian brother or sister enduring difficult times but hanging on to the grace of God. When we suffer, it's as though God is breaking us, as Jesus broke those barley loaves. But out of our brokenness, He can increase courage, hope, and blessing for others—proving to them that His grace is sufficient and inspiring them to persevere. Yes, it hurts to be broken, but what a privilege to be multiplied in God's hands!

Lord, let me be like that little boy who willingly gave up all he had into Your hands. He gave up everything but lost nothing! Before an hour had passed, he had more bread and fish than he had started with. I will never like the "breaking" part of life, Lord, but it's a great consolation to know I'm in Your loving hands.

God created you and me for one purpose: to showcase His glory—to enjoy it, display it, and demonstrate it every day to everyone we encounter. What does it mean to put His glory on display? It means highlighting His attributes and characteristics. It means making hard choices to do the right, or righteous, thing. It means keeping your tongue from gossiping, going out of your way for a neighbor in need, telling the truth even when it's hard, not snapping back when someone hurts you, or speaking freely and openly about your Father in heaven. In short, it's living like Jesus lived when He walked on earth.

In the Old Testament, God used visible things like a burning bush or a pillar of fire to show His glory. In the New Testament, God displayed His glory through His Son, Jesus. But Jesus doesn't physically walk on earth anymore. So how does an invisible God display His glory in this age? Through *you*. What a privilege!

Father God, what an honor I've been given! You no longer choose burning bushes through which to speak; You choose people like me. Point out ways I can showcase Your character and glorious qualities to others today. In so doing, I'll be glorifying You and living in the way I was created to live.

The reality TV show *American Restoration* features a team of ace mechanics and craftspeople who take rusty, beat-up items and restore them to their original glory. They'll tackle anything—from cars to bicycles to vintage slot machines. Each restoration is a high-stakes business project in which worthless junk is transformed into valuable collectibles. In our Christian life, that process is called *sanctification*. When God finally gets ownership over our lives, His purpose is to restore us from the inside out. He might use suffering to sandblast us, or disappointment to acid-wash our pride. Sometimes restoration requires being stripped right down to the chassis, to our very core. Today's Scripture reveals that God is into restoration. Israel was one of His ongoing projects. One day, He will reshape us into His original specifications. Like Adam and Eve before the fall? No, He has a far better glory in mind. He rebuilds us to be like His own Son, Jesus Christ.

Father, it's been quite a restoration project—years and years of stripping away the rust and peeling paint of my old life. And I know, since I'm still here and not in heaven, that You're not finished yet! Thank You for Your Spirit working in my life from the inside out, gradually shaping me to look more and more like Jesus.

Ask a veteran high school football coach what kind of young man he most enjoys training. Surprisingly, it may not be the five-star athlete who's loaded with natural abilities. In fact, it may be a kid with some good basic skills—coupled with a strong hunger to learn and get better. Sometimes the boy with all the talent thinks he's got it down already, maybe imagining he can cruise through practices and rely on his gifting rather than on hard work. In short, he doesn't want to grow. I think that's the thought behind Jesus' words in today's Scripture: "Blessed are those who hunger and thirst for righteousness, for they will be filled."

Are we hungry to do the right thing? Do we wake up with a deep-down longing to please God and a genuine fear of grieving Him? A lack of hunger for righteousness reveals we have stopped growing, which may mean we're slipping backward.

Lord, there's so much about me that needs to change—and I want to work with You to change it! Forgive me for imagining I can approach a new day on cruise control, relying on the grace, wisdom, and strength You gave me yesterday. Create a deep-down hunger in me to know You better and follow You more closely.

It's one thing to muster a submissive attitude toward God when we bring troubles on ourselves, but it's a different matter when we're hit with circumstances over which we have no control. These are the hardest to deal with. In today's Scripture, however, Paul writes, "That is why, for Christ's sake, I delight in weaknesses, in insults, in hardships, in persecutions, in difficulties. For when I am weak, then I am strong." Yes, this is a man who went through a mind-bending series of trials in life. And he didn't bring any of them on himself. Yet he could write that he *delighted* in these hardships, because he knew it was for Christ's sake. He was walking in the Lord's will and following the Lord's directions. The first thing out of his mouth when he was blindsided by troubles was essentially this: "This is for the Lord's sake. He is with me. I can deal with it." And so can we.

Lord God, for the sake of Your Son, Jesus, and for the sake of my friends and family watching me—as well as for the sake of the holy angels, who carefully observe our responses—I give You praise today in the midst of my hardships. I know I am walking in Your will, so I know You will bring me through today.

Today's Scripture affirms that God is a sun and shield, that He bestows favor and honor, and that "no good thing does he withhold from those whose walk is blameless." So why wouldn't that mean physical healing for someone who seeks to follow Him? Well, it might, if He so chooses; He is still the God of miracles. Even so, many broken things in this broken world will not be mended until Jesus returns or calls us home. Through it all, however, God will not withhold His wonderful, incomparable gifts. He won't withhold His grace and the provision for our sin. He won't withhold His kindness or His peace. He won't withhold courage when we need it. He won't withhold His Holy Spirit—our Counselor, Comforter, and Guide—who loves us and lives inside us. And when the time comes, He won't withhold eternal life or a room in His great house, where all will be set right forever.

Truly, Lord, You are a sun and shield to me. Your radiance floods my path, and You protect me from the arrows of the enemy. You have not withheld Your gifts or the sweetness of Your presence from me day by day. Never, not even once, have You left my side.

My friend Judy loves mystery novels. But here's the catch. To determine whether or not she will buy a book, she stands in the bookstore and reads the last few pages *to see how it turns out*. If it has a "good" ending, she'll buy it. But what about the mystery? What about solving the puzzle? She doesn't care about that; she simply refuses to invest time in a story with a disappointing ending.

When it comes to the story of our world and our destiny as Christians, we can look ahead in the book of Revelation to see how it all ends. Sin, death, and Satan are defeated forever. It's a *very* happy ending. And God tells us all about it. Today's Scripture reads, "I am God… I make known the end from the beginning, from ancient times, what is still to come." We know the ending to the story; we don't have to wonder. It's the promise of heaven, a glorified body, and joy forever.

Lord, there are so many mysteries in life as it is. But it fills me with joy to realize my eternal destiny isn't one of them. How joyous, how glorious to think about the new heavens and a new, restored earth! Thank You, Jesus, for salvation. Thank You for including me in Your eternal plan.

Sometimes God must look at us and say, "This is a *strange* lot I created." Take our reaction to the weather. Most of us delight in a warm, sunny afternoon with a gentle breeze. But how often do we express our gratitude to Jesus for great weather? Ah, but if hurricanes or floods come our way, then we go to God—but mostly just to complain. In good weather or bad, the Bible declares, "This is the day the LORD has made; we will rejoice and be glad in it." The Lord has made *every* day, and if we fail to give Him glory on pleasant days, how will we praise Him when highways are slippery or our flight is canceled by a blizzard? We need to make up our mind to rejoice every day, giving Jesus glory for good times and bad, knowing that all things come from His hand… and that He is good.

Lord, forgive me for withholding the thanks and praise that belong to You every day of my life, no matter what the weather. Praise You for the gift of life and opportunities to serve You. Praise You for family and for friends. Praise You for the wonder of forgiven sins. And praise You for the hope of heaven, just over the horizon.

Do your memories reach back to the tween years, ages ten to twelve or so? You felt almost grown-up at times, yet you were still very much a child—playing with dolls or Hot Wheels and not quite ready to let go of your favorite stuffed animal. You *needed* to grow up, but it took time to do so. That's what I appreciate so much about Romans 7. It gives me great hope to know that even Paul, the great apostle, struggled to grow in Christ. And if it was difficult path for *him*, you know it's a challenge for us! As Christians, however, we must continue growing. The Holy Spirit will help us and nudge us along into spiritual adulthood. But it means we've got to starve our old, sinful nature and feed the new creation we are in Christ. It's way past time for us to grow up!

Holy Spirit, draw me further into life—authentic life— today. If I've been playing with mud pies at the side of the road, help me to get back on the journey. I want to let go of the childish, unhelpful things I've been clinging to for comfort. I want to grow up into all You want me to be.

Have you ever tried to accomplish something for God without first seeking help from His Spirit? It can feel so desolate! Nothing is more mechanical than when we attempt to live a supernatural life apart from Him. I've done it. You do it too. When we live apart from Him, cruising along on our own self-sufficiency, prayer becomes dull, witnessing becomes burdensome, and relationships sag under the weight of selfishness. Our jobs drag us down; our smiles become plastic; our words about God begin to sound like a memorized script; performing an act of kindness becomes an unpleasant duty. Even our relationship to the Lord becomes a chore. In case you're feeling like you are fine on your own today, remember that in Him you live and move and have your being.[1] With His life flowing through you, you will accomplish more than you could ever dream.

Lord Jesus, how vain and foolish I can be sometimes! And what an empty experience it is to go through the motions of following You without experiencing the daily reality. I just need You, Lord. I don't want to attempt anything for You in my own wisdom or my strength. Please fill me with Your Spirit today, and empower me to be the person You want me to be.

1. Acts 17:28.

When I first became paralyzed, I thought it was hypocritical to express thanks to God when I didn't *feel* thankful. And it *would* have been hypocritical had I thanked God only to impress others. But I knew I had to move forward; I had to start somewhere. That's when I began loosening my tongue and mouthing words of thanks, hoping that somehow God would actually fill my heart with true gratitude. I wasn't hiding the hardness of an ungrateful spirit; I was desperately hoping for the in-breaking of the Holy Spirit!

After several months, a miracle occurred. I began to *feel* the emotion of thankfulness. I learned that doing the right thing was a way of placing myself under the shower of God's mercy. Thanksgiving with the mouth stirs up thankfulness in the heart. As today's Scripture reads, "Go through his open gates with great thanksgiving; enter his courts with praise. Give thanks to him and bless his name."

I praise You, Lord Jesus, for Your goodness and kindness to me through the years. You once said that if Your followers fail to praise You, the rocks themselves will cry out.[1] My heart was like a rock once, but You changed me. Continue to fill my heart with gratitude and joy.

---

1. Luke 19:40.

A life that pleases the Lord is never a smooth road. Today's Scripture tells us that our Shepherd guides us along the right paths—paths of righteousness. That is true, but sadly, we often shake off His guiding hand. His path might interest us for a while, but then we allow sin to beckon us down a detour. The old hymn writer wrote, "Prone to wander, Lord, I feel it, prone to leave the God I love."[1] It's true, isn't it? We are *so* prone to wander—so inclined to leave His path and run away from His lordship. But how gracious and patient He is with us! The psalmist David wrote, "He knows how we are formed, he remembers that we are dust."[2]

God is the One who forgives our sin time after time and makes available His grace that redeems every wayward attitude and action. He will hear our confession and will guide us back on his "right paths."

Lord God, You know me so well. I'm a sheep that keeps wandering away from the Good Shepherd, putting myself in danger and ending up in desolate places. Forgive me for taking detours from Your path for my life. Please help me not to wander! I want to be the sheep that follows closest to Your heels.

---

1. Robert Robinson, "Come, Thou Fount of Every Blessing" (1757).   2. Psalm 103:14.

We can't always see the good that comes from our ongoing trials and heartaches. We may see *some* good—a little more patience, maybe, or empathy for others. But on the whole, the good that we are able to tally in this life doesn't seem to outweigh the bad that we observe. We keep praying, but we don't see some of the answers closest to our hearts. Only heaven will reveal a clear picture of how the sweet fragrance of our faith in Jesus, even in times of grief and loss, influenced the lives of those around us. Only eternity will show how our fainthearted prayers changed the destinies of people on our prayer list. Great faith believes in God even when He plays His hand close to the vest, not showing all His cards. God wants to increase your "measure of faith."[1] He does this whenever He conceals a matter and you trust Him nevertheless.

Thank You, Jesus, for granting me faith to believe in You. I am making up my mind today to trust You with the things I don't understand. I know You answer prayer. I know You still work miracles. So I will keep on asking, keep on seeking, and keep on knocking—and trust You with the results and the timing.

---

1. Romans 12:3, NIV 1984.

I'm glad when I can wake up before my helper—my "get-up girl"—arrives to get me ready. I use that time to pray. I know myself too well—how easily my quadriplegia and morning stiffness can turn me into a sour, peevish person who lacks a smile for the day. My get-up-girl deserves a "better" me, and I'm always thankful that God pours out His abundant grace before she walks into my bedroom at 7:30 a.m. After I'm up in my chair, we'll read from a daily devotional. This morning, this prayer gave me a smile the entire day:

> Oh, give Thy servant patience to be still,
>   And bear Thy will;
> Courage to venture wholly on the arm
>   That will not harm;
> The wisdom that will never let me stray
>   Out of my way;
> The love that, now afflicting, knoweth best
>   When I should rest.[1]

Lord, the people in my life—my husband, coworkers, friends, and even strangers—need to see the best me I can be with Your help. Fill me with Yourself, so people who encounter me will see glimpses of You; hear Your kind, grace-filled words; and even catch Your fragrance.

---

1. L. B. Cowman, *Streams in the Desert* (Grand Rapids: Zondervan, 2006), 314.

Have you ever felt like throwing in the towel? Especially when an unresolved problem or a season of pain saps your energy? It happens to me all the time, given the decades I've spent in my wheelchair. For me, perseverance can often seem like an elusive thing out ahead of me, like a dangling carrot. And as much as I try to reach for it, I can't quite attain it. But then, before I know it, I'm there. I've made it to the other side. To persevere is to endure a hard thing for a long time, leaving the length of the trial totally in God's hands. The author of Hebrews writes, "Do not throw away your confidence; it will be richly rewarded. You need to persevere so that when you have done the will of God, you will receive what he has promised." And that promise is the incomparable reward of Jesus saying, "Well done, good and faithful servant!"[1]

Holy Spirit, You are the One who dwells in me, closer than hands or feet, closer than my breath. Infuse me with Your perseverance, patience, and determination today. I can only run today's race today; I can't do anything about yesterday's race or tomorrow's. I ask for the strength to run well this day, this hour, in Jesus' strong name.

---

1. Matthew 25:23.

As we live each day to please God, heaven takes notice, and we have the opportunity to earn eternal rewards. Scripture tells us, "We must all appear before the judgment seat of Christ, so that each of us may receive what is due us for the things done while in the body."[1] The way you live your life on earth *today* has a direct bearing on your capacity for joy, worship, and service in heaven. This is what makes our present life so exciting. It's a training gym! Your nine-to-five job isn't merely an occupation; it's a proving ground for your faith. Take a minute to think through the challenges facing you today, and remember this: Every earthly problem, affliction, task, household chore—and all the relationships that go with them—is a minor league exercise to prepare you for the major leagues in the next life. Stand firm, my friend.

Lord God, without Your help, without an infusion of strength and joy from Your Holy Spirit, this could end up being just another day for me. I don't want to spend these hours marking time and waiting for tomorrow; I want to please You now—today. I want these hours on earth to count for eternity.

---

1. 2 Corinthians 5:10.

In today's Scripture, Paul takes a moment to express awe and wonder about his God. He calls Him "God, the blessed and only Ruler, the King of kings and Lord of lords, who alone is immortal and who lives in unapproachable light." To be blessed is to be *happy.* Some scholars use the word *blissful* here for *blessed.* God is joyous and radiant. He is not a threatened, pacing deity starved for attention. He is not easily angered, touchy, or out of sorts on bad days. He isn't biting His nails or blowing His stack when the world goes awry. No, He is the exultant and rapturously happy God. And that is good.

People in distress need to reach out and find a strong, secure, and happy anchor. As my friend Steve Estes says, "Nothing we do can disturb the blessedness of God. We will always find Him full of compassion and tender mercies."

Lord, there is so much unhappiness in our world. So much disappointment and bitterness, so many broken dreams. Please carry me along on the overflow of Your joy today. May I see myself as blessed, happy, and contented in You. Let me show through my life how wonderful it is to have a joyful anchor and foundation in You.

Every human has one important thing in common: No one knows how much time he or she has left on this earth. It could be one day or a thousand. But whether you've been told you have only days to live, or you're enjoying robust health, each of us should learn how to make our life *count for eternity*.

Speaking to those who have faced the challenge of cancer, theologian and pastor John Piper wrote, "Satan's designs and God's designs... are not the same. Satan designs to destroy our love for Christ. God designs to deepen our love for Christ. Cancer does not win if we die. It wins if we fail to cherish Christ."[1] The point here isn't about cancer; it's about learning to live in such a way that *every* hardship helps us to focus on eternity. Our days, no matter how long or short, are opportunities to know Christ better and to invest in the life to come.

I ask, Lord, that You help me make the most of my time, the most of my days, and the most of my opportunities to know You, walk with You, and accomplish Your desire for my life. Paul was right—compared to the surpassing worth of knowing You, everything else is loss.[2]

---

1. John Piper, *Don't Waste Your Cancer* (Wheaton, Ill.: Crossway, 2011), 10.   2. Philippians 3:8.

In Luke 16, Jesus gives what seems to be a real-life account of two men who die and enter eternity. The man in hellish surroundings shows deep concern for his still-living brothers. If possible, he would have returned to earth to urge them to change their lives and turn to God. Here's the lesson: If lost souls can feel and care, how much more those who have died in the faith! Our Christian loved ones who have graduated into glory now live in the presence of the great I AM, the Lord of love. How deeply they must feel, pray, and see! How fervent and ongoing must be their love! After all, "Love never fails."[1] Love doesn't die, and it *can't* die, because it cannot fail. Our loved ones may very well love us right now with a holier, purer, and more intense love than they ever did on earth.

What an awesome thought, Jesus, to remember that I am one with my brothers and sisters who are now with You! It makes me feel closer to them and to You, knowing You are—at this moment—with the ones who have been so very dear to me. Help me to remember the "great cloud of witnesses" who are watching my life and my progress.[2]

---

1. 1 Corinthians 13:8.   2. Hebrews 12:1.

We behave differently when we know people are observing us. It's true, isn't it? We bite our tongues, try to smile, hold our tempers, and say kind, courteous words. That's why today's Scripture is so encouraging, reminding us "since we are surrounded by such a great cloud of witnesses, let us throw off everything that hinders and the sin that so easily entangles." If there really are people in the grandstands watching us, it moves us to make sure our walk matches our talk. Those in the stands could include departed family members and friends—a godly grandmother, a father, a sister, a teacher, or a coach. It may also include a host of Old and New Testament saints—Daniel, David, Esther, Mary Magdalene, Paul, and John. It may even include angels. They are our witnesses, urging us to persevere, reminding us that time is fleeting, and cheering us on to obedience.

Lord Jesus, whether or not departed saints are watching me from heavenly grandstands, I know You are watching me. Please let me remember this in my moments of anger or frustration or when I'm tempted to let my mind wander from You. I do want to please You. Thank You for watching me and guiding my steps.

California's Sierra Mountains rise abruptly from the floor of the Mojave Desert—a dramatic vista in whatever season you visit. Winter is especially lovely, when the mountains and surrounding desert are covered in snow. It's a quiet world. Not a stirring in the air, not the sound of a car in the distance, not the buzzing of an insect. In today's Scripture, the prophet wrote, "The LORD is in his holy temple; let all the earth be silent before him." The awesome display of God's creative power seems even more majestic when enveloped in silence. Find time to get outside today and quiet your heart before Him. You may not be near a mountain or in a desert, and you may not be able to shut out the sounds of traffic. But you can step away from the chatter of others' voices and electronic devices and invite Him to speak to you. "Be still," He may tell you, "and know that I am God."[1]

Lord of creation, help me not to rush into Your presence today, but to praise You with a quiet heart rather than in a tumble of words. Help me to find long moments to be silent before You. I've read Your Word, but I need to hear Your voice, sense Your direction, and enter into Your peace.

---

1. Psalm 46:10.

A few months ago, I met a young man who had been paralyzed in a motorcycle accident. Even though Calvin had lost the use of his legs, he seemed content and at peace with his wheelchair. "Right from the beginning," he told me, "it was clear God wanted me to testify about Him. I remember my surgeon telling me, right before they wheeled me into surgery, that he felt bad he wouldn't be able to give me use of my legs. But I smiled and told him it was okay. Then I shared one of my favorite Bible verses: 'God does not take pleasure in the legs of a man.'"

Calvin's story moves me. At his own point of disappointment and desperate need, he thought first about comforting his surgeon. What an amazing example. At this very moment, you may be disappointed and have great needs, but I urge you to find a way to fix your eyes on the needs of others.

Lord Jesus, this is so like You when You walked this earth. No matter how focused and goal-driven You were, You always noticed others, seeing their needs out of the corner of Your eye. Even on the cross, You thought of Your mother and the man on the cross beside You. Please open my eyes this day to the needs of others around me.

In John Bunyan's classic, *Pilgrim's Progress*, Christian reaches the shores of the celestial river with his companion, Hopeful. It is Hopeful who leads the pilgrim to the other side to the golden city. As Christian crosses the dark, turbulent river of death, he nearly drowns in the waves. The water is deep, and he loses his footing. Whirlpools sweep in circles, and he becomes disoriented, feeling like he has lost his way. Nevertheless, Christian keeps holding on to the shoulder of his steady companion, Hopeful. Hopeful keeps his eyes on the opposite bank of the river. Christian may have lost his way, but not Hopeful!

Hope in Christ never disappoints you, friend. Not in life, and not even at the prospect of death. If you have lost your footing and find yourself disoriented, hold on to the shoulder of Jesus. He is your Blessed Hope, and He knows the way. In fact, He *is* the way.

Lord, I'm so grateful to have my hope centered in You. Everything on this side of heaven is so uncertain. The world around me changes day by day; I can feel the very ground shift beneath my feet. But You are my Hope—now, tomorrow, and forever.

In Gethsemane, as Jesus agonized over the cross that awaited Him, He fell on the ground and prayed, "My Father, if it is possible, may this cup be taken from me."[1] Jesus asked the Father if there might be some other way. But in the next breath, He also prayed, "Yet not as I will, but as you will." Moments later, when the soldiers came to arrest Him, Jesus did not resist and told Peter not to resist either: "Put your sword away! Shall I not drink the cup the Father has given me?" Knowing He could not avoid the cross, Jesus was now ready to embrace it.

If you find yourself facing stress in your life that you just can't avoid, by all means pray that if it's God's will, He will remove it. But once you've prayed, be willing to take up your cross and follow Jesus down that hard path.

Lord Jesus, show me how to embrace those hard things in life I can't avoid. But I also remember how many weights, worries, dangers, fears, and impossible situations—beyond count!—You have already removed from my shoulders. You remove far, far more than You leave. And then You give me strength to persevere.

---

1. Matthew 26:39.

When we find ourselves in a very dark season of life, we long for someone to put an arm around us, assuring us that everything will be okay. We want assurance that our world is orderly and stable—not spinning off into chaos. We want to know that God is at the center of our suffering, not only holding our lives together, but also holding *us*. In today's Scripture, we have the massive promise of that assurance: "We know that in all things God works for the good of those who love him, who have been called according to his purpose." This is true no matter what we face in life. The robust hope of the believer is not that we will escape hurts and sorrows, but that God will make every one of them an instrument of His mercy to do us good—both now and in eternity.

Dear Lord, I really can't imagine how people get through life without You. What would it be like to believe that all of life is random, without plan or purpose, leading to nothing? I'm so grateful for You—the Way and the Truth and the Life.[1] I'm so thankful I can leave all the tangled details of my life in Your wise and loving hands.

---

1. John 14:6.

June

When you're bored, you can take it to God or you can switch on your "favorites" playlist. When you're depressed, you can run to the Lord, or you can run to the refrigerator. When you're working, you can ask Jesus for His guidance, or you can become frantic about deadlines. When you're between flights at the airport, you can spend a few minutes in prayer, or you can get absorbed in your iPhone.

All of us by nature are worshipers. The question is, do we worship God or the idols of our preference? We're doing either one or the other. Eventually, we will find that idols are utterly useless when we're facing the major issues of life. Today's Scripture is the closing line in the elderly apostle John's heartfelt letter to fellow believers: "Dear children, keep yourselves from idols." Today, make up your mind to take full advantage of God's favor, grace, and companionship. Find out firsthand the incomparable help that can be yours.

Father, in these brief moments of my day, I set aside other voices, other interests, other attractions, and all those nagging reminders of "things to be done." I turn to You. I open my heart to You. I release my anxieties and worries to You. In this moment, I want Your help— and Your help *alone.*

When King Nebuchadnezzar of Babylon created a towering gold image, he declared that anyone who failed to worship it would be tossed into a blazing furnace. Fearing God more than the king, Shadrach, Meshach, and Abednego refused, were bound hand and foot, and thrown into the inferno. That's when the king and his officials witnessed "four men walking around in the fire, unbound and unharmed, and the fourth looks like a son of the gods." Who was the fourth man? An Old Testament appearance of Christ! But notice this. These men were *walking* in the midst of the fire. We tend to think heartbreaks and tragedies will stop us dead in our tracks—and keep us from moving forward in life. But the truth is, a trial is one of the streets through which we move to reach our destiny, a road leading us deeper into the heart of Christ.

Lord, I have so often seen suffering as something to escape—a puzzle needing to be swiftly solved so I can "get back to normal." But maybe You are inviting me to *walk* in the fire rather than cower in self-protection. It's so good to know You will be walking with me.

You may or may not receive an earthly inheritance. Maybe your parents didn't have much at the end to give you, or maybe the government got most of it. Even so, as a son or daughter of the living God, you *do* have an inheritance. And it is glorious! Today's Scripture says this of our inheritance: It "can never perish, spoil or fade," and it is kept in heaven for us. What's more, *we can add to it* throughout the course of our lives. Jesus said, "Store up for yourselves treasures in heaven, where moth and rust do not destroy, and where thieves do not break in and steal."[1]

How do you add to your inheritance? By the way you live, by your faithfulness, by the way you choose to honor God in difficult situations, by the way you obey His Word, and by the way you serve Him for His glory rather than for your own self-interest.

Lord, just being in heaven with You and in a brand-new body that will never age, fail, or falter is more than I can wrap my mind around. But You have promised even more—an inheritance that will be uniquely mine and is even now guarded, secured, and waiting for the day I step through heaven's front door.

---

1. Matthew 6:20, NIV 1984.

I may not be in prison, but I understand a life sentence of confinement. Quadriplegia can often feel like incarceration, for I carry around my own set of bolts and bars wherever I wheel my chair. Yet here is something strange: My "prison" is the very thing God has used to set me free. It's why I am always buoyed by today's Scripture: "While Joseph was there in prison, the LORD was with him; he showed him kindness and granted him favor in the eyes of the prison warden." God did three amazing things while Joseph was in prison: (1) God was with him; (2) He showed him unceasing kindness; and (3) He granted him favor. If you are suffering in pain and confinement with patience and a godly response, God will do for you what He did for Joseph. Look to your Deliverer; He will always be with you, show you kindness, and grant you great favor.

Lord, I know Joseph didn't want to be in prison. But he knew he wasn't alone. You were with him. You hadn't forgotten or abandoned him. In spite of the harsh, gloomy conditions, he experienced Your presence, kindness, and favor. And so it has been with me. I can endure confinement if the unlimited Lord of All is with me.

"Now we see in a mirror dimly, but then face to face; now I know in part, but then I will know fully just as I also have been fully known." In Paul's day, Corinth was a famous manufacturing center for mirrors made of polished metal. By gazing intently into the surface sheen, the viewer could have a general—if vague—impression of what he or she looked like. But reflection was at best a dim shadow of the full-blooded reality. The word Paul used for *dimly* is the Greek term for a puzzle, riddle, or enigma. That's what life is like, Paul is saying. Even for a Christian. Yes, we have the Word of God and the Spirit of God to guide and teach us. But let's face it, we are only catching the merest glimpse of the full, eternal reality in Christ. Life on this side of heaven is only a dim reflection of the true reality yet to be.

Lord Jesus, help me to gaze and gaze upon You this day. You are the One who holds all the answers. You are the One who can fulfill each longing. You are my satisfaction. I know my earthly vision is often dim—but my prayer today is that I will see You more clearly!

In today's Scripture, Paul writes, "Our citizenship is in heaven. And we eagerly await a Savior from there, the Lord Jesus Christ." Some people have waited many years to become citizens of the United States. As the days and months go by, they eagerly watch the mailbox for the envelope that will bring them the good news. The apostle Paul's news, however, is even better than that. He tells us we are *already* citizens of heaven. There will be no need to fill out application forms, go through interviews with angels, present our papers, or get into a long line when we reach the other side. We will already be citizens of the eternal kingdom. Our passport has been stamped with the blood of Jesus Christ, and the door to heaven will swing wide open for us. Or maybe Jesus Himself will come for us, meeting us in the clouds with the believers of all the ages.[1]

Dear Lord, I love these thoughts beyond all others. Paul says we *eagerly* await our Savior from heaven, and my heart says, "Yes! Me too!" I am eager to watch and wait for Your return in the clouds. And if I die before that day, I'm eager to walk into Your presence and Your welcoming arms.

---

1. 1 Thessalonians 4:13–18.

When Jesus entered Jerusalem four days before His crucifixion and saw the joyous crowds worshiping Him, He knew very well what they were thinking. They expected an earthly king who would over-throw Rome and bring in the good life. In response, Jesus began to weep. Why did He weep? Pastor Ed Underwood notes that the Lord could see through their shallow praise.[1] He knew their hearts and their real and desperate need. In that moment they didn't need a Conqueror; they needed a Savior. They needed liberation from the penalty and power of sin. By dying on the cross for them, He would give them what they needed, not what they wanted. In a similar way, we might ask God to change our circumstances. That's what we *want*. But God knows what we need, and He may use those same circumstances to change our hearts, leading us into a deeper dependence on Him.

Lord, I know I'm sometimes like those fickle crowds in Jerusalem that broke Your heart. I want my life to be less troublesome, less challenging, happier, smoother, and easier to manage. That's what I *want*. But that may not be what I *need*. What I need most, Lord Jesus, is more of You in my life.

---

1. Ed Underwood, "Jesus and the Day after Election," http://edunderwood.com/tag/jesus-christ/ (accessed February 22, 2016).

Counterintuitive means something is counter to what intuition would lead one to expect. In other words, your logic and best judgment lead you in one direction, but reality is the complete opposite. For instance, to prevent the flu virus, doctors take a form of that virus and stick it into your arm. It shouldn't work, but it does. That's counterintuitive.

Jesus said, "Whoever wants to save their life will lose it, but whoever loses their life for me will save it." Really? I'm going to somehow find my life by giving it up? Yes, exactly. When you lose your life for Christ's sake, you think of others before yourself; you give generously even when you don't have much; and you make Jesus famous even when it diminishes your reputation and makes you look bad. When you live this way—for Christ's sake—you will begin to discover life beyond what you have ever experienced.

Lord, it so often seems like the way to save my life is to cling to it—by hanging on with my fingernails and toenails. It seems like the way to preserve my life is to protect myself, shield myself, and put my own needs first. That's the way it seems, but that's not reality.

Think of the times when you're nearing the end of a long, tiring trip. Maybe it's a familiar freeway exit, with home just five minutes away. Maybe it's the final approach to your hometown airport. Maybe it's the last quarter mile of a backpacking trip, and your car is waiting in the parking lot to return you to civilization—and a hot shower! Just knowing home is near can add a spring to your step and the stamina you need to keep going. So it is when we consider heaven. Every step, every day, every moment brings us closer. And just knowing our glorious home is near, right around the corner, gives us fresh courage to face the day. John 17 tells us that eternal life begins with the knowledge of God. So wherever you are in your journey, you can get a foretaste of heaven *today* by setting time aside to speak to Him and listen for His voice.

I think of those best-of-all words—"almost home!" What could be sweeter? Today, dear Jesus, I ask You to walk with me. You set the pace, and You lead the way. And if I begin to falter, remind me that heaven is near and that You are nearer still.

Reading the Bible, you can easily get caught up in what God accomplished long ago. You think of the Red Sea parting and the Israelites crossing it on dry ground. You think of King Solomon with his vast wisdom. You think of the apostle John, sitting close enough to Jesus to see Him breathe, to look right into His eyes. Yes… but… what about the mighty things He's doing in your life today? You may not see an ocean part, but think of the way He has made for you through impossible circumstances. You may not have the wisdom of Solomon, but think of the times when He gave you a cutting-edge insight at just the right moment. You may not see Jesus with your physical eyes, but you have God's own Spirit making His home *within* you. Today's Scripture reminds us that He's doing something new in *your* life, something mighty. Open your eyes to see it.

Lord, forgive me for thinking Your mighty works are in the past or imagining Your best plans for my life have already come and gone. Open my eyes to what You are doing in and around me this very day. Help me not to miss the stunning miracles taking place at work, at home, in my neighborhood, and in my city.

Like all married couples, Ken and I disagree at times. And sometimes we hurt one another's feelings in those disagreements. I remember the time a quarrel was still hanging heavily in the air, and Ken and I sat in stubborn silence. Finally, Ken spoke up. "Okay, so we don't measure up to one another's expectations." After a pause, he added, "So maybe we should pray." I knew he was right, but at that moment, praying with him or for him was the *last* thing I wanted to do. Yet as my husband began to pray, humbling himself before God, tears started flowing. And hearts started melting. Today's Scripture reads, "A gentle answer turns away wrath," and so does a gentle prayer! If you are in a disagreement with your spouse, family member, or close friend, take the first step. Take the initiative. Say something or pray something. It's not easy, but it will open the door to grace and peace, healing and forgiveness.

Lord Jesus, You were the offended one. You were the One who was rejected, ignored, devalued, and despised. But You weren't satisfied with the status quo. You took the initiative with us. You broke the impasse, coming to earth and giving Yourself for our sins. And now Your gentle voice says, "Come to Me."

When we load all our hopes, dreams, and expectations into the here and now, without taking eternity into account, we subtly ask people in our lives to be what they will never be and to do what they are incapable of doing. We make the mistake of seeing our relationships as ends in themselves rather than as means to ends. This is especially true of marriage. Don't think of marriage as a container for your happiness; think of it as a workroom for God to get you ready for the age to come. Don't think of marriage as the missing puzzle piece in your life that will magically complete you. Only God can complete you! Don't expect your spouse to make you happy, meet all your needs, or understand you through and through. Those are things only God is equipped to do. Place your hopes and expectations in Him. He will never disappoint you.

Father in heaven, You know my heart. You know my tendency to place such high expectations on the people in my life. If only I would turn to You first! Help me to release those unrealistic hopes and fantasies and simply to love and enjoy the companionship of the loved ones You have given me.

In the King James Version of Psalm 51:2, the text uses a word that doesn't even exist anymore: "Wash me *throughly* from mine iniquity, and cleanse me from my sin." If you type that verse into your computer, the automatic spellcheck will try to change that word to *thoroughly*. But that's not how the KJV has it. *Throughly* is an old English way of saying, "Wash me through and through from my iniquity." The old 1611 language may not be very popular anymore, but there's a good idea here and it's echoed in today's Scripture: "May God himself, the God of peace, sanctify you through and through." In other words, "I don't want God to do a surface job on my character—like sending me through an automated exterior car wash; I want Him to get rid of those deep-down, hidden sins that no one sees—and that I have possibly even hidden from myself."

Today, Lord, I pray with David, "Search me, O God, and know my heart; test me and know my anxious thoughts. See if there is any offensive way in me, and lead me in the way everlasting."[1] Thank You for forgiving me and cleansing me from all unrighteousness. Safeguard my heart and mind, and keep me pure.

---

1. Psalm 139:23–24, NIV 1984.

I wake up each morning with eternity in my cross-hairs. I have my sights on heaven. It's what keeps me going. True, nearly fifty years of living in a wheelchair is incredibly challenging—especially at my age. But I'm a little like Jesus who, as today's Scripture tells us, for the joy set before Him endured His cross. So, should I not endure mine? *Especially* when I consider the joy that is awaiting me, the happiness that my response to my wheelchair is accruing for me.

Look, friend, the Bible says your afflictions are winning for you a rich reward in heaven.[1] That means every time you muster a godly response to your trials, your eternal joy becomes weightier, bigger, happier, and much more glorious. The old Puritan Thomas Manton once wrote that a man's "greatest care should be for that place where he lives longest."[2] So join me in setting your sights on heaven and living for joy.

Father, give me a clearer idea of how grand and glorious heavenly joy really is. Show me Your gladness so I might better bear my sadness; reveal to me Your happiness so I might embrace my hardships; infuse into my heart Your joy so I can take up my cross daily and *smile.*

---

1. 2 Corinthians 4:17.   2. Thomas Manton, *The Complete Works of Thomas Manton*, vol. 6 (London: Nisbet, 1872), 182.

For some, flying thirty-five thousand feet above the earth in a quiet airplane may no longer seem like anything special. Even so, soaring over the mighty Rocky Mountains can remind you that many of the issues that have troubled and worried you really aren't very big at all. It's all about a new perspective. That's why I love David's words in today's Scripture: "From the ends of the earth I call to you, I call as my heart grows faint; lead me to the rock that is higher than I." When the world presses in on us, when deadlines circle like vultures, when people's expectations cut into our shoulders like a heavy backpack, we need a vantage point. We need to move higher and get above it all. Our God is the Rock that is higher than you or me. Spend time with Christ the Rock. Climb the heights. Breathe the clear, fresh air. Gain a new perspective— His perspective—on your life.

Lord Jesus Christ, You are the great and mighty Rock in my life, my Strength, my Stability. I worship You today. I want to climb as high as I can into Your vast strength and beauty. I want to see my world, with all of its anxieties and pain, through Your eyes and with Your perspective.

If you happen to be a little child riding with your daddy on a galloping horse, there is a way to stay snug and secure behind him in the saddle. All you have to do is wrap your little fingers around his belt and press yourself against the back of the saddle, and off you go—up and down hills, splashing through streams, charging into the day. In a spiritual sense, it's still the way to go. Today's Scripture reads, "Stand firm then, with the belt of truth buckled around your waist." In other words, if you're hanging on to God's truth—the precepts and promises of God's Word—nothing can shake you out of the saddle. It doesn't matter how winding or treacherous your trail is, you can move through anything—trials, hardships, disappointments, even death itself—and remain safe and secure. Just keep your grip on the truth and never let go.

Father, I'm holding on to Your Word today with all my heart. You have promised to be with me in every situation. You have promised to quench all the flaming arrows of the evil one. You have promised Your wisdom, Your strength, Your endurance, and Your peace when I need it most. Make my grip strong today, Father, because the trail ahead of me may be steep.

When you make your way into a kitchen and catch the aroma of chocolate chip cookies in the oven, you want to linger, don't you? You can easily imagine how one of those cookies, still warm with melty chocolate chips, will taste with a glass of cold milk. Or picture this: You're walking by a west-facing window and catch a glimpse of a sunset so bright and so vivid in its bands of colors that you hurry out the door to take it all in. That's the way it can be in our walk with Christ. We're reading in the Psalms and catch just a tiny whiff of His fragrance. And we want more! We've set aside a few minutes to get alone with Him in prayer, and we see a tiny glimpse—hardly a flash—of His glory. And our heart hungers to see more. The more we see of Him, the more we desire Him.

Holy Spirit, I know this is Your work. You whet my appetite to be with the Father. You grant me a tiny taste of heaven on the tip of my tongue and awaken my longing to experience more. You bring me into a moment of companionship with God's Son, and I want it to last all day.

In front of Rockefeller Plaza in New York City stands a famous statue from Greek mythology—Atlas, bearing the earth on his shoulders. The huge globe he holds looks terribly heavy. Even his mighty knees seem to be buckling under the weight. It reminds me of how people talk about Jesus bearing the sins of the world—as though He had a massive, invisible weight on His shoulders. But today's Scripture reads, "He himself bore our sins *in his body* on the cross."[1] He didn't carry our sins on His back; He took our sins *into himself*! It happened on the inside. When God saw Jesus on the cross, He literally saw our sin. Jesus experienced the full weight of God's anger meant for you and me. God "made him who had no sin to be sin for us, so that in him we might become the righteousness of God."[2]

Lord Jesus, there is nothing fair about this exchange. You took my sins into Your own body, paying my penalty. And in trade, You gave me Your righteousness, purity, and sinless beauty! You took on my death, allowing me to receive Your life. I will never comprehend this. I am in awe of Your love today.

---

1. Emphasis mine.   2. 2 Corinthians 5:21.

As followers of Christ, there is no end of things we *should* do or *ought to* do or even *must* do. There are commands we should cherish, goals we should embrace, attitudes we ought to cultivate. But the sad truth is this: In our basic human nature, in our flesh, we may not have any real desire to do these things at all. Oh, we might succeed in adhering to a list of "shoulds" and "musts" and "thou shalts" for a while, but if it's done in our own strength for the sake of duty, it will never last—and it really won't please God. The apostle Paul clearly teaches, "The mind governed by the flesh is hostile to God."[1] The good news is that the Holy Spirit within us will freely give us the desire to do God's will. He will supply the *want to*, which is far, far more compelling than the *have to*.

Praise You, God, for giving me the desire to please You, the desire to put others first, the desire to read Your Word, the desire to respond in kindness to others. Lord, I couldn't even follow You unless You gave me the *want to*. And You have! More and more, I find myself wanting what You want—and nothing makes me happier.

---

1. Romans 8:7.

We know from James 1:13 that God does not—will not—inject the idea of evil into anyone's heart. So how is it that we read in the book of Exodus that "the LORD hardened Pharaoh's heart" so Pharaoh wouldn't let the Israelites go?

God is constantly staving off evil, restraining the fury of Satan so that harm and calamity do not overwhelm us. The devil can only do what God allows. Every once in a while, however, God lifts His hand of restraining grace to allow evil people to carry out their wicked plans, but only as it serves God's higher purposes.

Has someone caused you harm? Hurt or maligned you? You can praise God today that He is in control of even *that* painful situation. If God allowed it, He has a purpose in it. We may not understand His reasons, but we know His intent. It is for our good and His glory.

Holy and righteous Father, I bow before Your infinite wisdom. I certainly can't trust my limited knowledge or my emotions in situations like these. Honestly, it sometimes doesn't make sense why You allow what You allow in this broken world of ours. But again, I will put my trust in Your wisdom and goodness and in Your love for me.

*J*une 21 | John 13:6–9

Talk to anyone who has experienced an extended stay in a hospital or rehab center, and they may tell you the thing they dread most is enduring a bed bath. All of us feel a profound aversion to being bathed by someone else. It's way too personal, too private. Taking a bath is a routine we would rather do ourselves—if we were at all able to do so. But listen to what David prayed: "Cleanse me with hyssop, and I will be clean; wash me, and I will be whiter than snow."[1] There was a time in David's life when he felt so soiled, so thoroughly dirtied by sin, that he cried out for a cleansing only God could give him. Jesus said, "Unless I wash you, you have no part with me."[2] You and I are in need of constant cleansing, and it's foolish to deny it. Come to God today and ask Him to make your heart clean.

Father, thank You for the most precious substance in the universe—the blood of Your Son, Jesus, poured out for my sins. Nothing else can make me clean. Nothing else can heal my wounded conscience. Nothing else can open the doors of heaven for me. I owe everything I am to Jesus.

---

1. Psalm 51:7. 2. John 13:8.

G. K. Chesterton once wrote, "When it comes to life, the critical thing is whether you take things for granted or take them with gratitude."[1] It's a great quotation, but the Bible was first to come up with the idea. God's Word tells us to "give thanks in all circumstances" and urges us to be "*always* giving thanks to God the Father for *everything*, in the name of our Lord Jesus Christ."[2] That doesn't leave much wiggle room, does it? In which circumstances? *All of them.* How often? *Always.* For what things? For *everything.* "But wait," you might say. "That would mean we're virtually giving thanks and praising God all day long for everything that happens." Yes, that's just what the Bible is saying. It doesn't have to be out loud or obnoxious, but from dawn to dusk, there ought to be an unceasing undercurrent of gratitude in all we do and say.

Lord, as in everything else, You will have to supply the *want to* as I consider these things. Sometimes there are painful, sorrowful circumstances that make no sense at all to me. If I am to live with an attitude of gratitude in "everything," it will have to come from a deeper source than me!

---

1. G. K. Chesterton, *Irish Impressions* (London: Collins, 1919), 24.
2. 1 Thessalonians 5:18; Ephesians 5:20, emphasis mine.

You're walking with a friend, who suddenly turns to you and says, "I don't get it. If things will be as they are going to be anyway, why should I pray?" We've all wrestled with such questions. Do my little prayers have anything to do with shaping God's will? If He's the driver of everything, does that mean I'm just along for the ride?

The fact is, we pray because God Himself commands us to pray. God's Word gives prayer a priority and urgency we simply can't ignore. When He was among us, Jesus prayed. It was the heartbeat of His life. Whether or not we understand how prayer fits into God's grand scheme of time and world events isn't the point. If the One who is all-wise strongly calls us to seek Him in prayer, we can be sure it's terribly important—for Him and for us.

Lord, sometimes I pray when worries and concerns weigh so heavy on my heart, and I try my best to leave those things at Your throne. But today I pray just because I love You and want to be close to You. You fill a place in the very center of my life that nothing or no one else can ever fill.

What do you really believe about God? Not what you *say* you believe or even *ought* to believe, but what do you actually hold to be true about Him. Here's how you can know. The next time you run into a difficult, painful, or even heartbreaking situation, *watch how you react*. Nothing reveals the stuff of which your Christian beliefs are made than tough times. Maybe that's why today's Scripture urges us to "glory in our sufferings" and James counsels us to "welcome trials as friends."[1] In fact, these hardships will teach you—as nothing else can—the real quality of your faith.

God, of course, already knows what's in your heart. He just wants *you* to know. Do you believe He is kind and good? In control of the details? Do you believe He is sovereign and has a purpose for your suffering? How you respond to your trial will make it plain to you.

Lord, I know how often my mouth gets ahead of the reality in my heart. I can say or write faith-filled messages by the dozen, but it all rings hollow if I don't cling to You when I suffer. I'm really tired of just talking about it, Jesus. I want a faith that runs deep and carries me through anything.

---

1. James 1:2, PHILLIPS.

In today's Scripture, we read, "Serve the LORD with gladness! Come into his presence with singing!" As C. S. Lewis reminds us, "Joy is the serious business of heaven."[1] Serving the Lord with gladness is a glorious occupation. On the other hand, those who do not serve God with a glad heart cancel out all the benefits their service could have won them. Charles Spurgeon put it like this: "Those who serve God with a sad countenance, because they do what is unpleasant to them, are not serving Him at all; they bring the *form* of loyalty, but the *life* is absent. Our God requires no slaves to grace His throne; He is the Lord of the empire of love, and would have His servants dressed in the uniform of joy."[2] Let our gladness prove that, yes, we serve a good and glad Master.

Father, I can imagine that Your mighty angels, along with all the redeemed saints in Your presence right now, sing for joy at the privilege of serving You. I ask today that just a little of that great gladness would filter down into my to-do list and put a smile in my heart.

---

1. C. S. Lewis, *Letters to Malcolm: Chiefly on Prayer* (San Diego: Harvest, 1964), 93.   2. C. H. Spurgeon, *Evening by Evening: A New Edition of the Classic Devotional Based on the ESV Bible* (Wheaton, Ill.: Crossway, 2007), 17.

Today's Scripture reminds us: "Reckless words pierce like a sword, but the tongue of the wise brings healing." How we need that reminder! Our words are incredibly potent. The words we choose will either nudge people closer to God or actually drive them away from Him. That is an awesome responsibility. When God created the world, He spoke it into being. When Jesus walked the earth, He spoke, and the lame were healed. When Peter preached his first sermon, thousands were gathered into the kingdom on one day. Powerful things happen when we speak. Our words can either accomplish great good or inflict unbelievable damage that may last a lifetime. Words can instantly create division. And with just the slightest inflection, just a subtle tone of voice, they can wound or create distance. At the same time, our words can lift people out of a pit of despondency or call them back from the cliff-edge of hell. Maybe Solomon said it best: "Words kill, words give life; they're either poison or fruit—you choose."[1]

Lord, today please show me ways I can speak words of healing and holiness into the lives of others. Most of all, help me to think—and to pray for wisdom—before I say anything.

---

1. Proverbs 18:21, MSG.

In today's Scripture, Peter addresses his letter "to God's elect, exiles scattered throughout the provinces." The apostle sent out his encouragement to believers who had been dispersed throughout the Roman world by violent persecution. But you don't have to face persecution to feel like one of the "scattered saints." Maybe you find yourself in a small apartment in a big city. You feel like a stranger in your own community—perhaps even distanced from other believers. You're out of the flow, jobless, single, maybe divorced, isolated. You may be in a lonely season right now, but read these verses again. You have been chosen by the Father, set apart by the Spirit for obedience to Jesus Christ. The entire Trinity—Father, Son, and Spirit—is actively involved in your life. And that, my friend, puts you in the mainstream of the main stream. You are deeply loved and treasured by your Creator.

Please give me peripheral vision today, Lord, to notice sisters and brothers who feel isolated and lonely, out of touch and out of the flow of life. Give me the grace and wisdom to encourage someone who feels unimportant to You and others right now. This is a lie of the enemy, Lord, and I need Spirit-empowered words to defeat this hurt and deception.

As David laid out his plans for building the temple of the Lord, he said, "I had it in my heart to build a house as a place of rest for the ark of the covenant... for the footstool of our God."[1] A footstool! David and the people of Israel were to worship in a place the king referred to as *God's footstool*. Frankly, it would be an incredible privilege to come anywhere near the footstool of the living God, the beautiful Creator of all that is. But think of the far greater access we enjoy because of our relationship with Jesus Christ. The Bible says we will one day join the angels worshiping God *before His throne* in heaven. What's more, Jesus says, "To the one who is victorious, I will give the right to sit with me on my throne."[2] What stunning grace and favor!

Even now, Father, You kindly invite me to come before Your throne of grace, bringing all my troubles, worries, sorrows, and burdens! Because of the cross of my Lord Jesus, I have been given access into the Most Holy Place. And I don't come as a fearful, trembling slave; I come as Your very own child. Who can imagine such privilege?

---

1. 1 Chronicles 28:2. 2. Revelation 3:21.

It isn't always easy to offer a disabled or elderly person a little help—even when it's obvious they could use it. It's easier to walk by—to pretend you didn't see. After all, what if you did something wrong? What if you created an offense? It's also true, however, that it isn't easy for the person needing assistance to ask for help. It's not fun putting someone out.

In both situations, it's good to remember that any act of help done in the name of Jesus will be richly rewarded in eternity. The apostle Paul speaks of "gold, silver, costly stones," but that's only a metaphor for something far more wonderful, valuable, and lovely that will shine throughout eternity. So when you help someone, you are rewarded. And when you ask for assistance, the one who gladly steps in to help will be rewarded. Either way, it's a win-win.

Lord Jesus, I'm so grateful for the way You have ordered our lives in this temporary world where we're camping out. We live within the borders of time, but You have given us glimpses of our eternal home just over the horizon. We sometimes need help in these failing bodies of ours, but You crown those efforts with heavenly motivation.

June 30 | 1 Corinthians 10:13

Some people find our Lord's approach to lust unnecessarily harsh. Jesus says, "If your right eye causes you to stumble, gouge it out and throw it away... If your right hand causes you to stumble, cut it off and throw it away."[1] He's not being literal here, but we get the idea. When it comes to lust, Jesus prescribes a severe, even radical operation. In other words, this is nothing to coddle or play with—just as one would not play with a venomous snake. If we don't deal severely with lust, then a glance becomes a gaze. A thought becomes an action. A casual fantasy becomes heartbreak and a nightmare. So, yes, be harsh with such inclinations. Walk away. Avert your gaze. Leave the movie. Turn off your computer. These actions will result in God's blessing—and spare you years of regret.

Thank You, Lord, for Your promise in 1 Corinthians 10:13. You will never allow me to be tempted beyond my ability to resist, and You will always provide a way of escape from every trap and snare of the evil one. Help me to quickly derail any train of thought that grieves Your Holy Spirit!

---

1. Matthew 5:29–30.

July

Drifting on a lake in a fishing boat is one thing; drifting in *life* is something else entirely. Fall asleep in a fishing boat, and nothing much happens. But if you try to sleepwalk through life, you *will* end up somewhere you never intended. Today's Scripture tells us that "we must pay the most careful attention... to what we have heard, so that we do not drift away." Sadly, drifting away from Christ comes naturally to us. But it is *supernatural* to anchor yourself to Him when strong currents try to pull you away. Every day of our lives we swim against the current, against the tide. And it is possible (don't imagine it isn't!) for any one of us to sink morally or spiritually.

Don't let yourself coast away from Jesus. Don't look up at the end of a day, week, or year, and be stunned at the distance between you and God. These are the times to anchor yourself to His Word.

Lord, I don't want to lose my love for You. I don't want to become distracted by all the bells and whistles of this life. I don't want my heart for You to cool off or become indifferent. Keep me close today. Anchor my heart and my affections in You.

The pool at Bethesda was a place where people waited—and waited! People with diseases and disabilities would crawl, hobble, or be carried there every day, hoping to be healed in the waters. One paralyzed man had been lying there for thirty-eight years. Think of it! That would be like lying by the pool from 1978 to 2016. When Jesus asked him if he wanted to get well, he responded, "Sir... I have no one to help me into the pool when the water is stirred. While I am trying to get in, someone else goes down ahead of me." His longing was fixed on a particular answer—someone who would carry him to the water. But the one He really needed was standing right in front of him— Jesus the Healer. It's a reminder: When things look especially hopeless, remember who stands between you and your need—the very One who will make you whole.

Lord, I know I have looked right past You many times in my life, hoping and longing for specific solutions to my problems. Sometimes I imagine some expert will have all the answers for me. But You have been with me all along. With the psalmist, I say, "But now, LORD, what do I look for? My hope is in you."[1]

---

1. Psalm 39:7.

As Jesus was approaching a village, He met ten men afflicted with leprosy. Following the protocol of the day, the hopeless men stood at a distance and called out in loud voices, "Jesus, Master, have pity on us!" When Jesus saw them, He said, "Go, show yourselves to the priests." And as they went, they were completely healed. As was true for Naaman in the Old Testament, they were given, we can imagine, the perfect skin of a young child.[1]

When you think about it, the men never asked for healing—just for pity. Maybe a handout of some money or food. But when they obeyed the Lord's simple instruction, He gave them much, much more than they ever requested. Here's the lesson: When God tells you to do something small, just do it! In your act of obedience, God may well surprise you, giving you more than you would have ever dared ask of Him.

Lord, help me not to overlook or procrastinate on the little tasks You ask me to do. I know, Lord, that following You means paying attention to the daily whispers and nudges of Your Spirit, as well as to the big crossroads of life.

---

1. 2 Kings 5:14.

July 4 | James 1:2–4, PHILLIPS

Why do some hardships never go away—even after we pray and pray? The pinched nerve doesn't heal; the job situation doesn't improve; the marriage doesn't get any better. Consider this: The core of God's plan is to rescue us from sin and self-centeredness. Suffering is one of God's choice tools to accomplish this. And it can be a *long* process. Some heartaches in our lives won't be like a 250-piece jigsaw puzzle that can be solved in a single evening. In today's Scripture, James writes, "When all kinds of trials crowd into your lives my brothers, don't resent them as intruders, but welcome them as friends! Realize that they come to test your faith and to produce in you the quality of endurance. *But let the process go on until that endurance is fully developed.*"[1] God has a long-term plan for your life to mold you into the image of Jesus. The results will be worth waiting for!

Father, help me embrace the ongoing difficulties and perplexities in my life. I want You to develop my endurance. I want to be stronger and wiser and more like Jesus. But honestly, I get discouraged. I feel impatient when things don't change. Please restore my faith and hope today.

---

1. Emphasis mine.

It's difficult enough trying to grab a quiet few minutes with God and His Word. But sometimes it feels like you're running through an obstacle course of distractions to get there. You head toward your Bible or the Bible app on your iPad, but find yourself checking Facebook first. Or the headlines. Or the latest sports scores. Or something totally unrelated to anything! Or maybe you think a cup of coffee will help your concentration, which leads to a snack—and before you know it, the time has flown and you have to move into your day without seeking the Lord.

Life has always been full of distractions. But we truly *need* to connect with the Lord and His Word every day. That's why today's Scripture gives such an effective reminder when distractions keep sidetracking us: "My eyes are ever on the LORD, for only he will release my feet from the snare." If we keep our eyes on Him, He won't allow us to become tripped up or entangled in trivialities.

Amen, Lord! I have spent too much time filling my mind with worthless distractions and the empty ways of this temporary world. Turn my heart! Draw my attention. Rule my heart. I need to spend time in Your presence, feeling Your nearness and listening for Your voice.

Jesus spoke of great faith during His years on earth, but He spoke far more about little faith. In today's Scripture, Jesus chides the disciples for their small faith. Then He gives them an illustration that must have stopped them in their tracks. He tells them, in effect, "Why, if your faith were as small a mustard seed, you could do *anything*!" Notice that He doesn't compare little faith with great faith; He compares small faith with tiny, barely visible faith. But even this microscopic faith, if genuine, can brush aside mountains in its path. Earlier in Matthew, we read that the mustard seed, even though tiny, grows into one of the largest trees in the garden.[1] It *grows*. It doesn't stay insignificant. You may feel your faith is small now, but persevere! Keep obeying, keep trusting, and your small faith will one day become something more than you could have imagined.

I know, Lord, that the main thing isn't the strength of my faith, but the strength of my God. Even so, I want to trust You more and more, because I know it pleases You. I want You to smile on my faith. And I want my faith to encourage others who are trying so hard to hold on to faith at all.

---

1. Matthew 13:32.

Even an old cedar tree can teach a lesson about life. The tips of this evergreen always point straight toward the sky, reminding us that "up" is the best direction of all. When circumstances close in, when disappointments darken our horizon, when pain slips into our world like a night marauder, we might find ourselves looking back to the "good old days." Or perhaps looking down in discouragement or despair. Jeremiah writes, "Let us lift up our hearts and our hands to God in heaven." David prayed, "To You, O Lord, I lift up my soul," and "I lift up my voice to the Lord for mercy." Jesus said, "When all these things begin to happen, stand and look up, for your salvation is near!"[1] We all need to look ahead in order to walk in this world, but true orientation happens with an upward glance.

Lord, be the Lifter of my head today. Open the eyes of my heart, like You did Elisha's servant's, to see Your horses and chariots of fire surrounding the adversaries that surround me.[2] I've spent too much time looking down at my circumstances, looking inward at my faults, or looking ahead at worries on the horizon. Today, Lord, I really need to look *up* and see You.

---

1. Lamentations 3:41; Psalm 25:1, NASB; 142:1; Luke 21:28, NLT.
2. 2 Kings 6:17.

Today's Scripture reads, "For us there is but one God, the Father, from whom all things came and for whom we live; and there is but one Lord, Jesus Christ, through whom all things came and through whom we live." Most of us understand that God uses hardships to improve our character, remove sinful habits, make us heaven-hearted, and instill compassion in us toward others. But refined faith should never be an end in itself—it should all lead back to God Himself. Stronger character isn't made muscular for its own sake, but for God's. A livelier hope isn't focused on "things getting better," but on God. It's all about glorifying Him. To forget this is to tarnish faith, weaken character, and deflate hope. The Bible never calls us to keep our eyes on suffering—or even on suffering's benefits. Only on God, the One "from whom all things came," including suffering. Consider the good benefits surrounding the hardships in your life. Let's take our stand with the apostle Paul, who wrote, "I consider them garbage, that I may gain Christ and be found in him."[1]

Lord Jesus, keep my focus off not only my hardships, but also even whatever benefits might come from those hardships. May my focus always and only be on You, especially today.

1. Philippians 3:8–9.

"When all else fails..." How would you finish this thought? Maybe like this: *When all else fails... I can always pray.* It's like one of those emergency panels in a building with the sign that reads, "Break glass in case of emergency." But you'd better make sure it's a real emergency before you do it. Yes, prayer should be your last resort. But it should also be your *first* resort—and all your resorts in between. In today's Scripture, Paul writes, "Pray in the Spirit on all occasions with all kinds of prayers and requests... Be alert and always keep on praying for all the Lord's people."

Turn again and again to the Lord, with prayers that are specific, on the spot, detailed, and out of the box. Pray when you pass an accident on the highway. Pray when you get into your car and out of it. Pray when a face floats into your mind. Pray when the Spirit nudges, and then pray some more. You can never pray too much.

Lord Jesus, I see people on their iPhones everywhere I go—walking, driving, waiting—whatever. I want to be attached to You like that—talking to You in an airport, in a mall, in a restaurant, and on my bed at night when the pain won't retreat and the morning won't come. The more I pray, the sweeter life becomes.

210

Jesus couldn't have made it any clearer. The words "follow Me" carry a strong and serious sense of mission. Today, though, in our age of easy believism, when Jesus says, "Follow Me," we imagine He is saying, "Try it out. See how it feels. See if it works for you. Give it a thirty-day, no-risk, free trial." In other words, though most of us wouldn't admit it, we follow Him incrementally, in little flashes of fervency. We're not really all in. This week, look through the gospels and study how seriously Jesus conveyed a call to His followers. Then shed any and all trappings of your old way of living. Disentangle yourself from every bad habit, and then turn and follow your Lord. You are a follower of Jesus, so don't look over your shoulder at what you might be leaving behind. The path ahead is so much brighter and better with Jesus leading the way.

Lord, today is all I have. I can't make up for not following You yesterday or last week. And I wouldn't presume to boast about how I will follow You tomorrow. Today You are saying to me once again, "Follow Me," and I am faced with the choice all over again. I choose, dear Lord, to follow wherever You lead.

A number of years ago, media mogul Ted Turner called Christianity "a religion for losers." He later retracted his comments. But when you think about it, wasn't he right?

To follow Jesus means to lose oneself to this world. It means losing all your winnings in this world in order to lay up treasures in the next. It means to negate your pride, subtract your fleshly wants, and be ready to release your carefully constructed plans. Jesus absolutely delights in reaching out to those who consider themselves the last, the least, the littlest, and the most lost without Him. Christianity is a faith journey of overcomers who learn to gain by losing.

You are my treasure, dear Lord. I lay my life at Your feet. Keep the tentacles of the world, the flesh, and the devil from entwining around my heart. I want to lose my life for Your name's sake.

Johan, a young man from the Netherlands, became a missionary to the Bedouins and nomads living near Israel's stark and desolate Sinai Desert—to a forgotten people in an overlooked corner of the world. Johan learned many lessons from the people of the desert, but one thing impressed him deeply. The Bedouins consider it worse than murder to know of a source for water in the wilderness and yet neglect to tell fellow travelers. Why? Because anyone going six hours in that harsh environment during the summer would perish.

People in today's values-vacant, anything-goes culture can't always hide a deep *spiritual* thirst. As Christians, we know very well where the water source is. In today's Scripture, Jesus says, "Whoever drinks the water I give them will never thirst." And here is the hard truth: If your neighbors, coworkers, and relatives don't know Christ, they will die of spiritual thirst. Today, then—somehow, some way—lead them to the Living Water.

Jesus, You are the artesian spring in my life, the head-waters of everything pure, fresh, and good. I have found refreshment in Your presence and satisfaction for my deepest thirst. Show me, by Your Holy Spirit, creative ways to shape conversations, write notes, give gifts—whatever it takes—to point people toward You.

In Job 38–41, the great Creator God takes His discouraged servant Job on a tour through the wonders of nature. In today's Scripture, the Lord points out that "the wings of the ostrich flap joyfully, though they cannot compare with the wings and feathers of the stork." Whatever else God intended to teach through this observation, one application seems clear: *Rejoice in who you are and with what God has given you.* The wings of an ostrich really don't do much of anything. Ostriches can't fly. But they can run like the wind![1] Even so, it's the glory of a bird to flap its wings, and the ostrich does so with pride and joy. We too can rejoice in both our strengths *and* our weaknesses—in our strengths because they are precious gifts from God, and in our weaknesses because God demonstrates His power and grace through them as we depend on and trust in Him.[2]

Father, forgive me for comparing my wings and feathers to those of others. I may not be able to do what others are able to do, but I am able to joyously let You shine through my life—and even through my imperfections and disabilities. My body may not work well, but my spirit runs with joyful abandon!

1. Job 39:18.   2. Thanks to my pastor, Bob Bjerkaas, for prompting this train of thought.

If you're shopping for an anniversary this month, you'll find a large selection of beautiful, expensive cards describing your spouse as the most virtuous, fault-free, brave, and lovely person on the planet. But the truth is—can I say this in print?—it's often difficult to love your spouse. This is precisely why 1 Corinthians 13, the famous love chapter in Scripture, begins its list of attributes with the words "love is patient." For the Christian celebrating decades of marriage—or just getting married—it's not about passion and romance; it's about patience in sickness and health, in wealth and want, for better or for worse. What's more, in any relationship, God asks you to show patience with others' shortcomings, to display mercy toward them, to release them from meeting all your righteous expectations, to bear with their weaknesses, and to not be itching to correct them. The fact is, when you love someone with patience, you love them as God loves you.

Lord Jesus, thank You for Your patient love for me through the years. You love me when I am unlovable. You watch over me when I am preoccupied with myself. You forgive me when I commit the same old tiresome sins right after I have confessed them. I don't know how else to say it, but help me to love like You do.

When you find yourself restless, lonely, or downcast, you may find comfort in singing an old, favorite hymn or Christian song. You sing it to yourself as a reminder that God is with you. And you sing it to God, praising Him in faith, even when you've left your feelings far behind. But did you know that God also sings to you? Today's Scripture reads, "The LORD your God is with you, he is mighty to save. He will take great delight in you, he will quiet you with his love, he will rejoice over you with singing." That verse may be the only happy moment in the entire book of Zephaniah, coming on the heels of image after image of gloom and doom. But it tells us that our heavenly Father will never let suffering, pain, and disappointment have the last word. The last note belongs to Him. Even in your hardship and sorrow, He sings a melody of hope, comfort, and victory over you.

What a wonderful thought, Lord God. The psalmist says You sing at night, in the darkest hours: "At night his song is with me."[1] I have heard Your voice, though sometimes in my pain it seems faint and far away. How I welcome Your songs over my life! I will listen for them and sing back to You.

---

1. Psalm 42:8.

The early Christians took Jesus' title as *Lord* very seriously. When Polycarp, the bishop of Smyrna, was arrested for refusing to bow and call Caesar "lord," city officials asked him to recant and reproach Christ. "Polycarp," they reasoned, "what harm could it do to say Caesar is lord and save your life?" But Polycarp replied, "Eighty and six years I have served Him, and He never did me any injury; how then can I blaspheme my King and my Savior."[1] And so, Polycarp went bravely to his death—a slave of Christ, but more free than any Roman citizen watching him burn at the stake. Today, how is your faith being put to the test? Where are you tempted to bend the rules, step over the line, or shade the truth? Remember that you have a *Lord* who deserves every bit of your love and loyalty. Do the right thing for your King.

Jesus, I may not be facing martyrdom for my loyalty to You, but I know I need to think seriously about what it means to call You Lord of my life. Forgive me for the "little" compromises that come so easily. Forgive me for being hesitant or embarrassed to boldly own Your name in public. You are Lord, and I want to live that truth as well as speak it.

---

1. Polycarp, "Epistle to the Philippians," *Apostolic Fathers*, vol. 1 of Ante-Nicene Fathers (Grand Rapids: Eerdmans, 1988), 89.

Sometimes when people say, "The Lord bless you," they may only be repeating some nice-sounding words to be polite—or to end a conversation. Even so, we ought to take every opportunity to receive God's blessings from every source we can. When someone says, "God bless you," we should reply, "I receive it!" We know from Scripture that God will impart special grace when He prompts another Christian to speak a blessing over us. In today's Scripture, the Lord tells Aaron and his sons to bless Israel by saying, "The LORD make his face shine on you." Paul echoes this theme when he writes that God has given us "the light of the knowledge of the glory of God in the face of Christ."[1] To be blessed, then, is to get a glimpse of the glories of God's Son. What a beautiful thing to do for someone you love, or even for an enemy!

Lord, I pray that You will hear me as You heard the prayer of your servant Jabez long ago: "Oh, that You would bless me indeed!"[2] I long for Your blessings— from sunrise to sunset and all through the night. May the glory of God in the face of Jesus shine on me.

---

1. 2 Corinthians 4:4, NIV 1984.   2. 1 Chronicles 4:10, NKJV.

One night after the accident that broke my neck, when things were as dark as they could be, when all hope seemed lost, I stared at the hospital ceiling from my bed and prayed, "God, if I can't die, please show me how to live." The prayer was short and to the point, but it left the door open for God to respond. Slowly, like someone coming up out of a coma, I felt something stir in my heart. It was a magnetic pull toward hope.

If you or someone you know are struggling against hopelessness today, if everything seems dark, follow the example of today's Scripture and pour out your heart to God. Ask Him anything, even the hard questions. Then leave room for Him to respond. The irony of questioning God is that it honors Him. Honest questions turn our hearts away from despair and toward the Lord.

Father, I don't understand why You do things the way You do, but I promise to bring my questions and heart-cries directly to You. Don't let me talk about You behind Your back or complain about You before others. Your Word tells us "the LORD is close to the brokenhearted and saves those who are crushed in spirit."[1] I count on that truth today.

---

1. Psalm 34:18.

With a recent pregnancy and health complications, Ashley found herself putting on more weight than she'd bargained for. She told a friend, "I want to be beautiful in God's eyes, but I really struggle with wanting to be beautiful as the world portrays women." Nearly two thousand years ago, the apostle Peter spoke to this issue: "Don't be concerned about the outward beauty that depends on jewelry, or beautiful clothes, or hair arrangement. Be beautiful inside, in your hearts, with the lasting charm of a gentle and quiet spirit that is so precious to God." God doesn't see you the way you see yourself. He doesn't think of you as the world thinks of you. So whether you are a woman *or* a man, don't be deceived by what you see in the mirror. Seek a calm, trusting, gentle spirit. It's what is lovely—and handsome—in the eyes of the Lord.

Lord, the images of beautiful people with perfect bodies and trendy clothing show up everywhere I turn. Help me to see myself as You do—a child of God, a daughter or son of the great King, a sister, brother, and friend of Jesus Christ Himself. Today I want to wrap myself in Your beauty and let Your radiance and peace shine from my face.

When we choose to follow Jesus, God enrolls us in the same school of suffering His own Son endured. Most of us really want to follow Christ and learn His lessons, but we squirm at the idea of picking up His cross every day in order to grasp those lessons. We want the deep insights of following Him, but we *don't* want the suffering that sometimes comes with it. We want intimacy with Jesus, but we don't want to make the tough choice to patiently obey Him in our hardships. So what does obedience look like? Don't complain when affliction comes. Don't grumble at life's disappointments. Forgive over and over again. Don't let the sun set on your anger. Rejoice in suffering. Consider others better than yourself. A list of dos and don'ts? No, you're following the Man of Sorrows and Lord of Joy, who gives you all the grace you need for every challenge.

Lord, I know all my words about loving and serving You fall flat if I neglect to obey You. But life is too short for empty words. Fill me with Your Holy Spirit so I will hear Your every whisper and respond to Your every nudge. At the end of this day, I want the sweet assurance that I have pleased You.

When life gets hectic or difficult, we sometimes wish we could just escape and get out from under the pressure. Someone once told David, "Flee like a bird to your mountain." And we want to flee too! We want to flee from the pile of bills, the irritating coworker, or the relentless grind of some chronic health issue. We might find temporary escape in a novel or movie, but sooner or later, reality intrudes again. We really can't escape from our problems. But here's the good news: We can't escape from our God either. The psalmist David wrote, "Where can I go from your Spirit? Where can I flee from your presence?"[1] Your situation won't change by wishing it away. But the very heart of your reality is that You have a God who loves you, who is present with you, and who has both the willingness and the power to help you face every challenge in your life.

Lord, I don't have to run away to the mountains to seek refuge, because You are my Refuge. You are My Mighty Rock. And You are always with me. I don't have to seek You in some foreign land or exotic temple. You have made Your home with me. Forever!

---

1. Psalm 139:7.

Today's Scripture tells a story about a man chopping down a tree with a borrowed ax. Suddenly, the axhead flew off the handle and landed in a deep stream. The man was distraught. What could he do? Wisely, he asked the prophet of God for help. Elisha made the iron *float*, and the man was able to reach in the water and retrieve it. That's quite a story! An axhead that floats? Everyone knows that's utterly impossible. But that's the point of the whole story. God wants you to know He is in the business of doing the impossible. If God is calling you today to undertake a work far exceeding your strength—if it seems absurd to even attempt it—remember that floating axhead, and let your faith rise to the occasion! The God of Elisha still lives, and He lives to help you. He'll provide the strength and ability—but He wants you to provide the faith. So believe God, move out ahead, and just watch the iron swim!

Dear Lord, please forgive me for giving up and walking away from situations that seem impossible to me. Forgive me for dropping certain people and certain problems off my prayer list because I can't imagine how to resolve the difficulties. You are God. You are mighty. Anything is possible for You.

You get home late and put a casserole in the oven—but then you get caught on the phone, and the whole thing burns up in the oven. So you whip up something else, only to have three out of five family members push it around the dinner plate. Before you know it, you're alone at the kitchen sink with your thoughts. Life can become hectic in ten thousand ways. So take a solitary moment in the midst of your whatever, and repeat the good words of today's Scripture: "For great is your love, reaching to the heavens; your faithfulness reaches to the skies." God is very great—and so is His love and care for you. Just for a heartbeat or two, let Him fill your field of vision to the exclusion of all else. God is bigger than His whole universe, but for some reason, it's easy to lose sight of Him. The big picture is *not* the frenzied details of your life. The big picture is a God who holds you in His loving hands.

Dear Lord, the events of my life loom so large. Deadlines. Relationships. Pressures. They become so big in my eyes that I can barely see You. But deep down, I know You are so much bigger than all these things. Right now, once again, I need to refocus on You, my Savior.

People who have a disability and can no longer use their hands can still compose and edit text with a voice-activation dictating program on their computer. You begin by saying, "Listen to me!" and the microphone comes alive. Then, when you speak naturally and smoothly, your words flow across the screen. This program is virtually mistake-proof and can be trained to recognize your voice—and your voice only. To the limit of its abilities, it will obey all your commands. Oh, that we Christians were more like this in listening to the Lord. In today's Scripture, Jesus says, "My sheep listen to my voice; I know them, and they follow me." We must train ourselves in godliness so we can quickly and decisively recognize our Shepherd's voice. When He speaks, we move. When His Spirit nudges, we respond. With an investment of time in prayer and the Word, you'll soon recognize every nuance of the Shepherd's voice.

Lord Jesus, I do want to learn how to hear You better and respond to Your direction more quickly. I know very well that this is where freedom lies—and great peace of heart. Teach me to listen today and obey, dear Shepherd.

Ever felt like you were up against a wall? Stuck? Stalled? Smack-dab against an unyielding barrier? You can't go back, sideways, over the top, or underneath, and there are no detours. What do you do? *Walk through it.* Whoever heard of anyone doing that? Well, Jesus did.

In the upper room after His resurrection, Jesus suddenly appeared in the midst of His frightened, discouraged disciples, who had been hiding behind locked doors. Jesus did the impossible, and He is constantly asking us to do the impossible. When we face a wall—whatever it may be—God wants to walk us through that wall. As we take that first step into impossibility, we will find Jesus there, in the most unlikely place in the most unbelievable circumstance. And then we will walk hand in hand with Him through that wall to the other side.

Mighty One, nothing is impossible with You. No situation is beyond Your help, Your counsel, Your strength. I choose to fix my eyes on You this day rather than on my obstacles. I don't know how I will get through the impossibilities that face me, but holding Your hand, I know I can walk through anything.

Which pain is worse—emotional or physical? We've all experienced both—and we'd rather have *neither*. We've had crushing physical pain, where we can't get comfortable; we've had devastating heartache, where the tears just won't stop. Many people find ways to cope with physical pain—if not through medications, then through mental disciplines that distract from the agony. But internal suffering is another matter.

You can't push mental anguish behind you. Emotional pain creates an emptiness that refuses to be crowded out of your heart. That's where our wonderful God steps in. He holds you in the palm of His hand. He hides you in the cleft of His rock. He shelters you underneath His wings. David—who would certainly know—wrote, "The Lord is close to the brokenhearted and saves those who are crushed in spirit." Remember that. He is never nearer than when your heart is breaking.

Lord, You know everything about me. I can't hide one thought from You or cover over a single emotion. You know exactly how I am formed,[1] and You know so well how to comfort me when I'm hurting. I will tell You all the things I can tell no one else, and You will put Your own shoulder under my sorrow.

1. Psalm 103:14.

In the classic devotional book *Streams in the Desert*, L. B. Cowman made a fascinating observation: "*Waiting on God brings us to our journey's end quicker than our feet.*"[1] In other words, if we want to get to the end of something quickly, then our best hope and solution are to check in with God. Today's Scripture puts it so well: "Wait for the Lord; be strong and take heart and wait for the Lord." There is no shortcut in life that will get you to your goals and heart's desire more quickly than putting your trust in Him. To wait for the Lord means to not rush ahead and not make rash decisions. It means refusing to settle for something satisfactory when something great is right around the corner. To wait on the Lord shows you are thinking of Him first. The Creator of time knows better than anyone how to maximize it.

I know, Lord, there are moments to get up and get moving—in Your timing and at Your direction. But I've wasted too much time rushing ahead on my own, trying to arrange life on my own terms. Instead of saving time, I've lost it—and found myself miles from the goal. Today, I will wait, watch, and listen for You.

---

1. L. B. Cowman, *Streams in the Desert* (Grand Rapids: Zondervan, 2006), 253.

Have you ever stood at the rail and overlooked Niagara Falls? Better still, have you taken the boat ride under the falls? If you could make yourself heard above the crashing water, you might shout, "God is so awesome!" The book of Job declares, "Listen! Listen to the roar of his voice, to the rumbling that comes from his mouth... God's voice thunders in marvelous ways... beyond our understanding." His voice is mighty. You can hear it in thundering waterfalls, cascading ocean waves, and rolling peals of thunder. But He also speaks in the quiet places of the human heart. And this very day, He is calling broken, unhappy, used-up, cynical men and women to Himself. He gives us the privilege of speaking to people who need Him so desperately. In the power of His Spirit, He gives us the right words at the right moments. But we don't have to thunder!

Father, I want to speak for You today. Bring me across the path of someone who needs to hear there is a God who loves and cares for them. If I can't give the whole gospel story, help me to at least point them toward Jesus. Speak through me—through my words and my smile with Your words and Your smile.

In your prayers today, remember your brothers and sisters across the world who struggle daily with severe, mind-bending, chronic pain. Even now, at this moment, there are those living very near you who are at their wit's end. No pain medication, no position in bed, no homeopathic treatment, and no surgery will help. Still, those who rely moment by moment on Jesus have not given in to despair. One woman in this condition quoted from today's Scripture: "Lord, to whom shall we go? You have the words of eternal life." It's true for all of us, no matter what situation we are in. At the end of everything, there is Jesus—Alpha and Omega, First and Last, Rock and Salvation. If you find yourself in a dead-end situation, don't run from Him. Don't turn your back to Him. Don't head in a different direction. Simply put, you have nowhere else to go. Trust anew in the One who has the words of life eternal.

Lord, how could I ever live a single day without You? How could I maintain hope for one moment? There are no dead ends with You. Even death itself is a gateway into real, glorious, never-ending life. And relying on You, day by day, moment by moment, means I must remain close to You.

"My, you are a strong person. I certainly admire your strength." If a compliment like that happens to come to you as a follower of Jesus in the midst of trouble or trials, remember that it's only a partial truth. Yes, we may show flashes of great strength in dark and desperate times—but it's not *our* strength. For those who battle daily with chronic pain or physical disabilities, the reminders of our weakness are even more stark; we can never really forget how powerless we are. But that's good!

In today's Scripture, Paul describes the cross of Christ as the "power of God." And weakness—that is, the empty-handed spiritual poverty that happens when we're down for the count with nowhere else to turn—that kind of weakness is the very key to God's power in our lives. It's why the cross cannot be merely taught or reasoned. It must be experienced.

Lord, what a transaction this is! I confess my sins, and You impart forgiveness. I acknowledge my poverty, and You bestow riches. I yield my weakness, and You give me strength far beyond my own. I come to You now, freely admitting that my physical and emotional reservoirs have run dry. I need Your river of life flowing fast and strong through me.

The Bible makes much of weakness. It constantly drives home the point: We are weak, and God is strong. He is able, and we are not. But then we come across the interesting wording in today's Scripture: "Those parts of the body that seem to be weaker are indispensable." Did you catch that? Weak people— that is, those who suffer, who are driven to the ends of themselves, who lack mind or muscles, gifts or talents—they only *seem* to be weaker. Yes, on the surface, they do indeed appear frail and feeble. But wait! These are the very people who are in the best position to comprehend the limitless power of Almighty God! In his second letter to the Corinthians, Paul writes that God's power is made perfect in our weakness.[1] So do what he did: Boast about your weakness and celebrate your limitations, for *then* Christ's power rests on you.

O God, I love how Your kingdom values turn earthly evaluations on their head! The high and mighty in our world, the gifted and talented, the well positioned and powerful, the "beautiful people," have no more access to the power and purposes of God than the weakest, most unlikely, most humble of Your servants. Truly, Lord, when I am weak, I am strong.

---

1. 2 Corinthians 12:9.

August

"For God so loved the world..." The well-known words of John 3:16 make the love of God sound so far-reaching, so big, so world-sized. Yet Jesus did not die "generally" for the "general" sins of the world. He died for *you*. He died for *me*. The early witnesses who suffered most for being Christians took the act of Christ's sacrifice *very* personally. They were captivated by the startling truth of today's Scripture reading: "I live by faith in the Son of God, who loved me and gave himself for me."

Jesus died specifically for *your* sins and *mine*. Jesus doesn't wave His hand over the entire earth, brush-stroking everyone with His love. No, *He loved me and gave Himself for me*. This is the way we should look at the sufferings of Christ. It wasn't just some historical event millennia ago that changed the world. It was for you. He died for you. He gave Himself for you. Because He loves you.

My heart is Yours, Savior, and I am overwhelmed by Your great love for me. I love the fact that You died and gave Your blood for the whole world. I love it that the door is open for anyone, anywhere, anytime, to believe and find eternal life, but today I am moved that You did it for *me*.

We know that God is *triune*—Father, Son, and Holy Spirit. But how does that work when we pray? In the New Testament, formal prayer is usually offered through Christ to the Father in the power of the Spirit. In today's Scripture, we read, "For through [Jesus] we both have access to the Father by one Spirit." But what about those moments when you want to address your prayers directly to Jesus? *You can.* Many New Testament examples show people praying directly to the Savior, including Paul, who pleaded with Jesus to remove the thorn in his flesh.[1] The Holy Spirit, of course, is very happy with our prayers to God's Son, because the Spirit never draws attention to Himself, but always points to Jesus. Just keep praying… and be assured that all three members of our triune God are listening!

Yes, Lord Jesus, there are times when I long to pour out my heart directly to You—my Savior, King, and Friend. I remember how You suffered for me on the cross, died for my sins, and then came out of the tomb on that best-of-all Sunday morning. I think of You walking on the water toward me in the storm and the night, and I want to come to You.

---

1. 2 Corinthians 12:6–9.

One August, I spoke at a conference in Palm Springs, California, and the temperature registered 118 degrees Fahrenheit in the shade. Due to my disability—and the fact that my body lacks any cooling mechanism—I don't deal with heat very well. To compensate, I have to drink gallons of icy water. Only when I super-saturate every cell in my body can I effectively deal with the heat. It's a good analogy for Christians facing the heat of temptation.

We don't have the resources on our own to successfully deal with the hot and pressing demands of sin. It's foolish—and suicidal—to imagine we could! The only way we can survive is by super-saturating every spiritual cell in our body with the Word of God. That's why today's Scripture reads, "I have hidden your word in my heart that I might not sin against you." So if you are feeling the heat today, don't sip, but *saturate* yourself with the Word.

Father, I really don't want to sin against You. I don't want to lose that sweet sense of Your nearness. I don't want to grieve the Holy Spirit You have given to me as Counselor, Comforter, and Friend. As I consider Your Word today, give me a verse to hold on to—one that will help me walk in the light.

After spending forty days on Mount Sinai meeting with God, Moses experienced a kind of transfiguration. Coming down the mountain, his face shone. God's people couldn't bear to look at the glory on Moses' face, so he had to wear a veil. But then we come to the gospel of Mark, when Jesus came down from the mountain after *His* transfiguration. In today's Scripture, we read, "As soon as all the people saw Jesus, they were overwhelmed with wonder and ran to greet him." Don't you love that? The glory of Jesus was far greater than the reflected glory of Moses, and yet the people weren't blinded. No, they ran happily *toward* the Lord. It just goes to show that the greater glory of Jesus always attracts, drawing people near. Our culture makes a show of rejecting Jesus, but whoever turns to Him will find wonder and joy… and eternal life.

Lord, do people see You in me? I want them to. Are they drawn to Your beauty and grace by any light escaping from my face? I don't want people to read disapproval, distaste, and judgment in my attitude, because they didn't read it in Yours! Shine through me, Lord. I can't shine on my own.

Today's millennial generation won't remember this, but people used to listen to the radio all day, hoping to hear a disk jockey play their favorite new song. When the familiar melody began—what joy! People would immediately sing along… and begin waiting for the next time it came over the airwaves. Now people listen to favorite songs whenever they want to on their iPhone's "favorites" playlist. But isn't it a little boring to get what you want, anytime you want it? It was better when the song was a surprise and the joy was spontaneous. Today's Scripture reads, "It is not good to eat too much honey." But in today's we-can-have-it-now culture, that's just what we do. No wonder so many people find life boring. Even Christians! It's why the Bible repeats over and over, "Wait on the Lord." Let good things come in *His* timing. Withhold a little self-gratification; trust in His goodness and provision… and life will always be an adventure.

Father, what sweet gifts You deliver—often totally unexpected. Like the days when I suddenly feel Your smile, on no special occasion and for no particular reason, shining down on me out of a gray sky. The good I hoped for may be delayed or withheld, but the good You give me in Your timing and wisdom is even better still.

Isaiah 54 is a favorite chapter for many people—right from the first verse: "Sing, barren woman... burst into song, shout for joy." Yes, it's a comfort for couples who have never been able to conceive children, but the passage speaks of much more than physical barrenness. There are times when we all *feel* barren. Times when our prayers feel lifeless, our love is cold, our faith seems weak, and we see no fruit in our lives. When we're in such a condition, what should we do? *Burst into song and shout for joy to God.* And if you are looking for something to sing about, choose Jesus. Even when there doesn't seem to be much to sing about as you look at your own life, you can focus on, sing to, rejoice in, and shout aloud to your Savior. In Him, you will find life for your prayers, love, faith, and—the best part—power to bring forth glorious fruit.

Yes, Lord Jesus, I can always, always sing about You. You are the Desire of Nations, the Bright Morning Star, the Lion of Judah, and the Rock of Ages. You have saved me from judgment and hell and opened the door of heaven for me. How could I be barren? You have made me an eternal child of the King.

Most of us have interests and potential projects that flicker across the screen of our imagination from time to time. *I wonder if I should learn Spanish. I could probably be a mentor to a troubled teen.* But we rarely get engaged in anything unless our heart is truly in it. When my heart is in something, I give it my full energy and affection. I can't wait to be involved in it. Today's Scripture reads, "Let the message of Christ dwell among you richly."

To follow Jesus closely, your heart must be full of Him. You can't get closer to the Person of Christ unless He has your heart. It's not enough to entertain thoughts of Jesus; He must grip your affections. It's not enough to meditate on Him; you must *feel* something for Him. That's what it means to love the Lord with all your heart, soul, mind, and strength.[1] And notice this—the heart comes first.

Dear Jesus, I hold You in my mind today because I have read Your Word and considered who You are to me. Now may those good and true thoughts of You flow into my deepest affections. There is so much more room in my heart to love You and adore You. Fill me, please, with the love I truly desire.

---

1. Mark 12:30.

Today's Scripture reads, "Taste and see that the LORD is good; blessed is the one who takes refuge in him." Jonathan Edwards drew a parallel between honey and this verse. You might conclude that honey is honey because it's golden, has a certain viscosity, or has bits of honeycomb in it. Or… just put a drop on your tongue! Truly knowing honey is to taste that it is sweet, delicious, and delightful. There's nothing quite like it.

The same can be said about our knowledge of God. We can conclude that God is God because we've read facts or heard sermons about Him. But even the devil knows the facts about God! We must taste and see that the Lord is good, sweet, and delightful. How do we do that? The psalmist wrote, "Blessed is the one who takes refuge in him." Crowd in close to Him. Open your heart to Him. Call on Him often. Linger in His Word. Lean on His strength.

Lord, Your Word is sweeter than honey, and I find You utterly delightful. Awaken my heart even more to Your beauty and splendor. And show me what it means to really take refuge in You today. To hide myself in You, to quiet my heart in Your presence, even in the midst of so much busyness and activity.

In high school physics, students get around to learning about geometric proportions—and how simple formulas, calculated out, result in fantastic numbers to the ten thousandth power and more. Perhaps the apostle Paul had something like this in mind when he spoke about "the unsearchable riches of Christ" in today's Scripture. We can study all we want, but Jesus will always be a greater Savior than what we think He is. He is more ready to forgive than you can imagine asking Him. He is more willing to supply your wants and needs than you are to declare them. He is so much more ready to give than you are to receive. Don't ever tolerate low thoughts of a barely adequate, minimalist Savior who might "keep you going" but not much more. Jesus has riches to bestow on you right now. He will not only give you heaven above, but also heaven-hearted joy in serving Him here on earth.

Lord, my thoughts about You are too small, too lean, too sparse, too thin, too colorless. Paul writes about Your unsearchable riches, but on some days, I barely even approach the treasuries. My mind is filled with too many smaller things. I'm in the trees and can't see the mountains. Lift my gaze to see Your greatness and majesty today.

The Bible calls us to take up our cross daily and follow Jesus.[1] But what does that really mean? How do we do that? Does it mean caring for a chronically ill family member, or maybe putting up with a melancholy spouse who doesn't communicate, or living paycheck to paycheck. It *may* mean some of those things, but it's also something more. Since Jesus died for our sins on the cross, then taking up *our* cross means dying to those same sins. Giving them up. Casting them aside. That's what it means when Paul in today's Scripture reading tells us to become like Jesus in His death. A cross is an instrument of death, and when we take it up daily, we learn how to die to ourselves, to our selfish wants and wishes. But take heart! The cross also means *life*. Not just life eternal, but joy and peace and power in the very midst of today's hardships and worries.

Lord Jesus, I'm so glad You spoke about taking up my cross *daily*. Each new day gives me a fresh opportunity to do that. Maybe I didn't pick it up yesterday or the day before, but I can pick it up today. Today, I will put You first. Today, I will place Your desires before mine.

---

1. Mark 8:34.

A lifetime in a wheelchair is a very difficult prop-osition. Impossible? No. But it can certainly feel overwhelming. How, then, can a Christian with quadriplegia—or any other disease or disability—keep a happy heart, a bright attitude, and a sharp focus? It's best explained in today's Scripture: "For our light and momentary troubles are achieving for us an eternal glory that far outweighs them all." I believe this to be *literally* true. Since it is actually our troubles that produce the glory, then the greater the afflictions suffered, the greater the glory these troubles create for us! The only catch is that we must trust God through it all. We must trust Him when life becomes terribly, even unbearably difficult. As we do, our very real hardships feel lighter and lighter—almost "momen-tary," as Scripture says. There is, for certain, a greater glory awaiting on our horizon.

Your truth, Lord, brings such comfort. I believe Your Word today, though it makes no logical sense to the world. If I endure troubles today, staying positive and trusting You, it's the same as depositing glory into my future account. And the glory will far, far outweigh, overwhelm, and surpass my heartaches and troubles in this brief life on earth. I believe it, Jesus, and I am content.

Maybe you're the type of person who doesn't handle change very well. It creates momentary vertigo, an unsteady feeling of imbalance, or a little wave of fear. You think, *What now? How will this work out? How will I manage?*

Thoughts like these should remind us to turn to today's Scripture to hear God: "I the Lord do not change." God's care and compassion for those in Christ will *never* change. He will always provide for us—even though it may seem to be in the very nick of time. What's more, His change in our lives may be exactly what we need. We have a tendency to hold on to old remedies, old patterns, old methods of coping. But the Lord says, "See, I am doing a new thing!"[1] Life changes and God's methods of provision change, but His care for us and commitment to us never will.

Father in heaven, I worship You today as the changeless one. You are ageless, undying, everlasting. You are "the Father of the heavenly lights, who does not change like shifting shadows."[2] The heavens will perish, "but you remain the same, and your years will never end."[3] I bring my fears and uncertainties to You and leave them at Your feet.

---

1. Isaiah 43:19.   2. James 1:17.   3. Hebrews 1:12.

In today's Scripture, God tells His people, "I will give you a new heart and put a new spirit in you; I will remove from you your heart of stone and give you a heart of flesh." So what does *that* mean? A heart of flesh is sensitive when it comes to sin and will grieve over its offenses against the Lord. A heart of stone, however, feels very little, if anything. A heart of stone is deaf to the Holy Spirit's voice, insensible to His nudges, and unyielding to His will. But a heart of flesh? It delights to be molded into the image of Jesus. A stony heart just doesn't get it when people exuberantly worship the Lord, but a heart of flesh cries out, "Oh, I love You, Lord. Please help me to love You even more!" Remember, we can't create our own pliable, sensitive hearts. That is a precious gift from God Himself.

Holy Spirit, I love that You often speak in a "still small voice."[1] It reminds me that surrounding myself with nonstop noise and distractions can keep me from hearing You. You know me so well. If You see areas where I have hardened myself, where I have resisted You, where I have neglected to listen, show me quickly. I want a heart of flesh!

---

1. 1 Kings 19:12, KJV.

If you linger past sunset at Niagara Falls, you can watch the colorful lights illuminate Horseshoe Falls, creating a mighty, cascading rainbow. Back at your hotel room at night, you might drift off to sleep thinking about the majesty of that display and hear its roar in the distance. Eventually, the colored lights blink out, the crowds disperse, the city is quiet, and everything stops. But the Niagara River doesn't stop. It continues to crash over the precipice; the waters continue to flow—with every bit as much force as they had during the day. This is a picture of God's grace, always flowing, always cascading, always constant, never diminishing. Speaking of the Lord Jesus, today's Scripture reads, "From his fullness we have all received, grace upon grace." You will never exhaust His fullness. You will never run out of His unmerited favor. Your teaspoon dipping into Niagara Falls will not reduce its thunder.

Lord Jesus, I am in awe of Your might. One day You will ride a white horse followed by the armies of heaven, bringing judgment to a world that has scorned and rejected You. But now I see Your strength and power poured out as grace—and grace upon grace—for me and for so many who desperately need You.

There is power in God's Word. When we search the Scriptures to find words to wrap around our disappointments, hurts, and worry, we are speaking God's language. And God *answers*. Jesus sets the example. When it comes to heartfelt questions and emotional pain, Jesus experienced both like no human ever has or will. He didn't linger in the damp fog of Gethsemane; He moved in the direction of His Father and proceeded to the cross. There He aimed His cries Godward, not choosing His own words to wrap around His agony, but the words of a psalm: "My God, my God, why have you forsaken me?"[1] Praying words of Scripture doesn't mean all of our questions get answered, or that the pain immediately fades away. But God *will* respond to His Word. Instead of answers, we find the Answer. When we turn toward God in our heartache, He promises our anguished hearts will find Jesus. And He is the One who holds all the answers—and all the questions—in His hands.

Lord Jesus, I especially love to wrap my prayers in the words of the psalms, just as You did on the day You gave Your life for me on the cross. Thank You for listening to me. Thank You for moving in my life.

---

1. Psalm 22:1.

God has said many things in Scripture that bring strength and encouragement to our hearts. But we can also gain comfort by what God has *not* said. In today's Scripture, He declares, "I have *not* said to Jacob's descendants, 'Seek me in vain.'"[1] In these very words, you have the assurance that God *will* hear and respond to your prayers. If you are seeking the Lord over some matter close to your heart, it will not be in vain. Let your doubts and fears say what they will, but if God has not cut you off from mercy—and He hasn't!—there is no room for despair. So today, seek Him with assurance; seek Him with all your heart. As Pastor Timothy Keller writes, "God will either give us what we ask or give us what we would have asked if we knew everything he knows."[2]

Again and again, Lord, I have poured out my heart's desires to You and You have answered in ways I could have never predicted. Your answers have far exceeded my requests. You have made my prayers and my seeking matter because You choose to respond.

---

1. Emphasis mine.   2. Timothy Keller, *Prayer: Experiencing Awe and Intimacy with God* (New York: Penguin, 2014), 228.

Could Jesus have limited the awful pain He endured on the cross? Could He have used His divine powers to somehow mitigate—even a little—the full force of spiritual and physical agony that fell on Him during those six hours? What guarantee do we have that Jesus plumbed much darker depths than the rest of humanity? The gospel writer Mark gives us that guarantee. In today's Scripture, we read, "They offered him wine mixed with myrrh, but he did not take it." To offer a sufficient sacrifice for our sins, our Savior had to go all the way, with nothing held back. Wine mixed with myrrh might have softened His misery, but He would have none of it. His work on the cross would be *complete*.

What work does God want to finish in you? It may, you must realize, involve some hardship and deep pain. But remember, you have a Savior who has gone deeper still.

Lord Jesus, You gave yourself completely for me, holding nothing back. Am I holding anything back in my commitment to You? Am I saving myself, shielding myself, sparing myself, as I seek to follow You? Life in these shadowlands will be over so quickly. Help me to love You and follow You without reservation today.

During His life on earth, Jesus was always thinking of others. As He told us, He came not to be served, but to serve. And He carried that determination all the way to His cross. There He was, in the midst of unspeakable agony, thinking of others—His executioners, His mother, even the criminal crucified next to Him. This example hits home for those of us who feel too sick, too disabled, or too weak to be thinking about others or caring for their needs. May it never be! In today's Scripture, we read, "To be sure, [Jesus] was crucified in weakness, yet he lives by God's power. Likewise, we are weak in him, yet by God's power we will live with him to serve you." Yes, you may be weak. You may be elderly or disabled. But like Jesus, we live by God's power. And we live with Him in order to serve others.

Lord Jesus, no one ever had a greater mission and urgency than You, and Your time on earth was brief. And yet somehow You always had time for people who needed You—children, prostitutes, religious leaders, people with leprosy, tax collectors. You were drawn to needs, to hungry hearts. Today, draw me out of myself and my own worries and difficulties to see people as You do.

You've heard the expression "she sings like an angel." Today's Scripture, however, is an actual quote from an angel—a mighty heavenly being with a "face like lightning" and "eyes like flaming torches."[1] He was giving the prophet Daniel a brief glimpse into his future… and ours: "Those who are wise will shine like the brightness of the heavens, and those who lead many to righteousness, like the stars for ever and ever." We will shine like stars? But what does that mean? Have you ever stood in the night wind and looked up at a blanket of stars? The blazing brightness of the heavens so captures you that words can hardly express the ache in your heart. In Christ, that glory will one day be yours. The ecstasy that captivates your heart at the sight of a night ablaze with twinkling lights—you will one day enter into that ecstasy. One day, you will put on glory like that, and it will be yours for ever and ever.

Heavenly Father, I want to live the truth of this verse today—right now. I want to be wise in You, filled with Your thoughts rather than the shallow wisdom of this world. And I want to lead people out of darkness, pain, and confusion into the light of Your righteousness—the life You offer in Your Son, Jesus.

---

1. Daniel 10:6.

God's children have no need to be enamored with gold—wearing it, flaunting it, hoarding it, or putting trust in it. But it wouldn't hurt to have a small piece around just to remind us of more important, eternal things. A gold nugget or coin might call to mind today's Scripture, where Peter writes that your trials "have come so that your faith—of greater worth than gold, which perishes even though refined by fire— may be proved genuine and may result in praise, glory and honor when Jesus Christ is revealed." Just think! We prove our faith to be genuine when we demonstrate confidence in Christ during a painful trial. What's more—and this is the amazing part—that same confidence will result in praise and honor and glory when Jesus returns. Are you looking for a golden gift to give Jesus on His coronation day? Let it be your genuine, tried-by-fire trust in Him!

O Lord, what will that day be like, when Your majesty and glory are revealed for all the world to see? I am awed and humbled to think that my faith in You will somehow add to Your glory and increase Your honor even more. Praise You for this privilege!

If you are serious about painting a fence, you have to prepare the surface of the wood. You scrape away the old paint—every fleck you possibly can. If you don't, you will simply be covering over weak spots. When the inevitable rains come, followed by baking sunlight, the new paint will bubble, blister, and peel, leaving your fence as ugly and exposed as it was before. In the same way, when the Bible tells us to repent, it means something more than just acknowledging wrong—more than changing our minds or our way of living. It means asking forgiveness or making restitution for the wrongs we've committed. Anything less is just covering up our old ways, and the changes won't last. Make your repentance deep—and it will bring a joyful and lasting change.

Thank You, Father, for making a way for me to know You and be near to You. Thank You that You don't require me to light candles, do penance, or make up for past sins by working very hard for You. You have simply forgiven me, head to toe, heart to soul, in Christ and through His blood shed for me—even cleansing me from a guilty conscience.[1] No words can express my praise and gratitude.

---

1. Hebrews 10:22.

Sometimes because of faulty decision making or maybe just the press of multiple circumstances, we find ourselves tired, discouraged, and a little burned-out. Yes, a vacation or a weekend away might help. But it may not be a change of scenery we need as much as a *change of perspective*. Today's Scripture provides that very thing: "Not only so, but we also glory in our sufferings, because we know that suffering produces perseverance; perseverance, character; and character, hope." Paul is saying, *Stand the test, friends. For the end is in sight. Hope is on the horizon.* Sometimes we think of the suffering in Romans 5 as huge life catastrophes. We forget that God's grace-giving power is mostly for everyday sorts of tests and trials. What are your tests today? Where do you need perseverance, staying power, and hope? Ask God to help you step back and see a bigger picture than the trial right in front of your nose. He uses everything in our lives to mold our characters and make us more like His Son.

I'm thinking of the words of that old hymn—"Just for today, Lord, just for today. Keep me and guide me, just for today." For the next twenty-four hours, fill me with the grace to face each setback and stress point with patience and joy beyond my own.

Many believers feel a little reluctant to wade into the mysterious waters of Bible prophecy. But today's Scripture reminds us that we all have a part to play as the time of our Lord's return grows near. A mighty angel looks John right in the eyes and says, "Worship God! For the testimony of Jesus is the spirit of prophecy." The New Living Translation reads, "The essence of prophecy is to give a clear witness for Jesus." There aren't many Old Testament prophets around these days, but their legacies live on. According to that radiant angel in Revelation, *we have that same prophetic spirit* when we speak about Jesus to others. Whoever shares Jesus with a neighbor or friend is a prophet. The history of our planet is winding to a close, and it is time for the Lord's people to declare Him! The Spirit of God will be working as you lift up the name of Jesus.

Lord, thank You for Your angel's clear, powerful words. You have given us the high privilege of identifying with the highest, best, brightest, loveliest Name in all the universe. Let me have that great joy today, Lord. Let me have the privilege of sharing some simple word, thought, or observation that brings Your name into the conversation. I want to be Your prophet today!

Jeremiah may have felt the arrows of disappointment and tragedy in his life, but they weren't fly-by-chance arrows from who-knows-where. They were *God's* arrows, and they were part of a sovereign God's greater plan for the redemption of this broken world. Our hardships and trials, our struggles and pain, are not random. Whatever happens in your life, it is not by chance. It is no fluke. It didn't result from some crazy, cosmic throw of the dice, or a divine game of Russian roulette gone awry. That means there is purpose—even in the darkness. There is meaning—even in the pain. There is a plan. And the great King over all will very soon bring all the loose ends, frayed threads, broken hearts, and incomprehensible events into a great conclusion that will reveal His glory and His all-surpassing love.

God, I don't pretend to understand Your methods or purposes, or why You allow what You allow in my life. But I trust You, believe in You, and choose to rest in Your sovereignty. Thank You for the Good Shepherd who loves me. Thank You for Your Holy Spirit—Counselor, Companion and Guide—to show me the way home.

In today's Scripture, the psalmist offers an honest reflection. "It was good for me to be afflicted," he wrote, "so that I might learn your decrees." He was looking back on a painful season in his life, when he faced real hardship and suffering. Later, however, he realized it was in those very days that he turned to God with all his heart and dug into the Word of God as never before. Suffering has that effect on some. Instead of turning away from God in bitterness, they fall into His arms and cling to His promises. The point is, you don't have to wait for some life-altering injury or personal tragedy to drive you into the pages of your Bible. It's wide open to you right now! All of its comfort, perspective, and unquenchable hope waits for your discovery. And the Holy Spirit Himself will come alongside to make God's truth come alive in your understanding.

Lord, I'm thankful for the afflictions that have welded my heart to Your promises and precepts. What if there had been nowhere to turn? What if I'd only had my own resources, my own wisdom, to rely on? How lost I would have been! Praise You for friends, mentors, teachers, and pastors who have pointed me to truths that shape my life.

There is nothing worse as a believer than when you deliberately, willfully sin—and then sense the withdrawal of the Holy Spirit's presence and power in your life. In today's Scripture, a brokenhearted David cries out to the Lord, "Create in me a pure heart, O God, and renew a steadfast spirit within me. Do not cast me from your presence or take your Holy Spirit from me." That's a good prayer for us too when we find ourselves in a similar situation.

It's time to freely confess our sins to the Lord, receive His boundless grace and forgiveness, and then invite the Holy Spirit to fill us afresh. And let's ask God to keep us from disobeying Him, even when the shorter, easier route seems so tempting. Today is the day to keep your heart pure, your spirit bright, and your conscience clear. Because no sin, no transgression, is worth risking the nearness of God's wonderful Spirit.

Thank You, Lord, for sending the Comforter to be with me forever. What an astounding thought to realize that I carry the Creator of all things within me wherever I am, wherever I go. Help me to live in a way that causes Your Spirit joy rather than grief. I praise You for this Companion and Counselor in my life.

*A*ugust 27 | Exodus 20:25

In today's Scripture, God tells His people, "If you make an altar of stones for me, do not build it with dressed stones, for you will defile it if you use a tool on it." In other words, the altar was to be God's work, not man's. Only natural stones were to be used, just as they came from the fields or streambeds, not custom stones shaped by a craftsman's chisel.

Isn't it funny how we always seem to want to improve on what God does? Our proud hearts are anxious to have a hand in God's gift of salvation. Human wisdom is always trying to improve on the gospel. We want to dress up the Good News of Jesus to make it sound appealing or contemporary. But let's learn what the Israelites of old learned: The altar is God's alone. Anything we try to add to the cross only obscures the work of Christ—and Christ alone.

There is such deep, deep power, Jesus, in the story of Your life, Your death, and Your resurrection. It's an old story, yes, and retold billions of times. But there is nothing in this sophisticated twenty-first century that can add to its authority, its might, or its limitless potential to change a man's or woman's heart forever.

Southern California is earthquake country. Those of us who love the sunny, Mediterranean climate must also accept the shaking and rumbling that occasionally awaken residents in the night. And, of course, we know that The Big One could be right around the corner.

In today's Scripture, God tells us that one day, all created things will be undone by a massive shaking "so that what *cannot* be shaken may remain."[1] And what are those things that can't be shaken? Consider this: You may lose your health, your strength, your home, or your retirement funds, but you have your salvation. You are forever a child of God. Friends and family may disappoint you or turn against you, but you have the constant love of Christ. You may suffer greatly on earth, but you have the unshakable promise that you will never suffer in heaven. This is a good moment to reflect on all that will not, that *cannot*, be shaken in your life.

Father, today I pray with David, "Though an army besiege me, my heart will not fear; though war break out against me, even then I will be confident."[2] What a wonder! How I praise You! You have given me an assurance deep within that nothing in this world—even death itself—can trouble or sway me.

---

1. Emphasis mine.   2. Psalm 27:3.

"The eternal God is your refuge, and underneath are the everlasting arms... He is your shield and helper." What a highly encouraging word about God's help and intervention in the lives of His sons and daughters! God definitely has something to say about the tragedies and awful situations that happen in our world and how they affect His own. God is constantly protecting us from the full force of the fall and the evil and suffering that go with it. He relentlessly shields us. Time and again, He drives the devil away and rescues us from his wicked schemes. This sin-stained planet would have been ripped apart at the seams long ago were it not for the restraining hand of God. The apostle Paul tells us how the Holy Spirit holds back the evil one, his lawless agenda, and the suffering he instigates.[1] Moment by moment, God is engaged with suffering—restraining it and only allowing those harmful things to reach you that ultimately fit into His plans.

Lord Jesus, bless You for protecting and preserving me today. Thank You for Your strong arms underneath me. Thank You for driving away the enemy from my door time after time and shielding me from his sharp arrows. I pray today, as you taught us to pray, "Deliver us from the evil one."[2]

---

1. 2 Thessalonians 2:6–7.   2. Matthew 6:13.

You're leafing through a desk drawer and come across a photo from years gone by. Maybe it shows a camping trip with your family, a special anniversary dinner with your "one and only," a couple little ones with tousled hair and mischievous grins, or the smile of a well-loved face no longer on earth. Gratitude wells up in your heart, just as it should.

Gratitude looks back on the many things God has done in your life and recalls how good and kind He has been to you, even through trials, challenges, and disappointments. It's why Psalm 105 tells us again and again to remember the wonders God has done. Through remembering, you gain a grateful heart. And then gratitude goes to work informing your faith, reminding you that you have *every* reason to trust God for the future. Gratitude looks back on the past to thank God—and then strengthens your faith to face the coming days with confidence.

Lord God, there have been so many wonders, kindnesses, and miracles. You have blessed me with such amazing, wonderful people throughout my life. Family and friends. Coworkers, helpers, and encouragers. You've given me the high privilege of declaring the love of Jesus in dark places. My heart overflows today. I am truly grateful.

My husband, Ken, keeps what he calls "the ten-second rule." When he senses the Holy Spirit prompting him to do or say something on behalf of the gospel, he will do it before ten seconds have elapsed. "No time like the present," he likes to say. He also realizes that to delay obeying the Lord sometimes means you never will.

Ken's attitude reminds me of Simon and Andrew in today's Scripture. When Jesus called these brothers, "At once they left their nets and followed [Jesus]." At once! Oh, that we would instantly obey when the Holy Spirit whispers a directive. When you hear a command from Scripture, put it into practice at once. On the spot. When you read a passage that pricks your conscience, confess your wrongdoing right then and there. Too many of us brush aside the Spirit's prompting, when the right and best course is to follow Jesus' lead… immediately.

Thank You, Lord, that You walk through my day with me, hour by hour, moment by moment. Help me to stay alert and watchful—with eyes open to opportunities to speak for You and ears open to the voice of Your Spirit. And when You do speak, Lord, remind me not to drag my feet.

September

September 1 | Mark 14:6-9

When it comes to the Christian life, the stakes are high. You and I only get one life on earth to please our Master. No do-overs. Do you ever wake up at night and wonder, *Am I doing this right? Am I making the most of the moments God gives me?* That's why I love today's Scripture. When the woman poured perfume on Jesus' head, some people went ballistic and criticized her. But Jesus rebuked them harshly. He said, in essence, "Back off! She did what she could; it was beautiful." Sometimes I look at my own service to the Lord and think it isn't much. I could have done so much better. And yet I did what I could. Really, that's all God asks us to do. We can only do what we are able to do in the moment. And inspired by the Spirit, it's always a beautiful thing in Jesus' sight.

Lord, You know my heart. You know I do want to please You. The results seem clumsy or ineffective sometimes (well, maybe *much* of the time), but You're not carrying around a clipboard making checkmarks. You are looking at my heart. And in Your great grace, You make beautiful, worthy things out of my awkward, not-ready-for-prime-time attempts to serve You.

Today's Scripture reads, "Blessed is the one who trusts in the LORD, whose confidence is in him. They will be like a tree planted by the water that sends out its roots by the stream. It does not fear when heat comes; its leaves are always green. It has no worries in a year of drought and never fails to bear fruit." That is exactly how Jesus satisfies and sustains us. To have Him near means you have it all. To know Him is to realize He is your dearest, most faithful companion. When life becomes difficult and anxieties press in, your spirit can remain fresh and strong as you send your roots deep into His hidden streams. The next time you pour a cold drink on a hot summer afternoon, pause and praise the Lord for the way He quenches your thirst. He, the Wellspring of Water, fulfills and satisfies like nothing else, like no one else.

Lord, I know these little roots of mine can go deeper into Your life, Your provision, Your companionship. Help me to stay fresh and alive and hopeful, even when my circumstances are hurtful and hard to bear. May the fruit I bear, even in a time of drought, bring honor to You.

Israel was under attack from a fierce enemy while Moses stood on a hilltop, overlooking the battle below. As Moses held up his hands in prayer, the Israelites gained the upper hand. But when he became weary and lowered his arms, the invaders surged back. That's when two men, Aaron and Hur, stepped in, one on each side, holding up their leader's arms "so that his hands remained steady till sunset."

The story reminds us that we all need help, especially when we're in a battle. Think of the times when a friend or family member came to your aid when you felt weary from struggling through some hardship. These people didn't just "happen along." God *sent* them, just as He sent Aaron and Hur. Take a moment today to thank God for the help He sends at just the right moment. Then be sure to show gratitude to the Aarons and Hurs in your life.

Lord, I have had strong helpers my whole life. When I've been weary and discouraged and I didn't think I could go on, You have always had someone who stepped alongside, helping me, praying for me, lending strength and courage when I had so little of my own. Thank You, Jesus. Now please help me to be an Aaron or Hur to someone in need today.

Parts of Southern California suburbia back up against dry mountain canyons where packs of coyotes howl at night. You don't hear them in the daylight, but when darkness falls, the desolate howls begin and often last until dawn. It's a reminder that for all our urban sophistication, wild things still prowl just beyond the light.

In today's Scripture, the prophet describes an invading army "fiercer than wolves at dusk." We all face such invaders—an army of dark, anxious thoughts that tear and devour all suggestions of comfort and calm. At such times, remember that your Good Shepherd stands guard. He never sleeps, never goes off duty. And even in the night shadows, He bids His sheep to lie down in green pastures, untroubled by worries and fears.[1] He is the only One who can slay fierce wolves that crawl out of hiding when darkness falls. Set your thoughts on Him, and the creatures of the night will slink back to their caves.

Lord Jesus, the wolves have been howling again, and my thoughts are troubled. As best as I know how, I rest my thoughts on You. Stand sentry outside the gate of my mind. Set up camp between me and the dark canyons of night. You have never faced a wolf You couldn't slay, and You never will.

---

1. Psalm 121:3–4; 23:1–2.

In today's Scripture, Paul commands believers to "do everything without grumbling or arguing." Seriously, Paul? *Everything?* Paul was writing to group of believers who were facing enormous hardships—and the temptation to murmur must have been great. But writing from jail himself, he wanted them to catch a bigger picture. He wanted the Christ followers to showcase the power of God to those lost in darkness. Nothing makes a scornful, cynical world sit up and take notice of God more than when it observes believers actually rejoicing in their hardships, without a hint of complaint. When we behave in this way, we "shine… like stars in the sky." Think of how complaints or grumbling may have diminished your witness to those around you. You will shine like a star in a dark world today as you put behind you any murmurings, disparaging comments, or negative communication.

Lord Jesus, for the sake of Your gospel and the advancement of Your kingdom—for the sake of this unhappy, cynical, sometimes hopeless generation in which I live—please set a guard at my tongue today. Keep me from complaining. Keep me from speaking empty, disheartening words that really don't help anybody. I want to shine for You today.

We may look strong and stable as believers. But any thinking Christian knows he or she can't survive apart from relationships with other believers. When bitter winds of adversity blow, we need each other's support. When our minds are gripped by perplexity and we don't know which way to turn, we need the counsel, the perspective, and the listening ear of a friend.

God engineered us so we require the intertwining of genuine give-and-take fellowship. Even Jesus needed this. On the last night of His life, when the storms of satanic opposition began howling around Him, He asked for help: "Stay here and watch with Me."[1] If Jesus sought support from his disciples in the midst of His trials, how much more do we need our brothers and sisters? Today's Scripture reads, "Encourage one another and build each other up." You need Jesus today. You also need His people. And they need you.

Father, keep me from living so independently, so separately from others. Show me how I might encourage, affirm, or build up the people I come into contact with today. I need discernment from Your Holy Spirit to know when to speak and what to say, and to know when to be silent and simply be there.

---

1. Matthew 26:38, NKJV.

Four determined friends brought their paralyzed buddy to see Jesus. But it wasn't easy, and it wasn't without great effort. The most critical thing in their lives at that moment was bringing their friend into close proximity with Jesus Christ. Mark tells us, "Since they could not get him to Jesus because of the crowd, they made an opening in the roof above Jesus by digging through it and then lowered the mat the man was lying on." Don't you love it? Faith found a way! A crowd may have jammed the front yard, treading on the flower beds; the house itself may have been a solid mass of people; and a roof with tiles may have presented a formidable obstacle. But there is always a way when it means bringing the needs of a loved one before the Lord. So run the risk. Make the effort. Think outside the box. Your loved one has needs, and Jesus can help. Your faith *can* find a way.

Father, I love the urgency here. These friends wouldn't be put off, sidelined, or delayed. They could have said, "Oh well, another time." But they persevered. They dared greatly. They found a way. Bring that urgency to my heart today, Lord!

Remember the great fish that swallowed Jonah whole?[1] Maybe you feel that way right now. But it isn't a sea monster that's treating you like fish food; it's a painful situation in your life—chronic pain, an illness, or a tough situation with a loved one. You try to think of something else and move on, but your circumstances won't let your mind rest. The truth is, you *can* change your focus. In today's Scripture, Paul writes, "We fix our eyes not on what is seen, but on what is unseen, since what is seen is temporary, but what is unseen is eternal." Speak your determination—out loud. Say to your situation, "You are *not* the focus of my life! No, I will fix my eyes on eternal realities, heavenly hope, and the overwhelming glory that awaits me, because I'm laying up the treasures of my heart above." Refocus your gaze on Jesus today... and find peace.

Lord, insistent voices shout for my attention today. I feel distracted, drawn away from that sweet walk with You that I value above all else. I'm not able to refocus in my own strength. Please draw my eyes, the gaze of my heart, away from all other diversions and demands. Fill my vision, if only for a moment, with heaven.

---

1. Jonah 1:17.

David, while still a young warrior and on the run from his enemies, stopped running long enough to issue a strong challenge to all comers: "Taste and see that the LORD is good; blessed is the one who takes refuge in him." A taste is just a brush across the tongue—a brief, fleeting impression of a full meal. In the same way, we may have tasted that the Lord is gracious, but we really have no idea *how* good and gracious He is. We're like the Israelites, who only tasted one cluster of grapes from the Promised Land they were about to enter. They had no idea how much abundance awaited them on the other side. Friend, we are still on this side of the Jordan, tasting God's goodness one grape at a time. But one day we will enter that Promised Land, and it will take an eternity to experience its true abundance.

I have tasted Your goodness again and again, Lord Jesus. I have tasted the sweet counsel and consolation of Your Holy Spirit. I have heard the Father say, "You are mine. You are loved." Even so, I know this is a meal of samples—a grape here, a bite of bread there. I long to taste more. Someday soon, I will.

Can you remember your first sight of the ocean? Maybe you were a child, camping at the beach. You ran up a little sand dune... and there it was, so impossibly big and wonderful. Or maybe you were older when you first filled your eyes with the wide Atlantic or majestic Pacific. The sight may have made you feel very small, and that diminished sense of self probably made the massive ocean seem even more regal.

Today's Scripture describes the first time God showed His glory to the elders of God's people. They, too, felt small in the presence of One so powerful and overwhelming. With Job, they may have said, "I had only heard about you before, but now I have seen you with my own eyes."[1] Take time today to fill your eyes with God. Empty your heart of cherished ideas of your own importance. Feel your smallness, and be glad you belong to Someone awesome.

Yes, God, I am a very tiny soul in Your vast universe. Yet for some reason, You have loved me and chosen me, and You call me by name. You have said, "Call to me and I will answer you and tell you great and unsearchable things you do not know."[2] I can lose myself in Your greatness, but can never be lost to You.

---

1. Job 42:5, NLT.   2. Jeremiah 33:3.

Living the Christian life is so opposite to, so against the grain of, our human nature. When today's Scripture exhorts us to "rejoice in the Lord always. I will say it again: Rejoice!" our first inclination may be to wave it off. We may prefer to fall into the easy rut of being negative or depressed. Common sense, however, warns us this will only make things worse. Today's Scripture is a triple whammy. We are to rejoice in the Lord *always*, and then *again*, and do so with an *exclamation mark*. Christians can rejoice because their ground for doing so is not in circumstances but in the Lord. How can we rejoice in chronic pain or rejection or bankruptcy? Paul goes on to provide reason enough: "The Lord is near." You can keep a bright outlook in the midst of any hardship; you can have peace of mind when you know that the Lord Jesus Himself is close at hand.

Lord, I know there's no getting around this command. It's as clear as any verse in the whole Bible. You want me to find courage, joy, and hope in You—all the time and in every circumstance. I may not find anything to sing about in my situation, but there are endless reasons to sing about You.

When you pray the Lord's Prayer, do you ever stumble over the words "give us each day our daily bread"?[1] Why should we have to ask? God *knows* we need it. Why doesn't He just supply it? And why ask every day? Why not ask for a whole week or month or year? The answer is, God knows us better than we know ourselves. He has determined we should feel and recognize our daily—even *hourly*—dependence on Him. That way, we will have to go often to His throne for help. We will be daily reminded that we are needy and that He provides. That we are weak, and He is strong. That we are nothing without Him and have everything through Him. Today's Scripture tells us that "each morning everyone gathered as much [manna] as they needed." A day's supply awaited them. But they had to get up in the morning and gather it in!

Lord, how foolish of me to imagine I can slip into cruise control and get by without coming into Your presence. I need fresh manna from heaven. I need a fresh filling of Your Spirit. I need a new set of directions from Your Word. I need a renewed sense that You are with me today, this moment, right now.

1. Luke 11:3.

Thousands of stately old oaks grace the California coast. Oaks may not have the iconic appeal of palm trees, but their twisted branches and gnarled trunks have a rugged beauty all their own—like trees out of a fairy-tale book. Those bends and twists tell a story of countless storms sweeping in off the Pacific and pummeling those trees. When you see the massive branches, you know the roots must run deep. So it is with the way God uses suffering in our lives.

Today's Scripture declares that after we have suffered a little while, God will make us strong, firm, and steadfast. But don't imagine you will be deeply rooted in Christ if you never experience any storms. It is only "after you have suffered a little while" that you become strong and steady in the faith. The wild and windy trials you face today mean deeper roots and staying power in the days ahead.

I feel battered by these storms, God. Be my strength today and keep me rooted in Your love, rooted in Your Word, rooted in the confidence that You have a purpose for everything that happens in my life. I want to draw on Your life today—from the deepest roots to the tip of my branches.

In the book of Judges, Delilah kept pestering Samson, saying, "Tell me the secret of your great strength."[1] She just *had* to know. In the same way, many people are curious about Christians who demonstrate strong faith in difficult times. How are they able to show such confidence in an invisible God? What's their secret? The answer, of course, is revealed throughout the pages of the Bible. The secret of faith is the food it feeds on.

As today's Scripture teaches, a person of strong faith lives "on every word that comes from the mouth of God." Strong faith first takes in the sweet milk of God's Word—and then cuts its teeth on the meat. Strong faith feeds on the Bread of Heaven. If you want great faith, then double-check the condition of your soul. Is it thin and frail? Weak and emaciated? Get away from the distraction of TV, phones, and devices and reengage with the Word of Life.

Lord, I have been feeding on the wrong things. Shallow things. Empty things. Things that won't fill me up and can't help me. And I seem to lose strength so quickly! I lose my grip on Your precious truths that have kept me going through the years. Open Your Word to me. Pour Your life into me. Renew my strength today.

---

1. Judges 16:6.

The prophet Habakkuk undoubtedly enjoyed many days of walking with God in sunlight, peace, and plenty. But then the day came when everything went wrong. There were no flowers on the fig trees, no grapes on the vines, no olives on the trees, no grains from the fields, no sheep in the pen, and no cattle in the stalls.

If you were a farmer surveying such devastation, you might have a difficult time rejoicing in the Lord. But not Habakkuk. He knew the very time to trust God in triple measure was on a day when everything bad happened at once and all his dreams came unraveled. He not only trusted God in the midst of crazy and bizarre disappointments, but he also determined to put a smile on his face. As a result, a very bad day on the Habakkuk ranch ended very well—with joy, trust, and thoughts of God's enduring strength.

Dear Father, I look forward to meeting Habakkuk in heaven. I'm so thankful for his faith and positive, upbeat frame of mind in the face of devastating events in his life. With this good man who loved you, I will also say, "Yet I will rejoice in the LORD, I will be joyful in God my Savior."

Have you ever put yourself in a situation where a non-believer turns to you and asks, "What are *you* doing here?" Maybe you showed up somewhere you knew you shouldn't be—and someone recognized you and seemed surprised. The very question is a rebuke. In the book of Obadiah, God confronted the descendants of Esau for standing by and watching Israel's destruction—and even cheering on the invaders. They were in the wrong place at the wrong time doing the wrong thing. It's as though God were saying, "Do you really want to be one of *them*?" When we claim to belong to Christ and yet sin willfully—even publicly—our sin is especially grievous. It's a double offense because we have been much forgiven, much delivered, much instructed, much enriched, and much blessed. Don't put yourself in a situation where the Holy Spirit has to ask, "What are *you* doing here?"

Lord, sometimes I've wished I could be anonymous and just go where I wanted to go and do what I wanted to do. But even if that were possible, I know You would be there with me. And Your Spirit would whisper, "What are we doing here?" I'm glad for that, Lord, because I really do desire to please You.

God promised to bless Abraham—and then He turned right around and told him he would *be a blessing* to all the nations of the earth. Although few of us today are called to bring God's favor to people across the globe, everyone can pass along God's blessing to a neighbor, a friend, or a total stranger. That's when you know for sure that heaven's blessing rests on your life—when you pass it along to someone else. It happens when you show a kindness or share a smile instead of complaining or grumbling. It takes place when you offer someone a helping hand or take time to listen and encourage them. Whenever you graciously tell someone what Jesus means to you and deliberately point people toward the God you love and serve, you *become* God's blessing to them. It will make their day—and yours.

Lord, it's easy to receive Your gentle love, Your quiet strength, and Your words of reassurance and comfort. I love to soak it all in. But I'm feeling Your nudge today. You don't want me to just take in Your blessing, but to *be* a blessing. And I will, Lord, as You open the doors.

One of my most precious memories of my father was having him tiptoe into the living room while I was playing the piano. For a long while, I didn't see him. Then I caught him out of the corner of my eye, sitting in the chair just behind the piano bench. Suddenly, the music I was making seemed much more important. I played with extra care and greater feeling—*all because I knew my daddy was listening.* Oh, friend, how much more important are the life choices you are making! Do you live out your confession of faith in Christ with carefulness and great feeling? If you knew—really *knew*—the Lord of the universe was near, cupping His ear to listen, would it change what you say and do? Of course it would.

Today's Scripture reminds us that "the LORD hears the needy." God is listening. May that knowledge inspire great joy—rather than fear—in your heart today. God hears *you!*

By faith this morning, Lord, I see You out of the corner of my eye. You are listening in to my conversations, observing my actions, and even considering the thoughts that pass through my mind. You hear my sighs and my songs. That makes me want to do my best today to please You and to bring pleasure to Your heart.

The gospels abound with parables of kings honoring servants for diligence, of landlords showering bonuses on faithful workers, of rulers placing loyal subjects in charge of many cities, and of owners of vineyards paying top wages to the lowliest laborers. These stories teach us that God *wants* to reward us. God is the King and Landlord who has every intention of lavishing on us more than we deserve. As we remain faithful in the midst of pain or problems, we are not only accruing eternal reward; we are giving greater glory to God. And He is worth it! The more faithful we are to Him, the greater will be our reward and joy in heaven. What will those rewards look like? Who knows? But it may include an increased capacity for joy, service, and worship through all eternity. God is more generous than we can possibly imagine, and He intends to more than repay us for every hurt and tear.

Lord, I know the world laughs at these thoughts. They call it "pie in the sky bye and bye." Sometimes even Christians dismiss Your promises as selfish or secondary. But in Your teaching, You never did. You want us to remain faithful. You want to us to hold on to our courage and faith. And You promise incomparable, indescribable rewards as we do.

When Danielle's car hit a patch of black ice, it skidded into a ditch and flipped upside down. Though her hand had been crushed in the impact, she was able to console her two little girls and call for help. It was clear, however, that she would lose her hand. She later wrote, "We have a new norm here, and it unfolds daily." We all face "new norms" after tragedy hits. It could be the loss of a job, a lingering illness, an unwanted divorce, or the death of a loved one. Yes, life moves on, but no, it's not the same. In today's Scripture, Paul writes, "One thing I do: Forgetting what is behind and straining toward what is ahead, I press on... to win the prize for which God has called me heavenward in Christ Jesus." Moving forward in Christ and pursuing His will for each new day are new norms we can all embrace.

Lord, I am so very thankful for the focus You bring to my life. In the words of T. S. Eliot, You are "the still point of the turning world."[1] No matter how many changes sweep across my world, I can fix my eyes on You, pursue You, and find all the purpose for living I need.

---

1. T. S. Eliot, *Four Quartets* (New York: Houghton Mifflin Harcourt, 2014), 15.

There is only one situation where weakness is a virtue. The Bible, of course, urges us to "be strong" again and again. Our culture celebrates powerful people and shows contempt for weakness. But in the presence of the Almighty, all-knowing, everywhere-present Lord of all, admitting weakness is both wise and appropriate. In today's Scripture, the Lord Himself speaks: "Be still and know that I am God." In Hebrew, the term translated *be still* could also be rendered "to be weak; to let go, to release." A paraphrase might read, "Let yourself become weak, and you will know God's power in your life." The apostle Paul agrees: "When I am weak, then I am strong."[1] Whatever adversity you may be facing right now, don't be ashamed if you feel weak or lack strength or resources. That's the best time to present yourself to God, so *He* can supply His strength.

Lord, I remember the story of David at Ziklag. He was defeated and heartbroken, and he had cried so hard that he had no strength left in his body. His men were so angry with him that they were about to stone him to death. But your Word tells us that "David strengthened himself in the Lord his God."[2] That is what I want to do, Lord, right now.

---

1. 2 Corinthians 12:10.   2. 1 Samuel 30:6, NKJV.

I happened to hear recently the old Beatles' classic "Here Comes the Sun"—a song I listened to when I was first injured. Thirty seconds into it, I broke down and sobbed. It reminded me of the dark, depressing days in the hospital when I thought I would never smile again, would never see the sunlight of hope. And now, nearly fifty years later, I still find myself thinking, *How in the world did I ever make it?* But here I am, living in joyful hope as though it were sunshine. How did that happen? Here's how: Day after day, month after month, year after year, I simply cast myself on Jesus. I clung to His name, crying out constantly, "O Jesus!" I'm reminded of today's Scripture: "For you who revere my name, the sun of righteousness will rise with healing in its rays." If you are struggling through dark times, lean on the name of Jesus, and you will also soon be singing, "Here comes the Son."

Lord Jesus, You are better than morning sunlight, more beautiful than summer sunsets, brighter than the billions of suns You scattered across the Milky Way with Your own creative hand. Your Word tells me to walk in the light as You are in the light, and that is my strong desire today.

A passage in the book of Exodus describes the garments of Israelite priests—in great detail![1] God wanted His representatives clothed in a very particular way, reflecting the dignity of their role and the beauty and purity of the God they served. There were regulations about tassels, turbans, breastplates, belts—and even undergarments. If these details start to overwhelm you, turn quickly to the New Testament book of 1 Peter, and read about *our* priesthood as Christians. Peter declares that "you are . . . a royal priesthood . . . that you may declare the praises of him who called you out of darkness into his wonderful light." And how are we to dress as God's royal priests? "Clothe yourselves with compassion, kindness, humility, gentleness and patience."[2] Rather than being compelled by Old Testament law, we are compelled by the liberating mercies of God. Dress yourself today in clothing that will draw attention . . . to Him.

Lord, I want to wear these clothes! I want to slip on compassion and kindness every morning. I want people around me to recognize the humility, gentleness, and patience that come from You. Please let the things I put on today remind people of You.

---

1. Exodus 28. 2. Colossians 3:12.

Today's Scripture reads, "We are happy to tell other churches about your patience and complete faith in God, in spite of all the crushing troubles and hardships you are going through." The Puritans used to say that assurance of faith comes to believers who endure great trials or testing. Of course, no one *wants* heartache or pain. No one in their right mind asks for disappointments or setbacks. But when trials come, God takes careful note of how you navigate them. When you go through hard times, your faith becomes stronger. Your spiritual understanding takes on a sharper edge.

Maybe you're still in the middle of it. Discouragement chills you like a winter wind, and you feel overwhelmed. If you hold on to Jesus through this stormy season, you *will* emerge with a stronger faith. According to Scripture, this enhanced faith is worth any amount of hardship. It's better and much more valuable than gold.[1] In fact, it will hold its value forever.

Thank You, Father, that trusting You through difficulty and pain is worth something. It isn't wasted. It isn't for nothing. The days of struggle, frustration, and tears aren't throwaway days. I don't understand why this refining of my faith has to hurt so much, but I'm going to trust You with all my heart for the outcome.

---

1. 1 Peter 1:6–7.

Enjoying a bit of junk food now and then in moderation is no sin. A little salty snack, a piece of chocolate, or the occasional Frappuccino won't do us lasting physical harm. But it isn't the same when you're talking about the spiritual life. There is no "moderation" when it comes to allowing "junk" thoughts or impure feelings or actions. In other words, God doesn't want us to tackle sin in moderation or by half measures. In today's Scripture reading, Paul writes, "Now you must also rid yourselves of all such things as these: anger, rage, malice, slander, and filthy language from your lips." Notice the word *all*. That means we must refuse to allow such things even the smallest foothold in our lives. It's really about seeking to love the Lord our God with all our heart, soul, mind, and strength.[1] When it comes to loving God and others, we don't do it in moderation. It's all or nothing.

Father, I so easily lose sight of Your holiness. I tell myself a few sinful thoughts won't hurt me. And yet I know very well how playing around with these sins gives them a foothold in my soul. With Your help, I refuse to allow room for thoughts and words that hurt my walk with You and grieve Your Spirit.

---

1. Mark 12:30.

The psalmist David writes, "God is our refuge and strength, an ever-present help in trouble." Nothing is more suffocating, more soul stifling, than hopelessness. This dark feeling spreads when we fail to sense God's hand or the presence of His help in hardship. It's demoralizing to feel as though He is off somewhere in His wide universe, distracted by a billion other needs bigger than ours. Hope, however, is built on fact. And the fact is, God *never* takes time off from tending to our needs. When troubles come, He doesn't back away to allow Satan a free hand. It isn't just God's assistance that's accessible at all times; the psalmist declares that *God Himself* is the always-present help in every trial. The Lord of light is your friend in darkness. The Lord of life stands beside you in death. The Lord of hope is your companion in despair. The Prince of Peace supports you when no peace can be found. The God of all comfort waits faithfully near you.

Yes, You are truly my refuge and strength, dear Lord. Thank You for always being present in my trials. When troubles cloud my horizon, when worries surround like a pack of wolves, when hope and courage drain away from my soul, You are as near as can be—as close as the air in my lungs and the blood in my veins.

After all the terrible difficulties in his life, mostly caused by his own brothers, Joseph told his family, "You intended to harm me, but God intended it for good to accomplish what is now being done, the saving of many lives." I like that word *intended*. The God of the Bible is a God of intention—even when (perhaps *especially* when) it involves accidents, mishaps, and attacks. Even in the face of unexpected twists and turns, even in unforeseen calamities perpetuated by people with evil motives, God *still* has a purpose, a target, a goal, and a plan. This means your trials have more meaning—much more—than you realize. Your problems have more purpose than you can imagine. Not because God merely uses bad things, but because He intends them for the salvation of others. He purposed your problems so your example of faith, patience, and a determinedly happy heart will bring others to Jesus.

Father, please show me how I can use my story—even the difficult and painful parts—to draw people toward Jesus and new life in Him. It's a great comfort to know You have purpose—and intentions beyond my understanding—for this season of pain. Be my help, my strength, and my song today.

Many of us at one time or another have wondered how God could love us and still allow so much pain in our lives. It really depends on how we view that word *love*, doesn't it? God's love is not an easy, breezy feeling of infatuation. In fact, God's love is always best displayed in the midst of pain and hardship. Just hours before the cross, Jesus told His followers, "Greater love has no one than this, than to lay down one's life for his friends." God loved us so much that He *died* to show it. And look what His love has won for us—escape from hell and a home forever in heaven. When we consider how God's love secured for us such awesome benefits and blessings, how dare we question His motives? If He loved us enough to die for us, then surely He can be trusted in the middle of our pain and problems.

Dear Lord, I know very well that Your love is vast beyond reckoning. But in these days of struggle, it's difficult for me to *feel* what I know. I choose now to simply rest on the biggest truths of my life: Jesus loves me, died for my sins, and has won a place for me in heaven.

We Christians shouldn't smirk at the misery of our contemporary culture or the frantic grabbing for diversions, attention, or pleasure. This is no time for smug self-righteousness. This is no time to get cranky that our country has been hijacked by this or that political movement. This is a season, perhaps like none other, to truly influence our nation, to showcase the love of Jesus through specific, practical acts of kindness. Others may whine and gripe about the world "going to hell in a handbasket," but, honestly, we know better. We know that good will ultimately triumph. So let's show what this ultimate good will look like by rolling up our sleeves and helping neighbors, feeding the hungry, and surprising people with courtesy and care in Jesus' name. If you find yourself overly discouraged or pessimistic about today's culture, then find a way to start serving that culture in ways that point to the love of Christ.

Lord, I admit it. I can get caught up in politics and negative talk about this culture and generation. Help me to remember You have put me in this place and time for a reason—and it isn't to complain or despair. Please open doors for me today to direct Your love to those who cross my path.

In a message years ago, missionary Elisabeth Elliot said she was sure her deceased mother still prayed for her. Does that statement startle you? Maybe create a little uneasiness? Here is how she explained it: "Since I know that Mother talked to Jesus about me all the time while she was here on earth, why should I think she'd *stop* doing this now that she is with Him face-to-face?" Paul writes in today's Scripture, "Love never fails." And if it never fails, why should we think that Elisabeth's mother stopped loving her when her spirit went to heaven? Yes, the current state of departed saints is cloaked in mystery. We know they're with Jesus and that they're happier, healthier, and wiser than ever before. Beyond that, who can say? It's not too much of a stretch to think their love for us and for the church brims over with wise prayers to our Savior.

Lord, it moves my heart to think that at this very moment You're in the presence of my dad and mom—and so many other friends and loved ones who have left this earth. I can't see them, but You can. I don't know if they're aware of my life and my challenges today, but I know You are, so I rest in that truth.

October

The word *happiness* gets a bad rap with some Christians today. They take great pains to separate it from the word *joy*. Joy, they patiently explain, is a gift of the Holy Spirit, but happiness is only a shallow, knee-jerk response to pleasant circumstances. The Bible, however, doesn't split such fine hairs. Today's Scripture reads, "May all who seek you *rejoice* and *be glad* in you."[1] The Bible uses the terms *joy* and *happiness* interchangeably— along with *delight*, *gladness*, and *blessed*. There is no scale of relative spiritual values applied to any of these.

Happiness is not a second-class emotion beneath joy. Are we really telling people the gospel won't bring happiness? Any perceptive listener would answer, "Then how is it good news?" Let's redeem happiness in light of Scripture and church history. Our message shouldn't be, "Don't seek happiness," but rather, "You will find in Jesus the real and lasting happiness you've always longed for."

Lord Jesus, in You I have found a happiness that goes way beyond the happenings in my life. I'm happy, Lord, even in my pain and trials, because I know that You are with me, that You love me, that every moment is in Your hands, and that one day soon, I will be with You forever.

---

1. Emphasis mine.

In the parable of the sower, Jesus described how "some [of the seed] fell on rocky places, where it did not have much soil." The gospel seed had nothing to root itself into, nothing in which to anchor. The soil was simply too shallow. And because Jesus taught that the soil represents our hearts, could it be that our hearts are too shallow? Is there enough soil? When fresh truth falls into your heart, is it able to take root? Does it find an anchor in your soul? The Bible calls us to go deep in our life in Christ. It starts with putting away a surface interest in God and fertilizing the soil of your heart through daily prayer and reading God's Word. As you do, you will become more and more occupied with spiritual reality and less and less distracted and caught up in the shallow trivialities of this life. The deeper your heart becomes, the more God's truth will take root, blossom, and bear fruit.

Lord, I know Your truth sometimes skips across the soil of my heart like a rock on a frozen pond. That's not what I want, Lord. I want to receive Your words, Your warnings, Your encouragements, and Your guidance. Open my spiritual eyes and ears, Lord. Deepen the capacity of my heart.

King David wrote, "The LORD will perfect that which concerns me." Maybe you resonate with that verse because, at this moment, there are *a number* of things that concern you. This passage tells us that God is in *all* of those concerns—and using them to perfect you. The Living Bible reads, "The Lord will work out his plans for my life." Since none of us know how long we will live, God may be close to completing His work, or He may have a long way to go. The encouraging thing is, He's at work in your life. In your triumphs and golden moments. In your hardships and disappointments. These are all evidence of the perfecting work of God in you and through you. Yes, afflictions—especially new and hard ones—will always be a concern. But they are never random. And God will use every one of them for your good.

Lord, I do have concerns. Of course I do. But I can smile, knowing that I am still under construction, and that when You have finished, You will take me home to be with You. I can have quiet contentment, even in my afflictions, because of the future that awaits me. Taking up my cross today leads to a crown tomorrow.

October 4 | Exodus 3:3

In today's Scripture, Moses catches sight of something totally unnatural—a desert bush in flames, which keeps on burning and burning—but never burns up! The text reads, "So Moses thought, 'I will go over and see this strange sight—why the bush does not burn up.'" Christians who suffer greatly and yet also graciously often cause the same curious response. They are a spectacle of grace to the church, like flaming bushes unconsumed, causing onlookers to ask, as Moses did, "Why is the bush not burned up?" Hymn writer John Newton has observed that the strength and stability of such believers—these fellow Christians who endure great pain yet keep their hearts bright and their smiles fresh—can only be explained by the miracle of God's sustaining grace. Friend, if you are suffering today, you are a fiery bush. You are also on display, causing others to marvel at God's grace in your life!

Father, part of me resists being a spectacle or drawing the attention of others. But if my life somehow draws attention to You, if the way I process suffering draws people to Your grace and strength, then I can accept—or even embrace—being on display. Thank You for sustaining me. Thank You that Your grace is enough for me.[1]

---

1. 2 Corinthians 12:9.

In today's Scripture, King Belshazzar sees a cryptic message handwritten on the wall of his banquet room. When he asks Daniel what it means, God's prophet replies, "You have been weighed on the scales and found wanting." Thinking about this reply might prompt us to ask, "Where are *we* found wanting?" To find out, look to Jesus and ask yourself how much you have been conformed to His likeness. Do you have His meekness? His humility? His gracious spirit? Do we, like Paul, consider ourselves "the worst of sinners" and least of all the saints?[1] Can we say with him, "For to me, to live is Christ and to die is gain"?[2] Let's ask God to bring us there. Let's ask His Spirit to rekindle our need for God, for deeper faith, for warmer zeal, and for more fervent love. Together let's cry out, "Please, Lord, if I am to be weighed on Your scales, may You never find me wanting."

Lord Jesus, I think about the way You spoke to Your church in the book of Revelation: "I know your deeds... I know your afflictions... I know where you live... I have found your deeds unfinished."[3] You examine my life and my words, my thoughts and my attitudes. That's why I humble myself before You, Lord, and ask for Your grace.

---

1. 1 Timothy 1:15.   2. Philippians 1:21.   3. Phrases drawn from the Lord's words to the seven churches in Revelation 2–3.

October 6 | Ephesians 2:6–7

Imagine receiving a personal letter from Queen Elizabeth, stamped in gold with a royal seal. And in that letter, the sovereign of the United Kingdom takes an oath on the blood of her son, promising to spend all of her vast wealth showing you as much kindness as she possibly can for the rest of your life. Wouldn't that get you excited? Consider, then, what God Himself promises in today's Scripture. We are told we have been seated with Christ in the heavenly realms "in order that in the coming ages [God] might show the incomparable riches of his grace, expressed in his kindness to us in Christ Jesus." God promises to spend the undreamed-of riches of Christ Jesus showing you as much kindness as He can for the rest of eternity. Today, reflect on the riches of grace, strength, mercy, salvation, favor, and one blessing after another—all of which are yours because God made you a co-heir with Christ.

Lord, I believe You. You will one day show me the limitless kindness of Jesus Christ through endless ages. But You also shower those riches on me today! I am rich in Your unmerited favor and mercy. I am blessed by Your counsel, provision, forgiveness, and sweet companionship. Your generosity awes and humbles me.

Today's Scripture reads, "Take delight in the LORD, and he will give you the desires of your heart." Sometimes we see the first half of this verse as a means of obtaining something. *Take delight in God, and you will get.* Get what? Well, maybe a husband, a wife, a child, a job, or a new apartment. The truth is, when we take delight in the Lord, *He* becomes the desire—the only desire—of our heart. The Christian who truly takes pleasure in God doesn't love Him out of compulsion. He doesn't feel fettered by his faith, driven to duty, or marched at gunpoint into right living. He doesn't think, *How near can I get to wrongdoing without becoming entrapped? How close can I dance to the edge of the cliff without falling over?* No, when we love God with all our heart, every obedience is a pleasure. And pleasing Him makes us ten times happier than pleasing ourselves.

Lord Jesus, I have seen this so often in my life—how You begin to replace my wants and desires with Your own. It isn't always easy to let go of my longings, as You know so very well. But what You leave in their place is so much better. You replace cheap, sparkly trinkets with pure gold.

If you have a job flipping burgers, you may find it difficult to look at your work as exalted. A stay-at-home mom who changes diapers all day, loads the dishwasher, and haggles with the appliance repair guy may look at her work as less than lofty or noble. But consider the potters mentioned in today's Scripture: "They were the potters... they stayed there and worked for the king." Although they were involved in menial labor and found themselves elbow-deep in mud all day long, they kept something very important in mind: They were working for the king.

It's always a great privilege to be enlisted in royal service, whatever your task might be. And so it is for Christians. No matter how lowly your occupation, "it is the Lord Christ you are serving."[1] Remember that. Remember to work wholeheartedly. The diligence and excellence you put into your labors have the attention of the great King of the universe.

Dear Father, help me to keep this in mind today. When the tasks seem long or tedious, when the demands begin to wear me down and I just want to be home, remind me that I am serving the Lord Christ, the coming King, not a job or even a ministry.

---

1. Colossians 3:24.

In the book of Acts, Luke describes the aftermath of a terrifying shipwreck that landed the apostle Paul and 276 frightened and shivering men on the beach of Malta. It was a cold, rainy day, and the men were bruised, battered, and exhausted from their ordeal. The sympathetic islanders quickly made a fire for the survivors, but one of them quietly left the warmth of the circle: "Paul gathered a pile of brushwood."[1] Think about that for a moment. There were younger, stronger men in the group, including soldiers and sailors. But Paul, an elderly missionary, gets up and begins serving the others by collecting firewood. What is the secret to such extraordinary service? Not cherishing inflated ideas of your own importance! The other secret has to do with focus.[2] As Paul later wrote to the Colossians, "Whatever you do, work at it with all your heart, as working for the Lord, not for men."[3]

I know, Lord, that I'm sometimes halfhearted about tasks in my daily schedule. I can be motivated about activities I like, but other obligations seem boring or tedious to me. I feel like I'm doing them out of duty or just so I can check a box. Remind me that I'm working for You—and because of my love for You—all day long.

---

1. Acts 28:3.   2. Thanks to my pastor, Bob Bjerkaas, for some of these thoughts.   3. Colossians 3:23, NIV 1984.

Memory is frequently the agent of misery. A sad frame of mind will easily call up every dark day in our past and every gloomy regret from days gone by. Wisdom, however, can transform memory into an angel of comfort. That's what happened to Jeremiah. In today's Scripture, he confesses, "My soul is downcast within me. Yet this I call to mind and therefore I have hope." Jeremiah had trained his memory to look on the bright side, the hopeful side—which is always God's side. He knew God was at work even during dark times in his past, and Jeremiah let that powerful truth bring hope and comfort to his soul.

Today, if you find yourself assaulted by sad memories, recall how God miraculously worked through even those losses, failures, and disappointments. Remember the loving-kindness of the Lord, and look for the trace of His hand in every downcast moment from your past.

Father in heaven, I have plenty to regret. And if I dredge them up, there have been long struggles, lonely hours, hurtful words, and dark times aplenty in my past. Today, I choose to remember how You have woven the tapestry of my life with dark threads and bright golden ones, creating a work of beauty, a masterpiece of grace.

October 11 | EPHESIANS 2:10

Have you ever watched a sculptor creating a statue from clay? She pushes against that clay with strong, skillful hands, working intently and often wetting it down so it might yield more easily. In today's Scripture, Paul writes, "We are God's handiwork, created in Christ Jesus to do good works, which God prepared in advance for us to do." Since we are divine works of art—still in process—the Master Artist will not be satisfied until our human clay has a certain character. He loves us and will take endless trouble to shape and conform us to the image of His Son, Jesus. We might wish at times that He wouldn't work the clay of our lives so hard, but God knows our limits. Through all our days and years, He works intently, with consummate skill, teaching us to yield to His divine pressure. Would any of us dare to wish for a less glorious destiny?

Since I'm still here on earth, Lord, I know Your creative work in me isn't finished yet. You're still shaping me. Still bending me to Your purposes. Still sculpting my destiny with infinite skill. Forgive me for the times I have resisted Your work and Your will. I yield to Your vision of what I can be.

Napoleon once wrote, "Conquest has made me what I am, only conquest can maintain me."[1] When it comes to the Christian life, we can say much the same. The battle never stops while we draw breath on this earth. And we will only conquer and receive a heavenly crown if we continue in our faith. This is what *perseverance* means—and no one said it would be easy! The world, the flesh, and the devil will try everything to discourage, dissuade, or distract us. Satan and his demons will whisper, "Oh, just give it up! The Christian life is too hard." But today's Scripture has stirring words for every conqueror: "Do not throw away this confident trust in the Lord. Remember the great reward it brings you! Patient endurance is what you need now, so that you will continue to do God's will. Then you will receive all that he has promised."

Lord Jesus, sometimes I think my worst enemy is just being so tired—tired of the physical hassles, tired of the pain, tired of fighting off the whispers and mockery of the enemy. My stamina is almost gone, and my tank is almost empty. Come quickly to my side. Be the strength and song I can't pull together on my own.

---

1. "Entries from the Diaries of Napoleon: Diary 1802," www.thecaveonline.com/APEH/napoleon.html#anchordiary (accessed February 25, 2016).

When you were a child, did you like to sleep with a light on? Somehow a dark bedroom doesn't seem quite so scary with a nightlight glowing softly in the corner or a door opened just a crack to let the light in the hall shine through. Light chases away fears and gives comfort. In today's Scripture, David writes, "The LORD is my light and my salvation—whom shall I fear? The LORD is the stronghold of my life—of whom shall I be afraid?" What a personal statement this is! The Lord is *my* light and *my* salvation. It's not that He gives light; He *is* light. He doesn't give salvation; He *is* salvation. Jesus is light within, light around, light reflected from you, and light to be revealed to you. Don't be afraid of what's out there in the dark. The powers of darkness have been utterly broken, and the grip of hell shattered beyond recovery. If Light itself is for you, whom or what in the world could you possibly fear?

Lord, You have rescued me—not only from the growing darkness in this world, but also from the darkness in my own heart and mind. You have lifted me into a light that never fades. Shine in me and through me today, Bright Morning Star!

The other day, I was backing my wheelchair out of my van on a very steep hill. Take my word for it; it was really scary. My husband, Ken, was behind me, saying, "It's okay, Joni. I'm here. I've got you!" Right then, I had a choice. I could either make my husband look good by trusting him and backing out, *or* I could make him look bad by giving in to my fear and refusing to budge. I budged! I put my power chair in reverse and proceeded down the steep ramp.

In spite of my queasy feelings, I wasn't about to convey to onlookers that my husband was untrustworthy or unable to help. In the same way, we glorify our God when we trust Him to do what He promises to do—especially when all human possibilities are exhausted. And the harder it seems it will be for Him to fulfill His promise, the better He looks when you trust Him.

Lord, I want others to see how much I trust and rely on You. I know it may mean being in some scary situations where my faith will be stretched and tested. But I want people to see how reliable and faithful You are—and how You answer prayers in ways I could never predict.

"I Left My Heart in San Francisco." Remember that old Tony Bennett classic? The last line speaks about coming home to the city his heart longs for. And in a way, that's the Christian's song, isn't it? When we came to Christ, the Lord freed us from the god of this age. You used to be kidnapped and brainwashed, made to think you were really a citizen of enemy territory. But then the King rescued you and shocked you out of your spiritual stupor. And now? You realize this world is not your home, and your heart longs for the city above. For now, though, the king tells us to stay here in enemy territory—with all its hardships and dangers—and live like an alien in love with the homeland. Friend, don't leave your heart in San Francisco—or any other city on earth. Wherever you live, let your heart walk the streets of heaven. And make it your aim to bring as many others to heaven with you as you can.

Father, I read in the book of Hebrews about believers who long for a better country and a heavenly city—and that is my heart too. How I praise You for such a hope! Help me to speak to at least one person today about my hope in Jesus.

Maybe you were blessed to have a dad or mom who read fairy tales to you when you were a child. Most of us can remember the last few words of each story: "And they lived happily ever after." No one had to explain what those words meant. We just knew. We understand those words because today's Scripture explains that "[God] has also set eternity in the human heart; yet no one can fathom what God has done from beginning to end." God has placed within us a strong sense of "happily ever after," and yet there are things about life today we simply can't fathom. Yes, we were made for eternity—and it's in the deepest places of our hearts. We were also made for earth, however, and earth is no fairy tale. But the true Prince has kissed you with His peace, and He has promised that, together with Him, you *will* one day live happily ever after.

Lord, we long for happy endings. We long for reconciled marriages, the return of prodigal children, and the cure for cruel diseases that tear loved ones from us. But many of those happy endings are out of reach. Fill my heart today with thoughts of my eternal home, where there will be no endings at all.

Will heaven's ecstasies really go on *forever*? Is it true we will never become bored? God sprinkles tiny hints of heaven on earth to give an inkling—just the briefest glimpses—of the wonders that await us. You may catch a suggestion of it in a magnificent sunset. Or hear a faint trace of it in the haunting strains of Dvorak's *New World Symphony*. Or smell it in the ocean air when dark, gray clouds blow in from the distance. Or recognize it in the soft gaze of someone you love. If these are mere flashes and keyhole glances of heaven, what will the reality be? Every earthly beauty that moves your heart is a God-sent gift to whet your appetite for the next life. Yes, the way here on earth can be terribly dark and difficult at times. But our Lord has left signposts pointing the way home.

Lord Jesus, I remember Your prayer: "Father, I want those you have given me to be with me where I am, and to see my glory."[1] I think that's the best thought about heaven. You want me there! You want to be with me forever! You're waiting for the day when I walk through the door.

---

1. John 17:24.

In today's Scripture, Jesus said, "No one who puts a hand to the plow and looks back is fit for service in the kingdom of God." It calls to mind the historical account of the Spanish conquistadors. In 1519, Hernán Cortés and a small army left Cuba and set out on a great conquest to find gold. To convey the seriousness of the mission, when Cortés landed at Veracruz (Mexico), he ordered his men to deliberately scuttle the ships that had brought them to land. There would be no "exit strategy"—no turning back for the Old World. Their destiny was now the New World.

The lesson for believers is unmistakable. We need to be just as committed about leaving our old world, old priorities, old habits, and old lifestyle choices. When Jesus asks us to follow Him, it means not even looking back. What do you need to destroy to make good on your radical commitment to Him?

Lord, I don't even want to look over my shoulder to see if I've scuttled my ships. Today is all that counts. You have called me to take up my cross daily and follow You, and that is what I seek to do. Holy Spirit, please give me a forward focus today, making the most of every opportunity You place before me.

I was discouraged one morning, but God had already sent His provision of encouragement to come to my aid. It came in a letter from a young man named Nathan. He wrote, "Joni, when God says anything, He is promising—which is as good as swearing. And what has God sworn concerning you? He says in Deuteronomy 33:25, 'As your days, so shall your strength be.' So are you feeling weak today? Just remember every hint of sadness or weariness only qualifies you all the more to lean on Christ with the full weight of your soul." I'd never even met this guy, but he followed a simple prompting of the Holy Spirit, enabling me to breathe in fresh courage.

Do you know someone who is feeling discouraged? Listen to the Spirit's prompting—and share a word of encouragement. Text it; email it; phone it; write it on a card; show up in person. Just follow through, and watch God work.

Dear Lord, this is an amazing prospect. To think I could be part of Your plan to breathe Your courage into one of Your struggling sons or daughters! I love that thought. Please nudge me into action through Your Holy Spirit and give me the very thoughts and words You want me to express.

You can't be a Christian. You're a nobody. God would never make time for the likes of you. It's an accusation the devil persistently throws at believers. Our adversary is constantly trying to get us to doubt our relationship with Christ and our citizenship in heaven. The same thing happened to Jesus. No sooner had the Father publicly declared, "This is my Son," than Satan countered with, "If you are the Son of God…" His strategy hasn't changed; he does the same with us today. Jesus' response was simply to say, "It is written…" The Word of God is called the sword of the Spirit because it is our main offensive weapon against the enemy.[1] Our Savior has given us the highest example—be ready to speak the Word of God. When Scripture is in your mouth, on the tip of your tongue, it will defeat the devil and doubts every time.

Lord Jesus, help me to be ready today when the enemy attacks. Thank You for giving me Your example in always using the Word of God to defeat the enemy's lies and tactics. Life is too short to fall for Satan's deceptions and to be discouraged and sidetracked by his attacks. Keep me in Your Word, Lord. And keep Your Word in me.

---

1. Ephesians 6:17.

"Come near to God," James writes, "and he will come near to you." What a sweet, simple thought! If we deliberately crowd in close to God, He will crowd in close to us. One woman used to describe such closeness as cuddling up in the Lord's lap, snuggling in tight, embracing Him, and feeling His nearness. But then, after a prolonged period of terrible suffering in her life, that picture changed. From then on, closeness to God meant collapsing, absolutely fainting, and falling back into God's arms—and then feeling Him carry her.

This may be a time in your life when you face emotional or physical pain. Take a minute to memorize James 4:8. Draw as close to God as you know how, and you will find He is also drawing close to you. As He does, you will sense His power and have the courage to keep going, carried along in His arms.

Lord, this sense of being close to You isn't something syrupy or sentimental. It is life itself! It's the reason for drawing breath each day. Please keep me from drifting from You because of unconfessed sin, neglect, or a hundred other lesser preoccupations. I need to sense You are carrying me today. Thank You for being so close.

October 22 | 1 Timothy 6:17, NKJV

If you tried to describe God's New Testament way of dealing with His sons and daughters, you might settle on the word *abundance*. Today's Scripture says that God "gives us richly all things to enjoy." It's true. All the time. No matter what our circumstances. He is always blessing. Always giving. Jesus is the sweet, wholesome manna always falling on the camp. He is the rock in the desert, sheltering weary travelers in its great shadow and sending out streams of life. He is the bronze snake—lifted up high; offering healing, hope, wholeness; and delivering from the deadly poison of sin and self-centeredness. He is the sun always shining. He is the wellspring of grace constantly overflowing. Who has ever returned from His door unblessed? Who has ever stood up from His table unsatisfied? Scripture says, "Bless the Lord, O my soul, and forget not all His benefits."[1]

Father, I don't have a reservoir big enough to contain all the ways You favor me, help me, and pour blessing into my life. I want to open the spillways today to let Your life flow through me and out of me so You can touch others who desperately need to taste Your goodness today.

---

1. Psalm 103:2, NKJV.

Any number of circumstances can unleash a flash flood of disappointment in our hearts. For the most part, we're able to muster emotional strength to stem the tide. But when one bad thing piles on top of the next, discouragement begins to overwhelm us. We wake up one morning to realize we've lost every bright prospect for a better day.

When our hopes are tied to our circumstances, in the way "life works out," we're bound to be disappointed. Because life on this side of heaven hardly ever falls together the way we wish, plan, or expect. It's a fragile house of cards, and we keep praying that nobody bumps the table. Real, biblical hope, however, isn't tied to circumstances. It is tied to God, the One who never changes, who loves us with an everlasting love, who promises to work through even hurtful and incomprehensible situations for our good, and who has reserved our new home with Him in heaven.

Lord, the psalmist David reminds me that You know how weak I am and You remember I'm only made of dust.[1] You know how I so foolishly tie my hopes and expectations to temporary, passing things. Help me to readjust my heart today. Help me to rest my deepest hopes in You.

---

1. Psalm 103:14, NLT.

The psalmist writes, "You have been my hope, Sovereign LORD, my confidence since my youth." These are the words of someone who has passed through dark places, challenging mountain ascents, and slippery trails with uneven footing. And yet he is able to say, "My hope is as steady as ever—not because of my life circumstances, but because of the God who holds me in His firm grip. I have all kinds of confidence, but none of it is in myself." Christian hope has an object of its focus, and it is God himself, the God who has revealed Himself in the Bible. To hope in God is to not feel consumed by difficult life challenges, because you know His mercies and compassion are fresh every day. To hope in God is to have confidence that one day when Christ returns, He will close the curtain on sin, Satan, and suffering and will make all things right.

Father, this is one of those times where I feel crowded, jostled, and boxed in by the troubles of the day. Right now, I choose to remember how You have helped me, comforted me, and provided for me in days gone by. I declare my confidence in You, in Your sure and steady love, and in Your ability to walk me through any circumstances.

October 25 | JOHN 15:15

Years ago, when I was first hospitalized after my diving accident, I dreaded the long, lonely nighttime hours when friends weren't allowed to visit my ward. So I comforted myself by imagining a personal visit from another Friend—the Lord Jesus. I was inspired to do that after reading today's Scripture verse, where Jesus specifically names His disciples as friends.

I pictured Him coming through the doors of my hospital ward, walking over to my bedside, and saying, "Hey, friend. What did you learn in physical therapy today? Was it nice to see your sister at dinnertime? Anything you'd like to talk about or get off your chest? Tell me all about it, Joni." Talking with Jesus like that strengthened my confidence in Him. He became my Friend who saw me through months of dark, suicidal depression. If you find yourself alone with no friends around, remember Jesus is your comforting friend. He will support you.

Dear Jesus, even though I can't see You, I know beyond any doubt that You are with me. Your companionship calms my anxious heart, stills my racing thoughts, and lifts the dread and worry from my shoulders. Thank You for being there, ready to talk about things great or small—or to just hold my hand—at two in the morning.

Most of us can get a little worked up when defending ourselves. Sure, we can handle "valid" criticism (or not!), but when someone attacks us unfairly or misrepresents the facts, we naturally have to speak up on our own behalf. In today's Scripture, as Jesus stood before a wildly unfair kangaroo court, He didn't defend Himself at all. After presenting false witnesses, the high priest yells in His face, "Are you not going to answer? What is this testimony that these men are bringing against you?"

Why didn't Jesus answer? Why didn't He defend Himself? Because it wasn't Himself He was defending. *His* guilt wasn't on the judgment seat; *our* guilt was. He was standing there in our place, taking the abuse, judgment, and scorn that rightly belong to us. In light of our sins and rebellion, it was fitting that He said nothing and gave no answer. The charges were all true, but they belonged to us.

Lord Jesus, You didn't speak for Yourself or defend Yourself against those hateful lies, because You had me on Your heart. You took the blame for me. On the cross, You willingly took the punishment I deserved and died the death I should have died. What a Savior! What a Friend!

Every believer has a story. Never doubt it! It may not seem dramatic. It may not raise goose bumps on a thousand arms. It may never be the subject of a book or movie. But we have all experienced rescue on a grand scale. God "has rescued us from the dominion of darkness and brought us into the kingdom of the Son he loves." God has saved us from a lifetime of futility and given us purpose, a destiny, and a reason to get up in the morning.

You may not realize it, but people love to hear that personal account. It's the story of redemption played out in each of our lives when we tell others how Christ has sustained us through the toughest of times. *Keep telling your story.* Don't ever stop. Even those who know it need to hear it again.

Lord, I'm truly stunned—sometimes overwhelmed—to think how You have used my story through the years. You have even taken the dark parts and low moments and somehow woven them into a story of hope, light, and promise in Your name. Please use my story as long as I live to show Your love and power to others.

The 1997 hit movie *Titanic* was a powerful metaphor of a frightening reality. This tiny planet has absorbed a mortal blow, a gash in its side. Rebellion against God has set it on a crash course with hell, and whether or not we like it, it's going down—dragging a vast multitude of people with it.

Stop and listen. Do you feel the tremors? The deep-down rumbling of something gone terribly wrong? Jesus said hell was "prepared for the devil and his angels."[1] It's unnatural for humans to be there, as unnatural as turning our backs on a Creator who loves us.

God takes no joy in anyone heading for eternal misery. His Son, Jesus, is the Lifeboat, big enough and wide enough to rescue the perishing. Ask the Lord to open your eyes to the urgency of telling men, women, and children about the Lifeboat that will take them safely into eternity.

Lord, You know how it is with me. I get so wrapped up in the details of my life, my responsibilities, my preoccupations, and my travels that I lose the sense of urgency about Your gospel and the crucial need for people to turn to You. Please forgive me for my nonchalant attitude toward the eternal destiny of my friends, neighbors, coworkers, and family.

---

1. Matthew 25:41.

Today's Scripture contains three references to *loss:* "Whatever were gains to me I now consider loss for the sake of Christ. What is more, I consider everything a loss because of the surpassing worth of knowing Christ Jesus my Lord, for whose sake I have lost all things. I consider them garbage, that I may gain Christ." Losses come in many forms. We can lose health... loved ones... financial security... valued relationships. All such losses touch us deeply—there's no denying it. But sitting in his prison cell, Paul took an inventory of all his earthly losses and insisted they didn't even compare to the *gain* of knowing Jesus Christ, walking with Him through life, and possessing the hope of heaven to come. Bring your losses to Him today, and lay them at His feet. Let Him heal your bruised heart with the profit, gain, and unquenchable hope of a relationship with God's powerful Son, who loves you.

Lord, as You know very well, the losses still hurt. As our High Priest, You experienced those earthly losses too. You had to say good-bye to friends and family and to all the sweetness of human life to embrace the cross. You gave Your everything for us so all our losses could be turned into eternal gains. I praise You today, wonderful Savior.

October 30 | JONAH 2:8, NIV 1984

Today's Scripture reads, "Those who cling to worthless idols forfeit the grace that could be theirs." We probably do this every day. We forfeit grace—sweet favor from heaven—that could have been ours. It's there for us, wrapped up in a beautiful package with a bow on top—strength, patience, endurance, supernatural insight, miraculous provision, and providential timing. The grace of God is abundantly available to us every day, but all too often we forfeit it, give it up, and let it go in order to invest in personal idols. What idols? It might be the idol of food, alcohol, TV, computer games, sports, Facebook, or certain relationships. When these things—not sinful in themselves—*replace* the time we might have spent seeking God in His Word and in prayer, we lose the grace that could have been ours. But when we loosen our grip on these things and stop clinging to them, we find the capacity and ability to accept His grace, letting it fill our hearts and minds.

Lord, it's no small thing to forfeit Your blessing on my life. I know there are days when I value certain comforts or preoccupations above time with You. It seems like a good decision at the time, but what have I lost? What have I forfeited? How I need Your grace! I want nothing less than the full measure today.

Years ago, I used to spend time with Corrie ten Boom, the much-loved Dutch Christian writer who, along with her family, helped many Jews escape the Nazi Holocaust during World War II. For many years, Corrie traveled and spoke around the world, sharing the gospel and her story of hope. Suffering a stroke, however, changed all that. Though her tired and disabled body was approaching the winter of life, her smile remained as bright as spring. She maintained her fresh spirit and happy countenance even as she reached the age of ninety. Corrie held on to the promise of today's Scripture: "The LORD will guide you always; he will satisfy your needs in a sun-scorched land and will strengthen your frame. You will be like a well-watered garden, like a spring whose waters never fail." Your body or soul may be in the grip of winter today, but as you stay close to Jesus, your heart can know the new life and the fresh hope of spring.

Lord, please flow through my life today like a fresh, clear stream. Wash away all the regrets and resentments, the anxieties and worries, the discouragement and negative thinking. Bring Your springtime, with its soft light, fragrance, and new life, into the very center of who I am. In You, Jesus, I am a well-watered garden.

November

Sometimes life puts you on the sideline. Because of any number of circumstances, you find yourself out of action, out of the mainstream, and out of the flow—and into an unwanted, unscheduled season of waiting. It might be an illness or physical condition that confines you—or a hundred other things. Whatever the cause, forced idleness can be tedious and boring. We don't want life to flow around us; we want to be right in the middle of it! In times like these we need to speak the words of today's Scripture directly to our own souls: "Wait for the LORD; be strong and take heart and wait for the LORD." It helps to remember you're not "just waiting"; you are waiting on God. Thinking about Him. Talking to Him. Anticipating His touch. You may find you really needed a time of quiet, a time to slow down and recall His promises.

Lord, help me to draw strength and courage from Your Holy Spirit in my time of waiting. I acknowledge that my life is in Your hands, and You are in control of my days and my destiny, even when I feel sidelined or on the bench. I trust Your leading today . . . and Your love.

Recently, a friend went through open-heart surgery and shared his amazement at the number of doctors and nurses who attended him in the operating room. It was an army of experts led by the head surgeon. The result? My friend's heart is all the better for it.

In the same way, when you suffer, God marshals enormous spiritual resources on your behalf. At no other time does the patient have more of the surgeon's attention than when he or she is bleeding beneath the knife of that expert. Psalm 10 says that when you suffer, you have 100 percent of God's concentration—*especially* when you are suffering. So if you are in the midst of a trial today, be assured that you have the complete focus of God's love, care, and attention. You may be sure that if you are suffering under the hand of God, you are in the crosshairs of his consummate compassion. And that is *great* news.

Father, you know better than anyone that I need all the help I can get—especially when a hard trial hits. I need every prop, every buttress and reinforcement available in your arsenal of support. Thank you for this reassurance that you're willing to throw open the floodgates of heaven's help. And I know I will be all the better for it.

November 3 | Isaiah 48:10–11

In today's Scripture, God says, "See, I have refined you... I have tested you in the furnace of affliction. *For my own sake, for my own sake, I do this.*"[1] In ways beyond our comprehension, God has His own great name at stake in our suffering. In fact, the cosmic stakes are very high. The way we respond to suffering isn't just for our spiritual benefit; God's own good name is on the line. When God tests us in the furnace of affliction, He has in mind to make Himself look good through the way we respond and continue to trust Him. Now, realizing this won't make the pain go away, but it will help us remember that our trials are never random and our pain is never arbitrary. The way we lean on God through the dark times will be told and retold when our lifetime on earth is only a distant memory.

Our Father in heaven, hallowed be Your name. Yes, Lord, I want Your name to be honored and blessed and celebrated—here on earth and among all the bright angels in heaven. Help me, please, to respond to You in trust and confidence, even on those days when I struggle to keep my head above water.

---

1. Emphasis mine.

In this era of omnipresent electronic devices, we might imagine "abiding in Christ" is similar to plugging a phone into an outlet. We sit down for our quiet time and ask ourselves, *How long do I have to be plugged into God today to get a good spiritual charge?* But Jesus never said, "I am the power cord, and you are the cell phone." No, He says, "I am the vine; you are the branches."

We don't get charged up in God in order to unplug and live on our own—until it's time for the next charge. No. We never disconnect from Him. We are living branches connected to the living Christ. His life is our life. Abiding is living in constant awareness of total dependence on Jesus. It involves a constant flow of life-giving sap from the Holy Spirit—not a spiritual charge that takes us to 80 percent. Abiding in Christ is a 100 percent relationship.

Lord Jesus, I don't want to deal with life in my own wisdom or power. I don't want to run on reserve energy. And I don't want to go out in public with my own life on display before others—what a futility that would be! Lord, I want people to see Your life and Your strength in me at every turn.

In today's Scripture, the psalmist declares, "This is the day the LORD has made; we will rejoice and be glad in it." The day begins with that first moment of consciousness when you're still in bed with the covers pulled over you. Before you even open your eyes, you begin to deal with the reality of a new day. Those brief moments are important. Even as your mind emerges from the fog of sleep, you have the opportunity to set your course for the rest of the day.

You *could* let your thoughts drift, thinking about aches and pains, deadlines and pressures, and getting your first cup of coffee. But you could also repeat Psalm 118:24, reminding yourself that this day of life is a gift from God, that He has all the resources you need for whatever you may face, and that He is worthy of your thanks and praise.

Dear Lord, how wise this psalmist is! Just as the sun clears the horizon, he is already declaring truth—and stating his firm intention to be positive and joyful. I, too, praise You for the miracle of life and for another opportunity to honor You and to walk by faith in a world that rejects You. I'm so very glad to be alive in Jesus Christ.

The author of Psalm 88 doesn't complain *about* God, but he certainly complains *to* God. Unlike many of the psalms that begin with sorrow and wrap up with hope and praise, this one stays dark right to the end. The writer is *really* down. In eighteen verses, he pours out his heart. And guess what? It was okay for him to do that. This psalm, too, is God's Word. What we learn is that God is big enough to take on our anger. He knows what kind of world we live in. He understands the brokenness, disappointment, and dysfunction. He wants us to move *toward* Him with our complaints, not away from Him.

Don't bring down your friends and family with your negative feelings; take them to God! Engage Him head-on. He can handle it, and He has all kinds of experience in bringing comfort to frustrated sons and daughters.

Lord, please let the hurt and anger I sometimes feel drive me into Your arms. When I am frustrated and bewildered, feeling lost and alone, remind me to pour it all out to You first before I unload on my family, friends, or coworkers. Thank You for the incredible privilege of calling You my Friend.

Phyllis is a Christian widow with a beautiful home and a large space to rent. When she met Nadine, a potential renter, and found out Nadine was a believer too, Phyllis was so excited that she offered a rock-bottom rental fee. Nadine, however, firmly but politely declined. It was a large space in a beautiful home, and Nadine didn't want to pay the heavily discounted amount. Instead, she thought it was important to pay for what the space was actually worth. Phyllis was shocked—but delighted—by Nadine's counteroffer. It spoke of Nadine's generosity, her sense of fairness, and a Christlike attitude, all of which touched Phyllis in a powerful way. Today's Scripture reads, "Turn my heart toward your statutes and not toward selfish gain." In other words, selfish actions and thoughts come easily for us; we need the supernatural help of God to respond with openhearted generosity.

Father, I understand that with many people I will only have one chance to make a first impression for You. Turn my heart toward what pleases You and honors You rather than toward what benefits me. Remind me by your Holy Spirit to be generous and patient with others, as You have been so exceedingly generous and patient with me.

Greg, a missionary to Africa, wore a bright polo shirt with an odd logo that read, "LIVE DEAD." But how can you live—be alive—when you're dead? As you might expect, Greg had a ready answer from today's Scripture: "I tell you the truth, unless a kernel of wheat is planted in the soil and dies, it remains alone. But its death will produce many new kernels—a plentiful harvest of new lives. Those who love their life in this world will lose it. Those who care nothing for their life in this world will keep it for eternity." Greg explained that we Christians are called to die to self each day—and that it's only by losing our lives for the sake of Christ that God increases His kingdom. But more than that—when we yield our self-centered desires for the sake of Jesus and His people, we begin to recognize that we're living the life we've always longed for but could never find.

Lord, it seems I have to learn and relearn this truth again and again. When I pursue what I want, what I desire, I end up with a handful of ashes. But when I deliberately yield what I want, seeking to follow Your desires, I end up with the best and sweetest times of my life.

I remember the time when my friend Charlie, who has cerebral palsy, asked me a tough question. Looking down at his twisted arms and legs in his wheelchair, he said, "What possible purpose could there be in my suffering?" I told Charlie his question couldn't be answered in a single conversation—or even in a book. That's because God's answers and purposes have to be *lived out* in order to understand them. And that takes time and trust.

Today's Scripture tells us there is a time for everything—and that includes understanding. If you have questions about suffering, or about why things have happened as they have, remember these two words: *time* and *trust*. Keep trusting in God, friend. Believe His promises. Act on His Word. Live out your faith. And in time, or perhaps beyond time, you will understand the heart of God in every one of your hardships.

Lord, it's difficult for anxious minds and heavy hearts to understand Your ways or discern Your purposes. I ask You to help me rest in Your wisdom and in Your goodness—and trust You in those events that make no earthly sense to me.

Whatever the time of year, most of us love the little, white LED lights strung around trees, porches, restaurant verandas, and the eaves of homes. Light is *so* connected with life, joy, and hope. *Even the tiniest lights have the capacity to change the character of surrounding darkness.* Today's Scripture reminds us that light—pure, divine, heavenly, eternal light—is part of our inheritance as sons and daughters of God. Paul writes of "joyfully giving thanks to the Father, who has qualified you to share in the inheritance of the saints in the kingdom of light." We have left the darkness behind us! We don't like gloominess, shadows, and dark corners, because we are children of light. It's a reminder that whenever we sense discouragement or depression casting shadows over our soul, we must immediately turn to the Light Himself. Seek His face in the Word and in wide-open, heartfelt prayer. Bask in His radiant presence. Let His light become yours again.

Lord, how wonderful to be a child of the Light. Even in this dark world, with so much heartache and evil, You have given me the privilege to shine. I pray that Your light in me—my countenance, eyes, words, smile—will be a sharp contrast to the cynicism and negativity of those who don't yet know You.

Are you experiencing hardship today? God promises that nothing will penetrate His sheltering hands to touch us except that which has been weighed and measured, so as not to ultimately harm us. And when troubles do come, God promises to flood us with His sustaining grace. As Jesus told the apostle Paul (three times!), "My grace is all you need. My power works best in weakness."[1] And though our world can be a dark and sorrowful place, we can still experience our Father's goodness in the simple pleasures of a rainbow burning against a dark sky, a honeybee exploring a daffodil, the soft morning sunlight, a cup of cocoa by a cherrywood fire on a stormy night, the whisper of a summer wind in the pines, the companionship of a loved one, and the hope of a wondrous new dawn in our heavenly home. Take a moment to think through the good in your life—the things and the people you love and value. Then spend some time thanking the One who sends us "every good and perfect gift."

Bless You, my Father, for guarding and shielding me from so much evil, so much harm and grief. Grant me a grateful heart through the hours of this day.

---

1. 2 Corinthians 12:9, NLT.

In today's Scripture, the psalmist declares, "If your law had not been my delight, I would have perished in my affliction." God may not have kept you from affliction, but He *has* kept you from perishing in your affliction. After all, you're still here! Think of the many times you have staked your life on God's Word and didn't even realize it. Every morning He awakens you with grace, washes away your sins, and grants you salvation. He has given you a home in heaven, escape from hell, and a purpose for living. He works everything for your good and grants you the honor of bearing His name and representing His character. God's Word tells you all this, creating delight at the very center of who you are. Once you delight in His ways, you'll be even quicker to follow them when facing affliction. He will keep you from perishing—until that bright, beautiful day when He takes you home.

How many times, dear Lord, have I turned to Your Word and found hope, life, light, perspective, and the courage to go on. I've been on the edge of despair, and Your Word pulled me back from the brink. Thank You for Your Holy Spirit, who brings Your words to memory at just the right moment.

Is it possible to head in two directions at once? Consider today's Scripture: "Therefore we do not lose heart. Though outwardly we are wasting away, yet inwardly we are being renewed day by day." As a follower of Jesus Christ, your outward self—your physical body—will eventually decline. But on the inside, your spiritual life experiences vibrant renewal each new day. Really, that's good news! You may be struggling with physical suffering. You may be diminishing outwardly. You may not heal as quickly as you used to, have the energy you had ten years ago, or get around as well as you once did. But inwardly? Your spiritual life can be more real, more alive, more vivid. You are being drawn so much closer to Jesus. As your physical strength and abilities diminish, your spiritual strength increases day by day. And in the moment your physical life gives out, your new life in heaven instantly begins.

Lord, thank You for this encouragement. Thank You for reminding me that even though this tired, broken body of mine is wearing out, I'm getting closer to You—and closer to heaven—with every passing day. Restore and renew me today as You promise. Keep my spirit bright today for the honor of Your name.

Today's Scripture reveals a fascinating side to God's character. The prophet Isaiah is reciting the goodness and kindness of the Lord toward His people, the Israelites: "In all their distress he too was distressed, and the angel of his presence saved them." The New King James Version reads, "In all their affliction He was afflicted." Don't you love that? It shows beyond a doubt that God's tenderness is aroused when His people hurt. He knows your suffering. He's touched by your tears. And He won't leave you alone in your misery; He will come to your aid. It may not be the exact remedy you want at the time you want it, but He *will* show up. He has a thousand ways of showing His care and His concern for your welfare.

Lord, I can't even count the ways You show up for me when I call to You in my trouble. Sometimes it's medical help. Sometimes it's a card in the mail, a friend at the door, an encouraging insight from the Word, or a phone call from someone in a distant place who has suddenly been prompted to pray. Thank You, Jesus, for all the ways You show Your tenderness to me.

In today's Scripture, we read these tender words: "It was I who taught Ephraim to walk, taking them by the arms; but they did not realize it was I who healed them. I led them with cords of human kindness, with ties of love." These verses reveal that God Himself is the One who helped you to take your first steps in faith. During times of confusion and tumult, He took you by the hand and led you. In your illness, He healed you. When you felt trapped by your circumstances, He lifted you. Best of all, He forgives your sin again and again. God is the One who hears your confession and gently guides you back on the best path for your life. What a wonderful Shepherd He is!

Dear God, awaken my memory to the countless ways You have tenderly guided and cared for me through the years. Forgive me when I take those stubborn and foolish detours away from Your paths of righteousness. What a mess I can make of things! I know Your path can be difficult, but I don't want to be anywhere else!

It was only our high school madrigal choir singing a Gregorian chant, but the haunting harmonies of the minor keys swelled my heart to the point of breaking. I had never been possessed by such glorious music before. The next week, I practiced my alto range and signed up for the choir. The joy, for me, was complete only if I could share in the beauty and power of participating in it. In today's Scripture, the Lord declares, "Be holy, because I am holy."

When the Holy Spirit awakens the heart of a person to please the Lord—to delight in His holiness—an urgent and aching desire is born, not only to behold that holiness, as from a distance, but also to *participate* in it. We're not just listening to the music; we're making it. We want to join in. And in our Lord Jesus, because of Him, we can.

Lord, there is nothing in all the world like the assurance of forgiven sins. A clean heart. A clean conscience. A fresh start in my walk with You. I want to walk in that freshness today. I know—and You know—how prone I am to stumble. But I want to walk in the Light as far and as long as I can.

The Holy Spirit will not only empower you to live a life pleasing to God; He will carefully, through the Word and through His gentle whisper, point out things that do not please Him. And what about those so-called "gray" areas of life? The Spirit will inform and instruct your conscience.

What is the conscience? It's the gauge on our internal instrument panel that shows us the difference between what pleases God and what doesn't. The Puritans believed the conscience was like a mirror, catching the light of God's Word and reflecting its concentrated focus onto our actions, desires, goals, and choices. We can suppress or stifle it, but its voice will continue to speak to us if its volume has been turned up through daily time in God's Word. Yes, it can also become *overly* sensitive as well.[1] But we can depend on the Spirit and the Word to bring it back into right alignment.

Spirit of the living God, please continue to inform and transform my conscience. I don't want to smother my conscience under a pillow, but I don't want to live timidly either—like I'm walking on eggshells. How can I know balance unless You bring me balance? With all my heart, I want to please You.

---

1. 1 John 3:19–20.

Lonely people sometimes develop the habit of looking *inward*, which only breeds more loneliness. God wants us to be looking *outward* to the needs of others. Today's Scripture reads, "Each of you should look not only to your own interests, but also to the interests of others. Your attitude should be the same as that of Christ Jesus." And what was His attitude? He prayed for the people around Him. He struck up conversations and asked people questions about themselves. He observed needs and met them.[1] So how do you react when you enter a crowded room? Are you fearful? Wondering what people think of you? Afraid no one will talk to you? You might start with thoughts like these: *Who seems to be in need of a little friendly conversation? How can I show Christ's love to someone in this room?* Start conversations that are focused on others rather than on yourself.

Lord, it's so difficult to forget about myself! I struggle sometimes to put my problems, worries, and concerns in the background in order to focus on someone else. Once again, I need You to enable and empower me to do something I don't feel very inclined to do. People need to see Your love and concern reaching out through me.

---

1. John 17:6; 4:7; 5:1–14.

Today's Scripture counsels us to "be wise in the way you act toward outsiders; make the most of every opportunity." It takes courage to reach out to others. It's always a risk, isn't it? *What if that person rejects me— or misinterprets my motives?* It helps to recognize that every acquaintance we make is a divine encounter. There's really nothing random about the people who cross our paths.

You can count on the fact that God has been at work in the one you meet, just as He is at work in you. When you approach new people with this outlook, you take a bold step beyond your feelings of insecurity. If the person you meet is an unbeliever, show an interest in their life, always looking for an opportunity to speak a word about your relationship with Jesus or show His love. If the person is a believer, find out what God has been doing in their life. And all the while, silently ask the Holy Spirit to show you how to open doors as it pleases Him.

Lord Jesus, I know You seek a relationship with every man, woman, and child on the planet. Help me to be wise in the way I treat people and speak to them. Help me to see people through Your eyes—and make the most of every opportunity.

Loneliness and discouragement are sad sisters who usually work together. When you feel lonely, discouragement quickly follows. Sometimes you can even be busy in God's work and find yourself discouraged. In the book of Ezra, we catch a glimpse of Satan's strategy against God's people. Today's Scripture makes it clear that the devil's plan is "to discourage the people . . . and make them afraid," and "to work against them and frustrate their plans." If the devil can, he will try to isolate you, to separate you from the rest of God's children. Once he gets you alone, he tries to make you feel as though your efforts are wasted and your life is useless. Don't let it happen! Stay active in a strong local church. Do your best to plug into a fellowship group or Bible study. Reach out to friends in Christ and spend time with them. It's not just "nice"; it is vital to our survival. The author of Hebrews commands us to "encourage one another daily."[1]

Lord, Your Word says You are "the God who gives endurance and encouragement."[2] I praise You for that truth and claim it as my own today. Help me not to withdraw and isolate myself during difficult times, but rather to find a friend and to be a friend.

---

1. Hebrew 3:13.   2. Romans 15:5.

Emotions are one of the most influential—*and least reliable*—forces we deal with in our lives. One day we're hopeful; the next day we're close to despair. Emotions are surging, restless tides that ebb and flow, drawing us up and then pushing us down. The psalms are gyroscopes for our emotions, keeping moving things level, like a ship held steady-on-course in turbulent seas. This is why the psalms often repeat the admonition to "remember the wonders he has done, his miracles, and the judgments he pronounced." The point? When dark and brooding emotions surge over you, threatening to drown you in doubt and fear, the only sure barrier against the flood is to remember what God has already undertaken and accomplished in your life. Remember the times you lived on His blessings, experienced His favor, and felt His everlasting arms underneath you. Those strong arms are still there!

Dear Lord, Light of the world, help me to remember Your great kindness and goodness to me when the horizon of my life begins to darken. Time after time, You have given me fresh strength in my weakness, brought loving friends to my side, and pushed aside the devil's attacks. And what You have done before—I know You will do it again.

Psalm 23 reminds us that our Good Shepherd leads us, guards our lives, and restores us. And then there's that scary part: "Even though I walk through the valley of the shadow of death, I will fear no evil, for you are with me." It's true—our Shepherd will sometimes lead us into and through some dark valleys. But that is where faith has a chance to grow and become strong. If God created us and saved us (and He did), then shouldn't He know best how to preserve, protect, and strengthen our souls? It's in those frightening, desolate places where His grace is abundant and His presence is especially near. It's where our need of Him becomes more desperate, and our dependence on Him becomes more urgent. Once we have passed through this shadowy place (and we *will* pass through), the memory of His presence, protection, and grace will assure us for the rest of our journey.

Lord, I remember the dark places and wouldn't want to go back to them. But I also remember how I was never alone. There were moments when it was hard to see You in the darkness, but I knew You were there and would once again guide me safely through. And You did.

When Jesus was in Gethsemane, He fell on His face and prayed, "O My Father, if it is possible, let this cup pass from Me; nevertheless, not as I will, but as You will." Jesus was asking, pleading, to not have to face the cross. Just moments later, however, when the soldiers came to arrest Him, Jesus didn't resist. He said to Peter, "Shall I not drink the cup which My Father has given Me?"[1] The Lord's mind was no longer set on bypassing the cross. No, in that moment He was unflinchingly ready to *embrace* the cross. That should speak to us as we face our own trials. If you find yourself in a distressing crisis, by all means pray that if it's God's will, He will remove it. But once you've prayed, leave the trial with Him. Be willing to take up your cross and follow Jesus down the hard, rocky path of surrender.

Lord Jesus, thank You for giving Yourself for me. Thank You for drinking the cup You didn't want to drink—for walking the road You didn't want to walk. You could have called twelve legions of angels to save You—in a heartbeat. But You accepted and endured the cross in obedience to the Father... and because of Your unwavering love for me.

---

1. John 18:11, NKJV.

I grew up in a little Reformed Episcopal church—evangelical to the core—where they read the Gospel, sang hymns from the heart, and kneeled in prayer. Our church even had kneelers. Sunday worship was a serious business, and I learned as a little girl what it meant to bend my knees in prayer before the Lord. For the last forty-nine years, however, since the accident that paralyzed me, I haven't been able to kneel. But the day is coming when I will kneel again!

On the day I receive my new body in heaven, I will rise up on resurrected legs and then drop down on grateful, glorified knees to worship before my Savior. Today, you can choose to do what so many who are elderly or have disabilities cannot do. Read Psalm 95 and—taking the advice of the psalmist—give an outward demonstration of your inward gratitude. Kneel before the Lord, your Maker.

Lord God, You know the secrets of every heart. I'm in awe of Your majesty and glory. I'm humbled by Your kindness, gentleness, and loving concern for me. You are the great King, and even though You have adopted me as Your child, I bow in Your presence—as low as I can.

We all experience dark passages, times when circumstances become so intense that we wonder if we'll even survive. The apostle Paul wrote about such an experience to some friends: "We were crushed and overwhelmed beyond our ability to endure, and we thought we would never live through it. In fact, we expected to die." Why would God put His apostle through such severe suffering? Paul himself provides the answer: "But as a result, we stopped relying on ourselves and learned to rely only on God, who raises the dead." Coming out of that experience, Paul would no longer cling to life and rely on his own strength. Instead, he fixed his eyes on God and His power. From that time on, he learned to delight in God alone and in the incomparable future God had reserved for him. That's what is known as dying to self. It's also known as really living.

Lord Jesus, I learn from Paul's words that relying on You is the bottom line in all of life. Suffering, perplexity, overwhelming circumstances, and even death itself are only temporary issues. We deal with them, leaning on Your strength and then moving on. How thankful I am for the inheritance that waits for me just over the horizon!

Today's Scripture tells us we should live "to please God" and that "it is God's will that you should be sanctified." The word *sanctified* means "set apart from sin." That's a tall order for any of us. But it is doable. Of course, this doesn't mean we will never sin or stumble—because we certainly will.[1] But it does mean that as our walk with Christ progresses through the weeks, months, and years, we will be less and less *inclined* in that direction. To accomplish this, you have help from out of this world! You are not alone in your struggle. God has placed within you His Holy Spirit, who empowers you to make choices that please God. When you obey the Lord, your focus isn't on some arbitrary list of dos and don'ts; it is on Jesus. You find yourself obeying because—first and foremost—you really do want to please Him.

Dear God, I want to fill my vision with You. I pause now to let my thoughts linger on who You are in Your kingly majesty...right at this moment...in the splendor of heaven...surrounded by angels and redeemed men and women from all ages. How good, how right, and how fitting it is to consider You and worship You!

---

1. James 3:2; 1 John 1:8.

When Chandler was nine years old, he lost his right eye in an accident. That was four years ago, and now thirteen-year-old Chandler is the starting quarterback for his middle school's football team. When people ask him why his eyesight hasn't hindered him, Chandler replies with a smile, "God is my other eye." What a perspective for such a young believer! It's a strong reminder not to allow our troubles to blind us to God's purposes.

In today's Scripture, we read about Hagar. After being mistreated by her mistress, Sarai, Hagar gave up hope and ran away into the desert. Out there in that harsh desert, however, God himself reassured Hagar, giving her hope for the future. She replied to Him, "You are the God who sees me… I have now seen the One who sees me." Both Hagar and Chandler came to see themselves and their difficulties through God's eyes. And that made all the difference for both of them.

Lord, I'm thinking about how the apostle Paul prayed for the eyes of the heart.[1] I know I need that. Sometimes my situation looks bleak to my physical eyes. I need Your perspective, Your viewpoint, and Your vision for my life today. The old hymn reminds me to ask of You, "Be Thou my vision, O Lord of my heart."[2]

1. Ephesians 1:18. 2. Unknown; trans. Eleanor Hull, "Be Thou My Vision" (1912).

When I first came to Christ, I underlined today's Scripture verse in my high school Bible: "For to me, to live is Christ and to die is gain." And I meant it—or at least as much as I was *able* to mean it. At that time, the verse translated like this: "I'll stick up for You, Jesus, if someone sneers at my Christianity. And I'll stick to moral standards when I'm with my boyfriend." (Yes, and how long did *that* last?) But then I broke my neck, and Paul's words meant more than I had ever imagined.

Paul ate, drank, and slept eternal life in Christ. Jesus was his very breath, the soul of his soul, and the life of his life. I couldn't have said those things before I suffered, but my quadriplegia utterly threw me into the arms of my Savior. Suffering does that. So today, don't despise it. It can help you to say, "For me, to live is Christ"—and you will truly mean it.

Lord Jesus, my life is hidden in You, and I can't imagine it any other way. You are my Strength, my Shield, my Helper, my Hope, my Song. As the psalmist wrote, "Your decrees are the theme of my song wherever I lodge. In the night, LORD, I remember your name."[1]

---

1. Psalm 119:54–55.

Remember in elementary school when your teacher planted a bean in a plastic container? You could watch the little bean sprout, sink its roots, and then finally break through the dirt. The funny thing about that sprout was that its roots were deeper and more complex than its little green leaf. In fact, it was only able to grow upward because it grew *downward* at the same time. Growth in Christ takes place the same way. But sometimes we make a show of Christlikeness without having an inner life that corresponds with it. And no Christian can ever hope to grow upward that way. Today's Scripture reveals that "the seed falling on good soil refers to someone who hears the word and understands it. This is the one who produces a crop, yielding a hundred... times what was sown." Sink your roots deep into Christ, my friend, and you *will* keep growing upward.

Lord, I have learned through the years that this is the truly joyous part. Yes, it's wonderful to bear fruit for You, as You intended all along. But I treasure the secret life even more than the visible one. I love sinking my roots deep into You, below the surface, in the quiet places where no eye but Yours can see.

The Bible takes great pains to remind us how small we are. In today's Scripture, for instance, we read, "'Do not be afraid... little Israel, do not fear, for I myself will help you,' declares the LORD." There's a reason God's Word makes so much of our smallness. It's that He wants us to remember and consider how big He is. And not only is He great and mighty; He is also willing to help us with every issue we face. After all, if God has done the greater—the bigger—things, then won't He attend to the smaller things as well? If He has saved you from hell and gifted you with eternal life, won't He also help and sustain you in the tiniest details of your daily struggles? Today, gather up all your wants and needs; collect your emptiness and your worries, great and small. The Lord of the universe, who bought you with His blood, stands ready to help you.

Heavenly Father, I love the last chapters in the book of Job, where the patriarch is overwhelmed with Your ability to move heaven and earth and yet keep track of the tiniest details in Your creation. And that's the way it has been in my life too. You concern yourself with what concerns me. Thank You.

December

Sometimes we can get lost in the flowery imagery of Song of Songs. Yes, it does read like a book of love poems, but there is more to it than that. Every follower of Jesus can identify with today's Scripture. It describes the heartbreaking moment when you realize you have lost the company of Christ. "All night long on my bed I looked for the one my heart loves; I looked for him but did not find him." Sadly, it happens. And nothing feels more desolate or frightening to the Christian. But take heart—Christ can and *will* be found. And you will find Him wherever it was you lost fellowship with Him. Was it in sinning? Then you will find Him by giving up that sin. Was it in neglecting the Word? Then you'll find Him when you delve back into the Scriptures. It can be hard work to go back and look for Christ. But if you seek Him, He *will* be found.

Lord, it's so easy to drift away from that sweet, soul-nourishing fellowship with You. I think of what Paul said about his once-loyal friend Demas, who "deserted me because he loves the things of this life."[1] Help me, Savior and Friend, to keep You first. To keep Your love in view through every waking hour.

---

1. 2 Timothy 4:10, NLT.

Have you ever felt completely hemmed in? As a quadriplegic, I can feel trapped by arms and legs that don't respond. Sometimes it feels like a dead end with no way out. I'm sure it was the same for the Israelites camped by the Red Sea. When they realized Pharaoh and his army were hot on their trail, they glanced at the crashing waves behind them and knew there was no way out. Yet it was God who had led them to that spot—just as God has led me into quadriplegia. And if God has led me here, it's to show me—as He showed the Israelites—His glory, protection, and provision.

God didn't lead His people to the Red Sea to destroy them. And God has not led me this far to destroy me. *Nothing* can hurt or harm my soul; not even death. At times you too may experience trapped, claustrophobic feelings. But God has you where you are so He can perform miracles you never imagined.

Dear God, You have been with me on those nights when the walls of my room closed in on me like a vise. I remember Your Word: "We are hedged in from every side, but we do not live cramped lives."[1] I may feel trapped, but I know You will make a way.

---

1. 2 Corinthians 4:8, MLB.

We have no idea—not even the smallest conception—of what we owe to our Savior's prayers for us. The Bible tells us Jesus lives in heaven to intercede for us.[1] And one day, when we look back from heaven's highest hill to see how God has led us, we will marvel at what we see: accidents diverted… wounding words silenced… mercy covering deep offenses… Holy Spirit encouragement coming swiftly to our aid in moments of great need. We may tire of praying, but Jesus doesn't.

Even before Satan begins to tempt, Jesus forestalls him by His prayers, just as Jesus did with Peter. In today's Scripture, Jesus tells Peter that "Satan hath *desired* to have you."[2] In other words, our Lord nips Satan's desire in the bud before our old enemy can clutch us. And it's all because Jesus prays for us—nonstop—before the Father's throne.

Lord Jesus, I'm kneeling beside You today before the Father's throne. I am praying and interceding for loved ones, friends, and hurting ones; dark, needy places in our world; and so many of Your sons and daughters who are even now undertaking risky kingdom ventures. Like You, dear Lord, I want to live to make intercession.

---

1. Romans 8:34; Hebrews 7:25.   2. Emphasis mine.

December 4 | Isaiah 40:31

Don't you love the way today's Scripture describes eagles and the way they soar? Author Ben Patterson once wrote, "As birds go, eagles' wings are big, but the muscles that make them flap aren't. Pound for pound, an eagle's strength is no match for the strength of a hummingbird. The strength of eagles is not in their flapping but in their soaring."[1] An eagle will perch on the edge of a canyon and then cast itself down into the abyss. With wings outstretched, it will then find the warm updraft from the depths below—an updraft on which it will circle and soar until it rises far above the canyon's rim. In today's Scripture, the prophet Isaiah says that those who trust in the Lord will soar on eagles' wings. May we Christians be known, not for all our frantic flapping, but for casting ourselves into the unknown and soaring upward on the wings of the Spirit.

Father God, I've done enough frantic flapping for a lifetime—trying so hard to do Your will and make things happen in my own strength and energy. How foolish I have been! I know I need to cast myself on You in faith before I will find those beautiful updrafts that lift me higher and higher.

---

1. Ben Patterson, ed., *Prayer Devotional Bible* (Grand Rapids: Zondervan, 2004), 849.

Again and again, the Bible speaks about the Father's love or the love of the Lord Jesus. But today's Scripture speaks of both the Father *and* the Son together: "May our Lord Jesus Christ himself and God our Father, who loved us and by his grace gave us eternal encouragement and good hope, encourage your hearts and strengthen you in every good deed and word." God never speaks words of fear or failure, hopelessness or frustration, into your heart. You'll never hear His voice counseling you to give in to defeat or despair. If you do hear such dark, negative, cynical words echoing in your soul, you can know for sure where they come from… and it's not from God. When the Lord whispers in your heart, He speaks words of hope and victory, rest and peace, joy and triumph. If your heart needs to be strengthened today, clear the clutter out of your mind, open God's Word, and listen for the voice of "eternal encouragement and good hope."

Because Your love is in my heart, Lord, I have something to give. Because You have infused "good hope" into my soul, I have hope to pass along to others. Because You have flooded Your light into the corners of my soul, I have light to carry where it's needed most.

Today's Scripture urges us to "put on the full armor of God." This is more than just picturesque language. It is life and survival for each of us. When you're walking in Christ, you quickly learn it means a fierce battle against the enemy. Every day—in a spiritual sense— swords are clashing, bullets are flying, and grenades are exploding.

Don't be lulled into a spiritual stupor, thinking your enemy hasn't placed a target on your back. If you name Christ as Lord, the devil has you in his cross-hairs. So don't let him decimate your faith, wound you with discouragement, cripple you with temptation, or take you out of the battle. In Christ, you are *more* than a conqueror.[1] God is with you! So strap on that armor and get a fresh grip on your shield and sword, taking God at His Word. Winning the fight doesn't require physical muscle, but a sharp, keen spiritual mind.

Lord, please deliver me from the fog of battle, when everything seems hazy and indistinct. Don't allow my anxiety or my struggle with pain to preoccupy me or make me careless. Open my eyes to the warfare around me, and help me to be ready when the missiles fly my way.

---

1. Romans 8:37.

December 7 | Numbers 21:6–9

Diana suffers from intractable pain. Recently she told me, "Joni, sometimes I don't have the strength to even lift my head. It's that painful!" I can identify with my friend. When I'm discouraged and besieged by pain, I can feel like my face is squished hard against the floor. But as I told Diana, I've drawn encouragement from a story found in today's Scripture. Out in the wilderness, God's people were in terrible trouble. But the Lord told them that if they would simply look at the bronze snake Moses had fastened to a pole, their rescue was assured. *Just look. Just lift your eyes.* Sometimes rescue is that close.

The beloved disciple John recorded Jesus' words: "Just as Moses lifted up the snake in the wilderness, so the Son of Man must be lifted up, that everyone who believes may have eternal life in him."[1] If you feel overwhelmed today, lift your eyes. Just *look* to Jesus.

Lord, if I had to go on some long journey or pilgrimage to find You, I'd never make it. If I had to look for You down every street and alleyway, I'd never track You down. But in Your love, You made Yourself accessible, reachable, findable. All I have to do is look up and call on Your name.

---

1. John 3:14–15.

Today's Scripture tells us, "Our light and momentary troubles are achieving for us an eternal glory that far outweighs them all." Don't you love that word *achieving*? Not only is your affliction momentary or temporary, not only are all your troubles "light" in comparison with eternity and the glory there, but all of it is totally meaningful. Your suffering is achieving something for you. Never forget this!

Every millisecond of your pain, every nanosecond of your misery in the path of obedience, is producing a unique glory that suits you—and you only. Think of the many times you've been bullied, slandered, or sorely abused. Think of your battles against illness or jaw-bending pain. None of it is random. None of it is meaningless. All of it is achieving, producing, and winning for you an eternal glory that *far* outweighs it all. So stay faithful, and take courage. The glory is coming. It is almost here.

Lord, how could I bear it if I thought for one moment that suffering is just random, with no meaning, effects, or results? How kind, how gracious, You are to give my disappointments and hardships a context, for framing them with eternal, significant meaning. How I praise You for 2 Corinthians 4:17! I cling to its truth today with all my heart.

With happiness and sheer abandon! That's how Linda worships God. Yes, she may be physically hampered by severe rheumatoid arthritis, and she has a difficult time lifting her arms above her wheelchair. But you cannot miss the unbridled passion in her worship. Linda demonstrates that faith-filled suffering is essential when it comes to intense, authentic worship. Pastor John Piper wrote, "When we are most satisfied with God in suffering, He will be most glorified in us in worship."[1] That's what you can see in Linda. Her afflictions have become the perfect display of the worth of God in her life. Today's Scripture reads, "Because your love is better than life, my lips will glorify you." Linda firmly believes that Jesus' love is better than a life filled with the unremitting pain of rheumatoid arthritis—and it shows in her joyous, unrestrained praise.

Dear Lord, if I had eyes to see, I think I would see angels worshiping You on either side of Linda's wheelchair. It's so clear at such times that she's occupied with You alone, paying little attention to the world around her. Thank You for her example! I want to worship You—declare Your worth—in difficult times as well as in easy times.

---

1. John Piper, *The Hidden Smile of God: The Fruit of Affliction in the Lives of John Bunyan, William Cowper, and David Brainerd* (Wheaton, Ill.: Crossway, 2008), 169.

Christians often try to forget their weakness; God wants us to remember it, to feel it deeply. We want to subdue and free ourselves from weakness; God wants us to rest and even rejoice in it. Weakness makes most Christians feel sad and short-changed; Christ teaches us to say, "I am glad to boast about my weakness, so that the power of Christ can work through me." Andrew Murray observed that "the Christian thinks his weakness his greatest hindrance in the life and service of God: God tells us it that is the secret of strength and success. It is our weakness, heartily accepted and continually realized, that gives us our claim and access to the [power] of Him who has said, 'My strength is made perfect in weakness.'"[1] The bottom line? Don't feel short-changed by your weaknesses. Join me in celebrating God's purposes in each one.

Father, You know my heart. Even after all these years of weakness, it never becomes easy to accept. It never feels natural to have someone do for me what I would so much rather do for myself. Even so, I praise You today for every weakness that keeps me leaning on the power of Your mighty Son, who loves me and gave Himself for me.[2]

1. Andrew Murray, *Abide in Christ* (London: Nisbet, 1888), 195–96. 2. Galatians 2:20.

Sometimes it seems as if my chronic pain has but one goal: to rob me of joy. When the agony bites with its sharp teeth, I can even lose the joy of my salvation. If I'm not alert to it, I can easily slip into a dusky, "coping" kind of Christianity, the kind that muddles through just to get by—and stops believing in God's deep concern or the hope of His deliverance. Don't go there! It is a white-hot lie from hell.

Certainly, pain may test any Christian's mettle, but it doesn't have to destroy your faith. Satan may whisper that God has abandoned you, but He hasn't. God is *with* you. Jesus endured pain beyond our comprehension, but He did so "for the joy set before him."[1] And He offers that same endurance to each of us. So make this your prayer today: "Dear Lord, restore to me the joy of your salvation and grant me a willing spirit, to sustain me."[2]

Yes, Lord, I do lose joy sometimes. Maybe Satan steals it, or maybe I just become so diverted and distracted that I forget where I put it. But praise Your name, what is lost can be restored and what is misplaced or mishandled can be found again. Please restore Your joy in me, deep in my spirit. Let the fountain flow again.

---

1. Hebrews 12:2. 2. Psalm 51:12.

On that bright eternal day when heaven's rewards are distributed at last, we will be stunned to see the vast and endless gains before us. Today's Scripture tells us our light and momentary affliction is accruing for us an eternal gain that *far* outweighs the inconvenience of earth's hardships. And when God says "far," he means *far*. Compared to heaven—our worst earthly pains will seem like a mere nuisance. When we stand amazed at the mountain ranges of joy and pleasures our response to suffering won for us, we will smack our foreheads, lamenting, "Why, oh, why didn't I trust God *more*?!" Saint Sebastian, an early Christian martyr, wisely observed, "When it is all over, you will not regret having suffered; rather you will regret having suffered so little and suffered that little so badly."[1] Such thoughts seem impossible to grasp when you're feeling demoralized by deep trials, but with God, *all* things are possible.

Lord, I'm reminded that Your Word urges, "Set your sights on the rich treasures and joys of heaven."[2] Be the lifter of my head today. Help me to fix my gaze beyond the troubles, disappointments, and heartaches of my current circumstances to the beauty and rewards and never-ending joys of the life to come.

---

1. Sebastian Valfrè, "Letter to an Invalid, 1690)," quoted in *The Quotable Saint*, compiled by Rosemary Guiley (New York: Facts on File, 2002), 265.   2. Colossians 3:1, LB.

A young Christian named Jennifer once confessed, "Joni, I can't believe how often I keep doing the wrong things. Honestly, the Lord must be so upset, so *disillusioned*, with me!"

I told her not to worry. I said, "Jen, the Lord can't be disillusioned with you, because He has absolutely no illusions about you. He knows full well the depths of your depravity, and He's not at all surprised by your sin." I could tell my words ruffled her feathers. But the sooner Jennifer stops "performing to impress God" and accepts His wise and good estimate of her life, the quicker she will grow in Christ. A sure sign of growth is knowing the dark sins of which you are capable, yet remembering you remain a glorious co-heir with Christ. If the Holy Spirit has made you aware of a sin, confess it to the Lord, turn away from it, and take a fresh grip on your eternal identity and destiny in Christ.

Yes, Lord, You know my sins and failures and see through my outward show. I may be able to deceive others, but never You. I confess and freely admit my transgressions today. Wash me clean, and put my feet back on the only road I want to travel, following You through life into eternity.

Have you ever been in a meeting where a coworker shares an idea—but it's something you'd thought of days before? When people comment on the brilliance of this concept, you feel like saying, "Yes, I thought of that already." Why do you do that? Because you want to share the spotlight, don't you?

Our fallen natures crave self-glory. We want our successes and strengths to be known, and our failures and weaknesses to be hidden. The apostle Paul could have been like that, but Jesus wisely gave him "a thorn" in his flesh to afflict him. Paul's thorn reminded him it's not human achievement that showcases God's glory; it is, rather, human want, need, and even helplessness. Paul could have said, "Well, when God called me up to the third heaven for a little visit, I learned thus and so." But the thorn kept reminding him, "Slow down, Paul. You're a man in great need." And so are we.

Dear Father, what a companion a thorn can be to me! Yes, it can bring grief and torment, but it can also be an unavoidable reminder of how needy I really am and how dependent I am on Your daily infusion of strength. For that reason, I thank You for the thorns in my life.

Long ago, whenever my daddy set up his easel and oil paints, I pulled out my cowboy coloring book and sat on the floor next to him, working with my crayons. Every once and a while, he'd glance down at my picture, smile, and say, "Nice job." But for the most part, hardly a word was spoken between us. An hour or two would pass—Daddy painting and me scribbling— yet I felt we were in perfect fellowship, both quietly delighting in each other's company. So it is between a contented Christian and the Lord Jesus.

A believer in fellowship with the Savior can move through a busy day, simply conscious that everything he or she does is blessed by favor and grace, as well as by a sense of God's pleasure and approval. Today, find delight in the company of Jesus. Cultivate that sense of His nearness. Remember that He takes great joy and pleasure in you.

As the psalmist wrote, "As for me, it is good to be near God. I have made the Sovereign LORD my refuge." Yes, Lord, it is good, sweet, satisfying, and peaceful to be near You. To crowd in as close as I can to You. To be quietly in Your presence as You go about Your work and I go about mine.

Amy Carmichael was a missionary to India who rescued hundreds of little girls from temple prostitution. Midway through her ministry, she suffered a terrible fall and became bedridden for the final twenty years of her life. In one of her letters to a friend, Amy wrote, "A day or two ago when everything was feeling more than usually impossible, I opened on Psalm 40 with its new song. 'He hath put a new song in my mouth, even praise.' How like Him it is to 'put' it there. We couldn't find it for ourselves, so He puts it. And when He puts it we can sing it."[1] He gives us words of praise that we can sing in His strength. So when your enemy comes like a flood, see it as a time to prove your faith in Christ and live out the song God puts in your heart. Remember, if He *puts* it, you can sing it.

Lord Jesus, I know Amy is in Your presence right now, perhaps with a song of faith and praise transformed into a mighty anthem for angelic choirs. How good You are to place words and melodies into my heart that I could have never found or sung in my own strength.

---

1. Amy Carmichael, *Candles in the Dark: Letters of Hope and Encouragement* (Fort Washington, Pa.: Christian Literature Crusade, 1982), 51.

Achilles was a ferocious Greek warrior, and legend has it that he died from a wound to the back of his heel. So when we describe someone's "Achilles' heel," it means a person's point of weakness that can lead to a downfall. But as pastor Jonathan Parnell writes, "That idea comes from Greek mythology, not Christian reality. God's wisdom gives us another picture. Believers in Jesus don't have an Achilles' heel—we *are* an Achilles' heel."[1]

Normally, when a person's weakness is taken advantage of, it can mean defeat and disgrace. But when we as Christians embrace our weakness, God exploits it for our triumph and His glory. It can happen for you every time you freely own and acknowledge your greatest weaknesses or vulnerabilities. When that happens, a flood of life-giving grace rushes in, seeking the lowest level of your weakness, filling you from the bottom up. In that moment, you have heaven-sent power to live, not in spite of your limitations, but because of them.

Lord, this is a message so at odds with today's culture. Our world teaches us to hide or deny our weakness, but You teach us to gladly own it and receive sufficient grace that more than compensates for everything we lack.

---

1. Jonathan Parnell, "Embracing Weakness Will Change Your Life," February 28, 2013, www.desiringgod.org/articles/embracing-weakness-will-change-your-life (accessed February 26, 2016).

December 18 | ROMANS 8:32

My husband, Ken, loves to present me with spur-of-the-moment surprises. He calls them *omiages*, a Japanese word meaning "a little gift you are not required to give, as for a special occasion." That's the way our heavenly Father is with us. He's not obligated to shower us with His gifts. He owes this rebellious planet nothing—and that's why His gifts are all the more special. Today's Scripture reads, "He who did not spare his own Son, but gave him up for us all—how will he not also, along with him, graciously give us all things?"

Thank God for His omiages the next time you're blessed by the sound of rain pattering on your window. Or a ray of sunshine on your kitchen floor. The smell of pine on a cold December day. The cooing of doves in the late afternoon. God gives gifts simply because He wants to. And they are *generous* gifts. Not little omiages, but big ones. What gift has God given you today? Praise Him for His blessings, great and small.

Dear God, You are the Father of Lights. Every good gift comes from You.[1] Thank You for Your kindness and generosity to me, shown in ten thousand ways every day. Today, I will count my blessings and be mindful to turn to You often and say, "Thank You!"

---

1. James 1:17.

In whatever circumstance we find ourselves—alarming reports on the nightly news, distressing physical problems, or the daily bumps and bruises of life in this imperfect world—Jesus tells us to "be of good cheer." The world may trouble us, but we can take heart. Why? Because Jesus has overcome the world. Our source of joy is always this: Christ is victorious over the world, the flesh, and the devil. *That* is the fountain of our happiness in this world.

This world may get you down. You may be constantly wrestling against the devil. Your emotions may be weary from dealing with difficult relationships. Your flesh may feel the crunch of older age or illness. But be encouraged by these words from the beloved disciple John: "Everyone born of God overcomes the world. This is the victory that has overcome the world, even our faith."[1] Take a moment to consider and savor all that Christ has accomplished for you—now and forever.

Stretch my faith, dear Lord, to be of good cheer in this dark, unhappy world. When people see genuine, unfeigned optimism and a hopeful heart, they can't quite make sense of it or figure it out. I want to be Your ambassador just by staying encouraged, keeping my spirit bright, and maintaining a thankful heart.

---

1. 1 John 5:4.

Because I deal with chronic pain, I'm sometimes tempted to imagine I'm the only one who suffers this way, this badly. That feeling of being alone in suffering is absolutely terrifying. Your world gets smaller and smaller as you tell yourself, *No one could possibly be hurting as much as I do.* In reality, I know better. Countless people all over the world suffer as much as I do—if not more. And people at my office, in my family, on my block, or in my church are carrying heavy weights of their own. These are people who will be encouraged by a phone call, a card in the mail, a thoughtful gift, an email, or a simple text that tells them you remember them and are holding them before Jesus in prayer. The more I reach out of my cramped world of suffering to encourage someone else, difficult as it may be, the less alone I feel.

Lord, I'm comforted to know You are well aware of my pain and difficulties. Please give me the grace and strength and initiative—in Your strong name—to bring a little brightness, a little courage, a little hope, into the life of someone else who is discouraged, anxious, or suffering today.

Many of us through the years return often to today's Scripture: "Let us then approach the throne of grace with confidence, so that we may receive mercy and find grace to help us in our time of need." And what are we looking for when we draw near to God—just getting our needs met? No, first we approach His throne of grace to receive *mercy*. Mercy always comes first. But we forget that, don't we? We tend to take *way* too much for granted, coming to God as though He were our personal butler or spiritual ATM. To fear or respect the Lord, however, is to first kneel before Him, acknowledging that in His mercy He rescued us, ransomed us, and offered us adoption into His very family. Then, while we're kneeling before this merciful God, we lay our cares and concerns at His feet—and find strong help and sweet provision in our time of need.

How kind You are to leave the door to Your throne room wide open, day and night, and invite me to come to You whenever I want to. Forgive me for just blurting out my needs and wants sometimes instead of taking time to remember who You are and how great Your mercy and grace have been toward me.

One of the Christmas classics you hear so often this time of year is "Have Yourself a Merry Little Christmas." The composer of that poignant song is my friend Hugh Martin. Years ago, when Hugh came to Hollywood after leaving New York, he fell on difficult times, which led this dear man to the feet of Jesus. And sometime after his conversion, Hugh went back to the piano and composed new lyrics to his beloved classic. This time, he wanted his Lord and Savior to be honored in the music. Hugh went home to be with Jesus in 2011 at the age of ninety-six, but before he died, he was a guest on our radio program, and I sang those new lyrics for him: "Have yourself a blessed little Christmas, Christ the King is born. Let your voices ring upon this happy morn."[1] The old lyrics were tender and sweet; the new lyrics may go on ringing into eternity.

Thank You, Lord, for the story of Hugh Martin's changed life. It's a story that can be told millions upon millions of times. You change lives, King Jesus. You lift up people from darkness, heartbreak, and impossible situations and give them hope, happiness, and a new song to sing.

---

1. Original words and music by Hugh Martin and Ralph Blane © 1943. Sacred lyrics by Hugh Martin and John Fricke © 1996, 1997 EMI Feist Catalog. All rights controlled. Used by permission.

December 23 | MALACHI 4:2

"Hail, the heaven-born Prince of Peace! Hail the Son of Righteousness! Light and life to all He brings, Risen with healing in His wings." Were you singing along with me? There's a reason this verse from my favorite Christmas carol means so much to me. Every time I sing the part about healing in His wings, I choke up. Many years ago, I thought it meant Jesus would heal me physically. I remember thinking, *Surely this Christmas He's going to raise me up out of this wheelchair!* Little did I know that, in due time, God would heal me—but in a way I never, ever dreamed possible. Because two years later, on another Christmas, I found contentment and joy, simply because I found I could embrace His will for my life. And what is His will? That we put ourselves in the best position, the best place, in which God can be most glorified.

Hail, the Son of Righteousness! Glory and praise to the Prince of Peace! Thank You, Lord Jesus, for coming to me with healing, grace, joy, and the hope of glory. As David prayed, "Keep me as the apple of Your eye; hide me under the shadow of Your wings."[1]

---

1. Psalm 17:8, NKJV.

Ken and I were keeping a holiday tradition by having a special dinner at an elegant restaurant. The tables were set with crystal, linens, silver, and candlelight. As we savored our meal, carolers dressed Victorian style—like a quartet out of a Dickens novel—came to our table. When they asked for a favorite carol, I requested, "Lo, How a Rose E'er Blooming." They looked surprised, but I could tell they loved singing all its harmonies.

This song pulls mysteriously on my heart, bidding me to go beyond, to "step into the other side" of Christmas—like an inkling, a hint, a whisper, of an even greater celebration yet to happen. Christmas is still a promise. Yes, the Savior has come, but the story isn't finished. Peace is in our hearts, but we long for peace in our world. Soon, though, the Rose of Sharon will return and with Him all the fragrance and joy of a longing fulfilled.

Lord, the glory and radiance of the angelic choir the shepherds witnessed that first Christmas night were just pinpricks from heaven into our dark world. If I had been there, I would have remembered it all my days. But in Your unspeakable grace, Jesus, I will see greater glory than this in the bright morning of eternity.

Today's Scripture describes Mary's reaction when the shepherds told her about the angels' announcement of Jesus' birth: She "treasured up all these things and pondered them in her heart." It's not the only time she responded that way. As Jesus grew older, there were other occasions when Mary treasured and pondered the meaning behind her son's life and ministry. Mary leaves us a great example. In the same way, we can treasure Christ when we rally our memory, affections, and intellect to understand just how supremely precious He is! When we weigh who Christ is and what He has done, not only are we enriched, but He is glorified as well. So train your memory to treasure up everything about Christ you have felt, known, or believed. Ponder the time you first heard of Him, and consider all He has done for you. Then you'll discover how precious Jesus really is.

Lord and King, what better way could I occupy my thoughts? I need a thought transplant today. I've been pondering the wrong things! I've been treasuring less worthy, less precious speculations and fantasies. With the help of Your Holy Spirit, I want to consider You in a fresh, new, worthy way. Please renew my thoughts today!

We often view our disappointments and trials as obstacles we just have to plow through in order to get back to "normal"—whatever that is. But it isn't so. Our trials have been purposed and intended by our wise God. If only we would recognize every hardship as something God has *chosen* to prove His love to us, then each trial can usher us into a place of His shelter, divine rest, and sustaining power. In today's Scripture, God says, "Have you entered the storehouses… which I reserve for times of trouble?" Job, of course, refers to weather storehouses stocked with rain and snow. But God also has vast storehouses of grace and hope, peace and mercy, reserved for you. Have you entered *those* storehouses? He doesn't give you the key until the moment of your need. Open the storehouse prepared and reserved for you before the world began.

Lord, I think I have rolled right past many, many storehouses of Your grace in my life. I have suffered alone in my pain and perplexity instead of entering what You have reserved for me in my moment of need. Open the doors for me today, Father. I want all that You have for me right now.

Today's Scripture declares that "the LORD hears the needy." When we bring our concerns and anxieties to God in prayer, He gives us His complete attention. How does He do that? How does He keep stars burning and galaxies spinning, while at the same time listening to the prayers of billions of people? We may not understand it, but it's true. When we pray, He "inclines His ear."[1]

He gets down close to hear every word, every inflection, and even the words you can't formulate. He isn't distracted by events in the Middle East, an urgent prayer from a mom in Indiana, or volcanic eruptions on Venus. He isn't wishing you would "wrap it up," isn't put off by repetition, and isn't looking for holes in your logic. That's because He loves you, cares deeply about your welfare, and actually looks forward to your company.

Father, I know how much I want to be near You and hear Your voice speak to me. But it staggers my faith to think You would want to walk closely to me, that You desire my company, and that You—to put it in human terms—actually cup Your ear and lean over to hear my words. What a wonder You are, God!

---

1. Psalms 40:1; 71:2; 88:2, NKJV.

I've always been flat-out interested in people and their struggles. If I meet someone in a wheelchair or dealing with chronic pain, I pepper them with questions: "How are you doing? What are your challenges? How do you cope? How can I pray for you?" I'm reminded of how Jesus took a personal interest in people when He walked this earth. He probed the deepest needs of a Samaritan woman at the town well. He invited himself to Zacchaeus's house for lunch and met all his friends. He asked the father of a young demon-possessed boy, "How long has he been like this?"[1] To this day, Jesus remains deeply interested in the lives and thoughts of every person you will ever meet.

Today, you will no doubt come across someone who needs a helping hand and a listening ear. Be a good ambassador of Jesus. Take time to ask questions and really hear their situation. Pray for them and, if you're able, lend a hand.

Lord Jesus, please love people through me today. Forgive me for being so wrapped up in my own stuff that I don't take the time for others. Forgive me for being so impatient and so intent on my own schedule. Help me to see men and women through Your eyes and to respond with Your heart toward them.

1. John 4:4–26; Luke 19:5; Mark 9:21.

Once my morning caregivers (I call them my "get-up girls") have me dressed and sitting up, once I've finished breakfast and am ready to head out the door, my friends and I take an important pause. We head for our favorite warm spot—the bay window seat in my bedroom, which looks out over my backyard and the San Gabriel Mountains beyond. It's one warm spot that invites sitting and lingering. In that cozy corner, the three of us open a hymnbook to harmonize together over some beautiful old hymns. Safeguarding a quiet moment, admiring God's creation, and giving God pleasure each morning with our song warm the soul as well as the body. Don't be in such a hurry with life that you rush past those warm, quiet places where you meet with the Lord. The peace and perspective that come from those few sweet moments will color the rest of your day.

Father, the Bible tells how You met with Adam and Eve in the Garden, in the cool of the day.[1] I imagine there were warm, quiet places in Eden where You loved to talk to our first parents. Help me to find those moments in my day. Please don't let me hurry past places and times where You seek fellowship with me.

---

1. Genesis 3:8.

Today's Scripture reads, "The Son of Man came to seek and to save what was lost." Jesus had a clear and concise ministry. To carry out His mission, He connected with virtually every person the Father put in His path—every kind of individual in every strata of society. He didn't bypass *anyone*. This included arrogant, self-righteous religious leaders, as well as prostitutes, traitors, people with infectious diseases, and even dangerous people inhabited by demonic spirits.

What about us? Every day we pass by people who are considered outsiders, oddballs, loners, foreigners, and second-class citizens. Yet God has placed these individuals in our neighborhoods, on our street corners, on our campuses, and in our mall parking lots. We may find ourselves tempted to relate only to those with whom we identify and with whom we are comfortable. But if we want to follow Christ's example, it will mean making inroads with people outside our normal circles.

Jesus, I've prayed this before, but I'm asking You again to open my eyes to see the people around me as You do. Help me to see beyond the externals. For Your sake, help me to venture outside my comfort zone to greet, speak to, help, or at least smile at the people I would normally avoid or ignore.

Today's Scripture gives the best possible word on which to end our year together: "Look, I am coming soon! My reward is with me, and I will give to each person according to what they have done. I am the Alpha and the Omega, the First and the Last, the Beginning and the End." In the course of this past year, we've heard countless voices and read material by dozens of authors. But after all is said, read, and done, Jesus is the first word in our lives, and He is the last word. What more can we say? Who else can we turn to? Where else could we go? There is no one like Jesus. It's my prayer that the plans you make, the ways you spend your time, the thoughts you entertain, the words you speak, the company you keep, and the manner in which you live before others—all of it—will point to Him.

As David prayed to You, dear Lord, "You are my God. My times are in your hands."[1] Oh, that I would remember this, from the time I open my eyes in the morning and in every minute as I go through my day. My life is not my own; my time is not my own; my opportunities are not my own. I belong to another—to Him who gave His life for me.

---

1. Psalm 31:14–15.

$\mathscr{B}$ible Translations Cited

ℳore for You . . .

If you've been blessed by this book, read more about Joni Eareckson Tada by visiting the Joni and Friends International Disability Center website.

www.joniandfriends.org

Or you can write Joni at . . .

Joni and Friends
P.O. Box 3333
Agoura Hills, CA 91376, USA
(818) 707–5664

The mission of Joni and Friends is to communicate the gospel and equip Christ-honoring churches worldwide to evangelize and disciple people affected by disability. Premiere programs include Wheels for the World, Family Retreats, and Joni's radio outreach aired on more than a thousand outlets across America. Through a network of volunteers and U.S. Field offices, Joni and Friends provides hope and practical help to special-needs families around the world. We invite you to partner with us, so contact Joni and Friends today.

Joni

An Unforgettable Story
Joni Eareckson Tada

It was more than a hot July afternoon on the Chesapeake Bay. For Joni Eareckson Tada, it was a moment in eternity. In a split second, a diving accident transformed her life from that of a vivacious young woman to one lived from a wheelchair.

Out of that incident has emerged one of the most remarkable stories of our time—a story of faith's triumph over hardship and suffering. With more than five million copies in print and translated into fifty languages, *Joni* continues to inspire readers worldwide with its message of courage, hope, and grace. This edition includes a new foreword from Francis Chan, a new sixteen-page photo insert, a new afterword, and an updated resource section.

Available in stores and online!

Joni & Ken

An Untold Love Story

Ken & Joni Eareckson Tada, with Larry Libby

God's immeasurable grace. It's the most important ingredient for the perfect love story.

Tragic circumstances often stretch relationships to their breaking point. But God's grace is always more than enough. For Ken and Joni Eareckson Tada, enduring quadriplegia, chronic pain, cancer, and depression only made their love more vibrant through thirty years of marriage. Discover a bond that has seen the worst and claimed the best. Discover God's amazing grace along the way, as their story enriches your own relationships.

A love untold. Until now.

In the midst of their deepest struggles with depression and pain, Ken and Joni return to the one true answer. One that is far from a denial of Joni's diagnosis or thoughts of how wonderful a quick exit to heaven would be. In their darkest hour, Ken and Joni encounter a heavenly visitation that changes their lives—and maybe yours—forever.

Available in stores and online!

Diamonds in the Dust

366 Sparkling Devotions
Joni Eareckson Tada

With more than 200,000 copies sold, *Diamonds in the Dust* has become a devotional favorite. Joni shows us precious jewels of biblical truth that lie scattered amidst the gravel of life's dusty road.

More Precious Than Silver

366 Daily Devotional Readings
Joni Eareckson Tada

More Precious Than Silver reveals surpassing wealth in the subtle things we overlook as we chase life's golden glitter. These wise, insightful devotions will show you why nothing can compare to the riches of a heart that's known the silver touch of God's Word. Includes photos and drawings by Joni.

Pearls of Great Price

366 Daily Devotional Readings
Joni Eareckson Tada

In a well-known parable of Jesus, a merchant sold everything he had to buy a valuable pearl. In *Pearls of Great Price*, Joni Eareckson Tada reminds you there is a spiritual treasure within your reach. Each day's devotion contains glorious pearls of hope and faith waiting to be claimed.

When God Weeps

Why Our Sufferings Matter to the Almighty

Joni Eareckson Tada and Steven Estes

If God is loving, why is there suffering? What's the difference between permitting something and ordaining it?

When suffering touches our lives, questions like these suddenly demand an answer. Suffering doesn't always seem to make sense, especially when we believe in a loving and just God. Joni Eareckson Tada's intimate experience with suffering gives her a special understanding of God's intentions for us in our pain. In *When God Weeps*, she and lifelong friend Steven Estes probe beyond glib answers that fail us in our time of deepest need to reveal a God big enough to understand our suffering, wise enough to allow it, and powerful enough to use it for a greater good than we can ever imagine.

Available in stores and online!

ZONDERVAN®
.com